The Trouble with Tom

If there is anything we wish to change in the child, we should first examine it and see whether it is not something that could better be changed in ourselves.

- Carl Gustov Jung

The Trouble with Tom

A Parent's Lesson on Letting Go

Susan Thomassen

SAGAMORE BEACH, MASSACHUSETTS

The Trouble with Tom

Cover Photo by Tom Noonan

First printing, February 2009
10 9 8 7 6 5 4 3 2 1

ISBN # 0-9818452-0-7
ISBN-13 # 978-0-9818452-0-3
LCCN # 2008910327

The Sandbar Press
P.O. Box 1547
Sagamore Beach, MA 02562
+1-774-413-9625

Visit our web site at www.thesandbarpress.com

For Tom:
It has been an amazing journey, one that I wouldn't change for the world. I look forward to the continuing ride, for the most part.

For Dave:
You make life wonderful. I don't know what I ever did to deserve you. You are my every breath. My heart. My soul. My love.

For Emma, my lil miss thaang:
Our ray of sunshine. Your smiling face makes every morning an exciting new adventure that we are thrilled to experience with you.

FOREWORD

by Shannon J. Scarry, MD

I didn't know Susan Thomassen for most of the years chronicled in her book. We met when she joined out Child and Adolescent Psychiatric Team almost 4 years ago, as the Registered Nurse who would provide the vital support for 3 Child and Adolescent Psychiatrists, and a Child and Adolescent Nurse Practitioner. She's been an invaluable member of the team, and is beloved especially by the parents of the very sick children we treat. She listens, explains medications and their side effects, consults with us about problem solving, and is our link to the families when they are not here, but at home or school, or in Court, wherever the "trouble" is. She knows and helps care for ALL of our patients, and brings both her expertise, and wealth of personal experience, which has taught her wisdom, to her job.

Her book explores the difficulties, as well as the delights of motherhood, but more than that, she tells her story of learning to grow up herself as she raised her son alone, and how hard it is to know when to "let go." All good parents want the best for their children; it is extremely hard to learn that the "best" isn't giving in, not setting limits, or being overprotective.

The "best" is being able to teach your child how to behave in the world at an age appropriate level, to the best of their ability. It is knowing your child better than anyone else, and using that knowledge to foster psychological, social, and physical health. This book is about how Susan learned to do that.

Some people mistakenly believe that every child is born with the same developmental potential, but that clearly isn't true. Each child is unique, but a blend of its parent's genetics, experiences, and circumstances. Susan writes poignantly about finding out what her own son is like, his strengths and weaknesses, and how to help him grow. The themes of this book are individual and universal. Most of you readers will see a lot of yourselves in this book–if you are a parent. D.W. Winnicott, MD, the great Pediatrician and Child Psychiatrist, wrote about a parent's need to be only "good enough," and that's what you will find in this book.

Shannon J. Scarry, MD
Child and Adolescent Psychiatrist
Cape Cod, September, 2008

ACKNOWLEDGEMENTS

Thank you Dr. Natalie Belkin, my brilliant friend. Without you, this wouldn't have been possible. Your support and confidence in my writing gave me the courage to move forward in publishing my story. Thank you for holding my hand through the editing process, for asking for more when I didn't think there was any more to give and not accepting no. For questioning, at times, what my true feelings were. You were right. You helped to bring clarity to my story.

Thank you Clifford Bowyer, Managing Director of Creative Strategist, for walking me through the entire publishing process. Your patience with my endless questions, concerns and changes was very much appreciated every step of the way. Your knowledge and experience in publishing has made me feel more comfortable and confident in learning new things.

Thank you Alison Novak, editor at Creative Strategists, for polishing up my work and transforming my story into a refined narrative. Your frankness and requests for more where more was needed gave me the push I needed to make the necessary changes and additions.

Thank you, Dave, for your never-ending support and encouragement, and for always believing in me, even when I didn't. Your unwavering honesty is exactly what I needed. I am eternally grateful for your devotion to me and my endeavors.

Thank you Dad for your words of wisdom, and Mom, for believing in me so strongly. Thank you both for believing I'm the next best thing to sliced bread in whatever I do.

The Trouble with Tom

Prologue

I sat on the edge of Tom's bed feeling beaten and tired, wondering where I had gone wrong with him. Was it something I had done? Was it something that was out of my control? I thought I had done everything right, but I had this nagging feeling that there was something I was missing. Something I could have done differently. I racked my brain for answers. I couldn't stop thinking about how ruinous his life had become. My mind wouldn't allow me to let go. I was determined to make things better. Tom's life had started out a little less than perfect, but I thought that I could make it work. My thoughts flashed back to the beginning.

1

The Players

Claustrophobia was setting in again. Loneliness started to creep back into my brain. I couldn't stand sitting in Phil's bedroom any longer and there wasn't much television worth watching. I didn't know where Phil was. I didn't know when he would be home. It could be hours. It could be days. What I did know was that he was out running around with his friends, as usual. Spending time with his girlfriend was low on his priority list.

I tried to occupy my mind with redecorating ideas. Phil's bedroom was all the space that I had. It wasn't really my space. I felt more like a long-term visitor than a resident, but it would have been nice to make the room feel a little homier. The plain white walls would have felt more inviting with some color. The full size bed would have felt more comforting with new pillows and down blankets, with curtains to match. I knew I couldn't really change things. The redecorating was only a temporary diversion for my mind. I knew my ideas might be interpreted as too much of a commitment and would be a waste of my time, so abandoning my notion was the only option.

I wasn't sure where I would be a few months down the road. I didn't think I would be living in Phil's grandmother's house, but I didn't know where else to go. I couldn't live on my own. I wasn't able to support myself yet. Moving back to my parents' house was an option. My mother would be supportive, but that would feel like I was giving up what independence I had. I didn't want to let go of that. It would feel like I was moving backwards, and I didn't want to be dependent on anyone but myself.

I couldn't let go of Phil. I wanted to be with him. I wanted him to want to be with me. I thought, in time, things would change for the better and he would want to settle down. I couldn't give up on us yet. For the time being, I would stay in the lonely, drab, messy bedroom.

I went downstairs to say hello to everyone; to see my friends that, at one time, I had loved hanging out with. I needed some company in order to ease my boredom. I didn't feel like I was missing out on anything. Partying was a thing of my past. I was done being irresponsible. It was just nice to have some human contact once in a while.

Company was never far away in Phil's house. It was a good thing, because Phil wasn't around very often. I found myself waiting for him far too often. It was mostly my fault. Phil never gave me any false hopes. It was what it was. He didn't tell me to leave. He didn't tell me to stay. I chose to stay. I was going to make him love me. I didn't like to think about it too much, though. I just wanted to forget. I wanted to laugh. Phil's brother Danny was usually the person everyone sought out for a good time, so that is who I went to see to ease my loneliness.

On my way down the stairs, Danny's song began to resonate in my ears, planting a grin across my face. "Oh no, no, no, it smell like haddock, haddock, haddock. No, no, no, no, it smell like cod, cod, cod." The house filled with laughter. Exactly what I needed. I hadn't heard the vulgar comment that prompted Danny into song, but I had had a good idea of what he was referring to.

I stood at the end of the long island that ran the length of the kitchen. The island turned the kitchen into a galley, except for the addition on the far end. Everyone was sitting around the kitchen table when I got downstairs. All my childhood friends. They were drinking beers and being loud. It was always good to see them, even if I didn't want to drink with them. It was a typical Danny night. He had some friends over to get drunk. He never had a chance to feel lonely because he made sure there was always someone around.

Suddenly, Nonie appeared in the doorway between the kitchen and dining room. Nobody heard her coming. She startled me. I jumped at her bellowing voice. She was just there, out of the blue, screaming for everyone to get out of her house. "Ya'all bess git movin on! Now! Or someone's gitten a bullet in their hide!" There was a moment's hesitation while everyone had a chance to comprehend what was happening.

A numbness spread up my body, until it reached my

brain. I began to tremble. Nonie looked crazier than I had ever seen her. She was standing there in her long, cotton print nightgown. Her grey and auburn hair was wildly standing on end. Her eyes were so wide; the amount of white took all focus off any color that may have existed. Nonie was holding a shotgun across her chest like a well-trained soldier. The larger-than-normal fingers on her left hand were wrapped tightly around the wooden stalk. Her right hand gripped the long, metal barrel with confidence. Nonie swung the gun up, as if she would fire a warning shot if need be; or keep swinging until the end of the long barrel found a target in the center of someone's back. I was closest to her. I didn't notice if her focus was on me. I didn't take the time to find out. It was more urgent that I just get out, fast.

There was no explanation needed. Nonie didn't leave any questions in anyone's mind. We knew exactly what she wanted so we cleared the kitchen in seconds. I was the last in the pack, praying, as I ran, that I wouldn't get a bullet in the back. It wasn't a good position to be in, but I was grateful that I didn't have to pass her on my way out. The door to safety was right next to the table that everyone was sitting around. I prayed that the obedience Nonie commanded and received was enough to keep her from pulling the trigger.

I didn't think Nonie was intending to target me. She knew I wasn't part of the problem at the time. I was not going to take the time to reason with her, though. I was scared half to death and didn't want it to be my time to die. I had a lot ahead of me. I knew that there were a lot of difficult times coming, but I was willing to embrace them and make something of my life. So, I joined the fleeing crowd and out the door I ran.

I sprinted across the lawn and jumped behind a car that was parked in front of Nonie's house. Most people headed for the woods. I wasn't in the condition for a marathon, so I took the closest cover that I could find and secured my position behind the car, hoping for the best.

I found myself lying on my back, on the pavement, with my chest heaving from the short sprint across the lawn. I tried to focus on slowing my breathing. I could feel the tiny, protruding pebbles pressing into the side of my skull as I lay there. Sweat began to pool between my shoulder blades, helping to cool my shocked body. I lay as still as I was able. I watched Nonie standing in the doorway, with only her feet in my line of vision. I knew I had to move without being noticed. I slowly rolled onto my stomach and rose to a crawling position. I quietly moved to the front of the car, staying as low to the ground as I could. I had to get a better view. I could see Nonie sweeping the shot gun back and forth, scanning the width of her property. "Don't ya all come back, ya hear!" She meant business. Nonie was a large woman. She was big-boned. It wasn't an excuse for being overweight. She really was big-boned. Her hands were the size of a football player's hands. She stood about six feet tall. In her crazed state, she appeared to top eight feet.

I remained squatting in front of the car, too scared to make a noise. My thighs began to burn. I didn't know how long I could stay in this position before my legs gave out. I had to keep an eye on her. I needed to know if she was coming my way. I would need every possible second available to stay ahead of her. I didn't know what I would do if she did decide to approach. I wasn't exactly agile at the time. I could stay crouched and move around the car as she came toward me, I thought. I could make it to the thin wood line that was about twenty yards behind me, I thought. What would I do when I got there? The trees weren't big enough to hide behind. I couldn't be running through the woods and chance hurting myself, so I decided to wait it out behind the car. I eased my knees down to the pavement to relieve the burden from my thighs. I could feel the full weight of my body grinding my knees into the tar. It was more forgiving than the burn. I waited.

Nonie didn't come out of the house. She just stood in the doorway, shouting threats in her best southern accent. Her accent was always thicker when she wanted to make a point. Point taken. She didn't want anyone back in her house. That was clear.

Danny and I waited for hours before we went back in. We wanted to make sure Nonie was asleep before we reentered the house. I knew once she slept, it would all be forgotten. She would be a different person in the morning. She would act like nothing happened.

Nonie had never threatened me with a gun before, but it wasn't the first time she had acted crazy either. I would never forget that night. Nobody would. Nonie may have been harmless most of the time, but most of the time wasn't good enough for me anymore. I had to get out for good.

Nonie

Most neighborhoods have a party house. In my neighborhood, it was Phil's house. His house was one of the most popular party houses in town. Despite the night with the shotgun, Nonie usually didn't mind us drinking in her house, and it didn't matter to her how old we were. The house was always full of under-age kids.

Nonie drew the line at drugs. Surprisingly, she wouldn't stand for drugs in her house. Some people had to find that out the hard way. Most of the time she didn't know when there were drugs in the house, but when she did find out, she would get violent if you didn't take immediate action to rectify the situation. I've seen Nonie beat up some pretty large guys with whatever weapon was closest to her. It was usually the broom at the top of the cellar stairs that she would grab on her way down. Her glaring, dark eyes told the whole story. She wasn't taking any shit.

Nonie would just stand quietly, scanning the basement. If she saw something she didn't like, it was time for people to take action. If they didn't, there would be trouble. There were a couple of guys who thought they could ignore her. I guess they figured that it was a party house and it was their right to party. They thought wrong. She beat on them all the way up the stairs, out the front door, and into the street. She would not be ignored. She had no fear. She had an unnatural strength when she got angry, and it wasn't always because people didn't hit back. Most kids respected her. A few didn't. The ones that mistakenly felt they should retaliate with physical aggression realized their mistake quickly. Nonie never lost a battle. Her opponent was never welcomed back, by anybody.

Nonie was unpredictable. We couldn't always count on her being okay with us partying. Sometimes she got fed up with all the kids in her house. The noise would get to her, and when it did, there was never a warning. She would let us know, in no uncertain terms, that it was time to go. Her wrath would come down hard and fast, but it was a risk worth taking. There was nowhere else to go during the winter.

Nonie wasn't Phil's mother. She was his grandmother. She raised him and two of his siblings from the time they were babies. She loved them. She probably wasn't the best parent, but she was the best option in the family. Nonie did her best. She kept a roof over their heads, food in their stomachs, and she sent them off to school when it was time. I'm not sure how they survived sometimes because Nonie was a little crazy and the kids ran wild.

Danny

Phil's brother Danny was just a wild, partying, good-natured drunk. He had a great sense of humor and a good heart. He was the funniest person I had ever met. I had been laughing at his jokes from the time I was ten years old. He was one of the first kids that I had met after moving to the neighborhood.

Danny was an average-looking kid. He always thought he was much uglier than he actually was because Phil got all the girls. Phil was popular. He was a great-looking guy with a hot rod. Danny was resentful of his older brother's striking physical attributes. He was resentful that I had picked Phil.

It didn't help that Danny wasn't the most popular kid. He rode the short bus to school, and spent his days in the resource room. He thought he was dumb because he was raised to believe that he was dumb. Nonie wanted to keep him dependent on her forever. He was the youngest of the grandchildren she had raised. I imagine she was afraid that she would be alone one day, so she mentally disabled poor Danny. He did the only thing he could. He stayed at home, had a lot of friends, and drank himself into oblivion at night. He depended on Nonie for everything else.

I've never met anyone who could remember as much information as Danny could. He chose to mostly remember the information that he could make people laugh with. It was a waste of a good brain, but Danny would never think of his brain as "good."

Danny made me feel comfortable when other kids didn't. I was painfully shy. It was hard for me to make friends. Danny didn't care about popularity or being cool. He was just nice to everyone who wanted to be his friend. The adults in the neighborhood would describe a completely different person. He was not nice to his neighbors.

One night, while Danny was drunk, he thought it would be funny to cut down his neighbor's prized Blue Spruce. It stood tall in the center of the elderly man's front lawn, towering above the roof of the house. In the middle of the night, Danny took a saw to the tree as quietly as he could. He sawed and sawed until his arms were burning and weak. Just as the tree started to fall, he screamed, "tiiiimberrrrrrr!" Then he ran back home, three houses away. We could hear the man crying for his tree from Danny's front lawn. I thought it was mean. The man who lived there was mean, but he didn't deserve that. He just wanted peace. Danny didn't like the man because he was always yelling at Danny for making too much noise. Danny wanted to get even. He didn't want to be bothered by this man anymore. After he cut down the tree, the man never spoke another word to Danny. Danny won his battle.

Danny didn't get caught, but everyone knew who it was. It was the kid from the party house, the kid who terrorized the neighborhood. The kid who was always causing trouble, the kid who created all the noise.

When Danny had no money, he would do anything to get alcohol. He loved being a witness in court. Any time a friend got in trouble, they would name Danny as a witness, whether or not he was present. Danny would collect his nominal witness check and head for the package store for a bottle of Mad Dog 20/20 or Wild Turkey. The most he could get for his money.

Danny couldn't always count on witness fees to provide his alcohol. He would become desperate sometimes. One night he was so desperate, he broke into his next-door neighbors' house because they had a bar. The man knew who it was, so he went to speak to Danny. He told Danny that if he really needed some alcohol, he should just ask and he would give it to him as long as his house never got broken into again. Danny could relate to that, so he decided to test the rules. He asked. He received. He never asked again. Danny liked the man so he never broke into the man's house again.

From the first drink Danny took, he spent his entire existence figuring out a reason to get drunk. Any excuse would do. He thought up more reasons to party than actually existed. He didn't really need a reason. It was just more exciting that way. Danny would call me to ask if I wanted to drink with him because there was a storm coming. He would get so excited about the storms, he would gather up all the candles that he could find and place them on the table next to his thirty-pack of beer. He was always prepared. In New England, the storms usually rolled in much milder than predicted, but that didn't deter him. Danny would be drunk before the storm hit, or didn't hit. His excitement never dwindled, but I think it was the drinking that he found exciting, not the storms.

As much as Danny laughed, he could just as easily fall into a deep depression. It was usually over a girl. His depression usually only lasted a night or two. Everyone thought Danny had abandonment issues because of the way he attached himself to girls. He would never break up with a girl, and he was devastated when they broke up with him. He had a funny way of showing how upset he was.

One night, after a girl broke up with Danny, he decided to get as hammered as he could. He wanted to forget all of his woes. He bought a half gallon of cheap vodka for himself. He didn't buy any mixer. He didn't feel that he needed any. Danny drank the entire bottle straight down in about ten minutes.

What I didn't know was that Danny had gone into the house and had called 911 right after he finished his vodka. He came running outside, as fast as he could, and rammed his head into a snow bank. He stayed there until the ambulance came. My friends and I couldn't pull him out because we were all laughing too hard.

The EMTs pulled Danny out of the snow. They said it was a suicide attempt. I could understand the vodka, but the snow bank was baffling to me. It was a good thing that Danny had a sense of humor because his friends never stopped making fun of him for it.

Danny quickly recovered from his break-ups and was often on the look-out for the next love of his life. They were all, immediately, the love of his life. Danny was an interesting character. There was never a dull moment with him. He fit right into the family.

Anita

Phil's sister Anita wasn't around as much as the boys were. She was the middle child in the house. She lived at Nonie's house less and less as she grew older. Anita was busy finding a man. She would move out for short periods of time when she thought she had found the right one, but she would always move back, sometimes with her man. When Anita was single, she was around a lot more often. There were always plenty of Phil's and Danny's friends to pick from.

Second to men, Anita loved animals. She always had a dog. She usually had more than one pet and she took good care of them. Anita also loved children. She, Phil, and Danny had a younger brother and sister who lived with their father. She loved to take Robbie and Tina for the weekend. She would spoil them with love and toys with the never-ending supply of money she seemed to have. She didn't always work, but she somehow always had money. She was a good-hearted person. She was loving and generous. She just seemed unable to control her desire for men and money. Anita was manic.

Anita's generosity was usually spurred by someone else's money. That girl could smell money. She could find it anywhere. Phil couldn't find enough hiding places to keep her hands off of his money. He worked hard. Well, maybe not hard. He worked a lot of hours and he made good money for a young guy. I don't know why he didn't put his money in the bank. You would think he was raised during the depression. He had to keep it in his room. It would have been safer having his money kept by a bill collector.

Phil had to be creative when looking for new hiding places for his money. He always thought he had found the perfect spot. One time he separated his carpet at the far end of his bedroom, slid his money as far under the carpet as he could get it, and left the edge looking as if it had never been touched.

Anita found it anyway. She always did. It was never a small amount of money either. Always hundreds of dollars. She wouldn't take it all. She wanted to make it look like nobody had touched it. Phil always knew how much money he had, down to the dollar, and he always knew how much was missing.

When the carpet method failed, Phil tried the light switch compartment. He folded his bills as flat as he could, removed the cover of the light switch and concealed the money in his new, foolproof spot. Anita was no fool. She found it again. Phil was no fool either, but I couldn't understand why he insisted on keeping his money in the house. It became a game that Anita was happy to play. Phil wasn't happy about it, but he kept on playing.

Anita had other talents. She knew how to get money out of an ATM machine before I knew how to use one. I don't know if she took people's bank cards or she just knew how to manipulate the machine. It must have been the former because she wouldn't have been the only person to figure it out. If she had bank cards that belonged to other people, why would they give her their password? If they didn't, how did she figure them out? Nobody ever knew how she did it. She never gave up her secrets.

Anita wasn't exactly an upstanding citizen. She was not the type of person that I would leave a child with. I never knew when she was going to end up in jail. I did feel bad for her when the military showed up and took her out in shackles for embezzling money from the United States Navy. I liked her.

She had a good heart. I just couldn't trust her actions.

Aunty-Sister Sarah

Aunty-Sister Sarah was Phil's aunt. Nonie's daughter. He called her his sister because his grandmother raised him. He called all of his aunts, his sisters. It was very confusing to me. It took years to figure out who was really who. I was determined to keep it straight. It seemed more important to me than it was to Phil's family. Of course, they all knew who was really who. They were just okay with the way it was. I found it bizarre. I grew up in a place where an aunt was an aunt and a mother was a mother. Phil and I were from two different worlds.

Phil called his brothers and sisters what they were, even though they were half-siblings. Most of Phil's siblings never knew who their fathers were, which simplified the process of figuring out who was who.

Aunty-Sister Sarah was a bit of a grounding force for me in Phil's chaotic family. She was Phil's grounding force. I didn't see her much when I was growing up. She lived far away from the family, and she wasn't interested in spending much time in Nonie's house. She loved Phil, though. He would go to her house to visit once in awhile. She came to visit him on rare occasions. Usually just for the holidays. When she did visit, it was brief. She preferred Phil go to her house. She was always nice when she came; she just had her own life. A different life than she found at Nonie's house.

Aunty Sister-Sarah had a quiet life. She seemed more

normal than the rest of the family. She had a family of her own. She was settled. She didn't drink or do drugs. She didn't chase men. She had a long-term husband. I liked her because she seemed stable.

Phil loved his Aunty-Sister Sarah. Her house was a respite for him, a place where he could get away from all the chaos. Phil did have good judgment once in a while. He was grateful that he had a normal place to go to get away from it all, but his quest for normalcy was always short-lived. He had become accustomed to the chaos. He could never stay away too long, no matter how much he had protested.

Aunty-Sister Linda

Aunty-Sister Linda was Phil's aunt, another daughter of Nonie's. Her family was too V.C. Andrews for me. Aunty-Sister Linda had a husband named Harry. Harry raped their daughter Kim from the time she was a small child. When Kim got older, she became pregnant with her father's child. Harry's granddaughter is actually his daughter, or so they say. Poor Kim was mentally challenged because she drank turpentine when she was a baby. She didn't have the mental capacity to defend herself. She was left unprotected from her own father's evil ways.

I believed the story. I had a gut feeling about Harry. He always gave me the creeps. Every time they came to Nonie's house for the holidays, he would look at me funny. Never in the face. Always at my chest, or lower. Chills literally ran up and down my spine every time I saw him. That would happen before I ever heard about what had happened to poor Kim. It had happened from the first time I met him. There was no way in hell that I would ever leave a child anywhere near that man. How Aunty-Sister Linda didn't see it that way was beyond my comprehension. Maybe she did and just didn't care. They were creepy.

Aunty-Sister Linda was a hypochondriac. From the time I was a teenager, she was crippled and in a wheelchair. I'm not sure why. I know she fell off a bus while it was stopped. I remember she had a brace on her leg after the accident. People usually recover from that type of injury, but she never did. Maybe it was her weight. It was too much for an injured body part to hold up. She was on disability for years and it all started with the fall.

Aunty-Sister Linda had sleep apnea before any of us knew what that was. She carted an oxygen tank around with her. One end hung from her wheelchair; the other end hung from her nose. I didn't know the difference back then, but I've never heard of anyone being on continuous oxygen for sleep apnea. She seemed to love the props. She loved the attention and special arrangements people had to make for her disabilities.

My favorite ailment was her sudden and complete deafness. I'm not sure how she went deaf. I don't remember any story about the cause, but she did say it was a familial condition. I remember because her grandson was also losing his hearing. Nobody else in the family had any hearing problems.

Aunty-Sister Linda had to learn sign language to communicate with the world. One day, she just knew how to sign. It wasn't long after the deafness struck. I didn't know sign language, but I had seen it on occasion. I remembered learning some basic signs on Sesame Street. Her signs were nothing I had ever seen before. Danny had a very funny imitation of this strange sign language, and he wasn't too shy to let her know about it. Danny's imitation was even more bizarre than hers.

He didn't believe that she was deaf, so he would sit behind her and put his mouth as close behind her ear as he could get without touching her. Danny would call her names and say rotten things until Aunty-Sister Linda became agitated. She squirmed in her seat and let out big sighs of air, but she was too stubborn to verbally admit to her charade.

Danny had quite an endearing description of Aunty-Sister Linda's family. He called them the Addams Family. When they would pull up to the house, Danny would pop in the tape of the theme song to the Addams Family. He would crank up the volume to ten. You could hear the music down at the end of the street. <u>Da da da da... neat, da da da da... sweet, da da da da... petite.</u> Danny had a dance and his own words to go along with the chorus. At just the right pause, Danny would call out one of their names while displaying his impression.

For Harry, Danny would hike his pants up to his chest, flatten his black hair straight down onto his forehead, and protrude his upper jaw as far out as he could push it. It was an uncanny impersonation of Harry. <u>Da da da da... Harry.</u>

For Aunty-Sister Linda, Danny would hold his arms out

away from his body, mimicking her large shape. He filled his cheeks with air. Then he would stomp around the porch with large, pounding steps. The porch vibrated under everyone's feet. Da da da da... Linda.

When Danny imitated the grandson, Chester, he would hold up his crossed fingers to his forehead because that was the sign he was taught to represent Chester's name. He would continue on down the family. They heard and saw all of it. Danny wasn't trying to hide anything. They would get mad and threaten never to come back to the house. They always came back. I always hoped they would follow through with their threat.

Mama-Sister Karen

Phil called his biological mother, his sister. It would have been more appropriate to call her nothing. Mama-Sister Karen didn't deserve either title. The only impact she had on her children was negative and abusive.

Mama-Sister Karen caused a lot of heartbreak for everyone she came in contact with. She would make up stories just to get people fighting. She was the meaning of shit-stirrer. She thought nothing of causing trouble for her own children. She would tell them that their significant others had cheated on them, or vice versa. Then she would sit back and watch the fireworks. I don't know why anyone listened to her. I knew better, but knowing better didn't keep me from getting angry at her.

When I was younger and hanging out at Phil's house, she would show up once in a while and try to join the party. Nobody ever wanted her around accept Anita and Nonie. I guess they couldn't see her for what she really was. Maybe they didn't want to. Anita couldn't get past the fact that no matter what Mama-Sister Karen did, she was her mother. The same for Nonie. Karen was her child. Nobody else had a problem writing her off. They preferred it when she wasn't around.

One night, when we were all sitting around the kitchen table, Mama-Sister Karen came strutting in the house. She was sporting her way-too-tight, unflattering jeans, and a tube top that was never meant to be stretched that far. Her large stomach was indecently exposed. Her hair was bleach-bottle blonde, with a short, choppy cut. She was convinced that every endless inch of her was sexy. She thought every man wanted her. She would say so herself. No matter what anyone said to the contrary, she went right on believing in herself. She had very inflated self esteem.

What Mama-Sister Karen did that night will be forever burned into everyone's mind, especially poor, unsuspecting Danny. She strutted around the table and came to a stop right behind Danny. Danny barely noticed her as he chugged another beer. All of a sudden, she pulled up on Danny's chin, tilting his head backward, and planted a kiss right on his mouth.

We knew she had tongued him by his reaction. Danny shoved her away hard, and took off running for the bathroom. He was sick. Literally sick. He gagged and spit into the air as he ran to the bathroom. I could hear him heaving so hard, I thought his toes were going to come up through his throat and out of his mouth. Vomiting wasn't enough. When Danny was done in the bathroom, he went upstairs to take a bath. I felt so bad for him. He kept saying that he felt dirty and he just wanted to get clean. Danny didn't come back downstairs. It didn't take long to get rid of Mama-Sister Karen that night. Nobody wanted her around.

Another night, we were having a party down in the cellar. There must have been a storm coming because Danny had everyone over. I remember that he was exceptionally excited. It was a good time, until Mama-Sister Karen showed up. She came after everyone had fallen asleep. I had settled on one of the two couches for the night. My friend Stew was sleeping on the floor about five feet away from me.

I awoke to the sound of Stew's muffled screams. When I turned my head to see what the commotion was, my brain instantly wanted to reject my eyeballs. I saw Mama-Sister Karen squatting down over the area where Stew's face once lay. All I could see was her nightgown hiked up to her waist. I could no longer see Stew's head. His arms and legs where flailing wildly. He was desperately trying to escape his horror. She thought it was funny. I found it utterly disgusting.

I wanted to move out of Phil's house. I had to move out. It wasn't the place for me. Living there was okay for a while, but I knew it was time for me to go. I wasn't into the crazy scene anymore. I had grown up before my friends. I loved them, but I couldn't live that life any longer. I wanted to move on.

Phil had no plans to get an apartment. He didn't need to. He had it made living in his grandmother's house. It was cheap. He didn't have to make a commitment. Nonie promised him that she would leave him the house if he stayed and helped with some of the bills. Phil stayed, even though everyone was promised the house at one time or another. Sometimes more than one family member was promised at the same time, but he believed that he would be the one to inherit it. He also preferred the freedom of cheap rent and living close to his friends.

I gave it my best shot with Phil. I really wanted our relationship to work, but we were looking for different things in life. We would be tied to each other in some ways for the rest of our lives, but I knew on some level that it would never be what I wanted it to be. I just wasn't ready to accept that. I couldn't completely let go, even though I had to leave that house.

I didn't want to move back to my parents' house, but that is where I would have to go in order to make my new start. I tried not to think of it as moving backwards. It was a good home, a safe home. It was my only option, so I decided to call my mother. I knew she would take me back in. It wouldn't be for long. I was determined to find a way to get my own place. That was the only way I would allow myself to go backwards.

2

New Beginnings

The pain tore across my midsection, seemingly crushing every one of my internal organs, as I lay there soaking and sticky despite the cold December air. I wasn't prepared, even though I knew it was coming. Nobody could ever really prepare themselves for that. I had to keep reminding myself to breathe. Every time the pain intensified, I became unwilling to let go of my air. It was all that I felt I had control of.

Trying to distract myself, I looked around the childish room that I had recently returned to despite my wish for independence. It wasn't much of a distraction, but it would have to do. It was all I had. My thoughts were invaded by painful circumstance. The white, chubby, caricature bunnies were all around me. They were pleasant enough. Their faces were smiling. Their legs were dancing in a pasture along the papered walls. It didn't look like a bad place to be. Better than the place I was in.

I had no idea where Phil was. There was no sense in trying to make my way to the phone. He couldn't be my first priority. I was lucky to have good parents. They were in the next room. I knew they would help me. I just needed to get to their bedroom before it was too late. Before it got worse. That was hard to imagine, but I knew it was true.

I pulled myself up to a sitting position, using the knob of the bedpost as a counter-weight. I needed a minute to recuperate before I could get myself into a completely upright position. I eventually made my way to my parents' bedroom door and banged forcefully so that I wouldn't have to do it a second time. I was trying to remain calm. I kept my voice steady as I called for my mother, but my heart wasn't as easily controlled.

My mother jumped out of bed and reached the door in an instant. Her usually jolly expression had turned serious, promising control. The soft lines of her Irish face had provided the maternal comfort that I needed. My father was on her heels. His six-foot-four stature had always made me feel safe, as opposed to the fear others often experienced when seeing him. The carved lines in his forehead and bushy clumps of wiry hair that sat atop his eyes had only served to make me feel secure in his wisdom. His large, right hand rubbed his beard; a familiar gesture he used during tense moments. My parents delivered me to the living room as quickly and as carefully as they could. The sweat was trickling from my forehead. I needed a cold cloth to ease my discomfort. I didn't have to speak the words. "Don, get me the phone and a damp cloth. Cold water." My father silently left to fulfill his duties.

I sat in the corner of my parents' living room, knowing the time had come. I looked around the room where I had grown up. It hadn't changed in years. The brown-stained, once light-blue carpet had been torn up long ago, leaving the plywood exposed, except for the red paint intended to be a temporary interior design. It was a poor idea. It was long past temporary. The unfinished, horizontal barn board still sat half nailed to the walls. The railing leading up the stairs of the split-level ranch was still missing. The lattice stood in its place. Another poor idea. I sat in the mismatched, orange and gold floral recliner, thinking that my life was about to be changed forever. I was afraid of the pain. I was afraid Phil wouldn't be there. I was ready for everything else.

My mother knelt at my feet, trying to be supportive. I could always count on her. I would be even more grateful for that later on in life. My father was milling around in the kitchen. He was quietly trying to calm his anxiety. I knew many things would not ever change. As much support as my parents provided, it wasn't the support that I craved. I supposed I would have thought differently about that if I had no support at all. I was young; only seventeen years old.

I sat in the recliner with the cordless phone clutched tightly in my hand, wishing, praying. I wanted, more than anything, to hear some good news about Phil coming before I had to leave for the hospital. The time was getting close, and the pain was getting worse. The periods of relief were becoming shorter. I was afraid to wait. I needed the comfort of medical professionals. My mother was calm. She knew better. She knew better about a lot of things.

Phil was nowhere to be found. He knew this time was coming at any moment. He knew that I needed him there. I wanted him there. I don't know why; I shouldn't have. Everyone was out looking for him. Every one of his friends and family members who I was able to contact was involved in the search. They were all racing from one location to another as I periodically took the reports from them. The search was narrowing. There weren't many places left to look, at least not places that anyone knew about. He could be anywhere. He could have picked up some girl at a bar and gone back to her house. That wouldn't have been unusual. The only thing we could do was to try to find one of his friends who might know something.

I sat in my chair and cried, wondering why I even cared. This was not supposed to be about Phil. I was not supposed to let it be about Phil. I couldn't let go for some reason. I was still trying to force him to be someone that I wanted him to be. I was still trying to force him to be someone he was not.

Just as my mother helped me to my feet, the phone rang. My pain started to ease again. Maybe it was just the distraction. "We found him, Susan. He's on his way." It was Danny. His voice sounded pressured, relieved in some way. He sounded happy–excited, like it was okay because Phil would now be there. Maybe he was just happy for me because he knew that was what I wanted.

"Where was he?" I shouldn't have asked. It didn't matter. I didn't need to make myself feel worse. I chose to want him there. I needed to know. I always needed to know. Maybe it was so I would have plenty of ammunition. If that was the reason, it wasn't a conscious one at that moment. I had other things to worry about.

"He was passed out on Steve's living room floor. I had to bang on the windows forever to wake him up. Nobody would answer the door. He finally heard me."

"Thank you, Danny." It could have been worse, I thought. That scenario was also typical of Phil, but one of the better ones. Once he had been found, my fear of being alone quickly turned into anger. I suddenly no longer wanted Phil with me, but it was too late. They had found him. I had made them find him. My only choice was to accept the situation as it was. I had to put my anger aside and focus on other, more important things.

I could hear a car pull into the driveway as I walked toward the stairs. I couldn't wait any longer. I could see that it was Phil as I passed the living room picture window. He had just made it. I headed down the stairs for the front door. I knew that, suddenly, all would be forgiven again. The excitement in Danny's voice was not unwarranted; I was happy because my new family would be together. I decided to ride with Phil and have my parents follow us. I knew Phil would want his car at the hospital. He would want to make an escape if he needed to. I just hoped it wouldn't be too soon.

My contractions were getting closer and closer together. The pain was getting more intense. Phil was nervous. Suddenly, I wasn't. I was excited. Billions of women had gone through this. There was no reason that I couldn't. I was young, but my mother always told me that my hips were made for having babies. It was the only time I would be grateful for that.

We arrived at the hospital a couple of hours after my contractions started. They put me in the labor room right away. Only Phil was allowed to come with me. He was my coach, even though he had made it to only a few of the classes. The rest of the family would have to wait outside the labor and delivery unit.

The labor room was plain. There were no pictures on the walls or color to the paint. The bed was just an average hospital bed with no comforters or fluffy pillows. There was a chair for Phil and a small, rectangular hospital table that he would later eat his lunch on. Nothing to help me feel more comfortable. Nothing to make me smile. The room was cold. It was sterile. It was all business.

The further my labor progressed, the more I started to regret my decision to deliver naturally. I didn't know if I could take any more after eight hours of agony. My parents told me later that they could hear me screaming through the labor room doors, down the hall, and through the double doors leading to the waiting area. My father was angry. He wanted them to give me something for the pain. It was my decision. A decision thought out without firsthand knowledge of what I was getting myself into.

I couldn't wait for the baby to come. I couldn't wait for the pain to end. Even more, I couldn't wait to hold my child in my arms. I had waited for that moment for so long. Eighteen days longer than I should have. I tried to take a walk to speed the process along, but I didn't make it very far, only a few steps. The next contraction gripped me with an inhuman force.

I needed something to help me get through the last stretch. The nurse told me that I had waited too long for an epidural. The only thing they could give me was a shot of Demerol. I didn't care what it was at that moment. I would take anything. A shot sounded better to me anyway. It would still be considered a natural childbirth, and I needed something to ease my pain. I was completely exhausted. I needed a rest, so I took the shot.

I no longer had the short respites between contractions. Suddenly, I was nauseous. I began to sweat profusely. I felt dizzy. The room was spinning. My thoughts were jumbled. I was miserable. I wanted to give the Demerol shot back. It was a big mistake. It was the last thing that I needed. My experience went from bad to worse. Then, the next contraction came. That ripping, torturous pain that would take me much longer to forget than it took many women.

In a strange way, the contractions were somewhat of a relief from the nausea, the confusion, the spinning. I couldn't think straight. The contractions forced me to focus. I needed to be present for the most important moment of my life.

Almost twelve hours from my first contraction, I was being wheeled into the delivery room. It was almost over. The lights overhead sent me into a faster spin as I rushed by on my stretcher. I wanted to vomit, but I had more important things to do. The baby was coming. Any moment, it would soon be over.

The nurses and the doctor kept telling me not to push. All I wanted to do was push. I had to fight my body's natural reactions. I had to fight what my mind so desperately commanded my body to do, but I did what I was told. I didn't need anything else to go wrong. I waited for the words that I longed to hear: "Okay, push."

Phil stayed by my side. He tried to be the coach he was taught to be. I wanted to tell him to get lost, but I needed his hand to squeeze. I needed the cold cloths held to my sweaty, burning forehead. I needed the man that I loved to be there with me. I didn't need him telling me to breathe. I knew how to breathe. Everyone knew how to breathe, for God's sake. Breathing wasn't helping me. His words were not helping me, but his actions were. I was glad that he was there.

December 29, 1985 was the day my little Thomas entered the world. Twelve hours after my first contraction. Forty-nine days after my seventeenth birthday. I had a beautiful, bald, curious baby boy. As soon as he entered the world, he had a big stretch and scanned the delivery room with his eyes. It was the happiest moment of my life. I couldn't wait to hold him. I just wanted to touch every inch of his precious little body. I wanted to make sure he was real. I wanted to make sure everything was there. I wanted to make sure he knew that I loved him.

I was second in line, after Phil. He was so excited; tears were streaming down his face. I knew how intense the moment was for him when he kept looking at the ceiling as he spoke—an old habit learned when overcoming his stutter. Phil grabbed his son right out of the nurse's arms and immediately relieved anyone of the decision of who the baby should go to first. I was still trying to recover from the Demerol. The only thing I could do was wait. He was worth it. There never was a more precious moment than when Phil laid my child across my chest. I never wanted to let him go. It was true love.

Thomas was a perfect, eight-pound, twenty-one-inch, healthy baby boy. I loved every inch of him. From the top of his cute, bald head, to his tiny, ten toes. I couldn't get enough of him. I thought my Thomas looked more like me than Phil. He had my blue eyes, although they were mostly black at the time. You could see a blue hue mixed in with the dark coloring. His little head was bald, but you could see a little bit of blonde fuzz. It was unlike his father's long black hair. His skin was pale, unlike his father's dark, Portuguese skin. Thomas did have his father's long fingers and body. Any other of his features would have to wait to be revealed.

Contrary to what the maternity nurses believed, I loved caring for my son more than anything in the world. If they could have gotten past the stereotype of a young mother, and the signs they were taught to look for in the bonding of mother and child, they would have found out that I was struggling to recover from the side effects of the medication they gave to me.

I don't remember much of the next day. That's how long it took for the Demerol to wear off. I had a lot of difficulty with basic daily functions, like getting out of bed without the floor wanting to come up to meet my face. I was dizzy and confused.

It took longer than usual to formulate a plan, like how to get the toothpaste on the toothbrush to brush my teeth. I was afraid to handle my son unless I was lying in bed.

The nurses looked at me with disgust. I knew what they were thinking. They thought that I didn't want to take care of my own child. I tried to tell them what was wrong. I tried to tell them that I wasn't feeling right. They didn't listen. They never asked how I was feeling. They never tried to help. They barely spoke to me. I couldn't wait to feel better and leave the hospital. I couldn't wait to be the best mother that I could possibly be.

On the third day, I was finally leaving the hospital. I was feeling almost normal again. Normal for a woman who had just had a baby. I was able to stay out of bed without the fear of losing my balance. The medication had left my system. I was ready to go. I gave Tommy his first bath and made sure the receiving blanket was tight enough to make him warm and comfortable. He had his first pictures taken. Then I sat, with my child in my arms, waiting for Phil to come and take us home. There was no need for Tommy to go back to the nursery again. There was no need for him to leave my arms. He was mine to care for. Mine to love forever.

Phil showed up with the car seat secured properly in the back seat. I sat in the back so I could make sure Tommy was okay. I wouldn't be able to see him from the front seat. It was nice to get outside in the fresh air. It was cold, but it was better than the inside of the stuffy hospital room. I couldn't wait to get to my mother's house. I was grateful to be living there so she could help me with the baby.

I loved every moment of my new role as mother. Tommy made it easy for me. He slept through the night in those first couple of weeks. He had no colic. He ate well. He hardly cried. I was worried he wouldn't develop his lungs enough because he was so quiet. Tommy was a content baby, and I was a content mother.

My mother told me that I acted like I had five children the way I took care of Tommy. She said I was a natural. It felt natural to me. Being a mother was easy. All it took was love, and I had plenty of that to give him. I gave it my all. My heart was stolen. He would become my whole world for far too long.

I was blown away by how powerful this love was. A mother's love. There is nothing else like it in the world. I was going to love this child unconditionally for the rest of my life.

Mothering was easy when Tommy never left my arms. It was easy when he was dependent on me to be fed, comforted, clothed, and protected. The only part that I considered difficult at times was the physical part; the lack of sleep when he was sick, pacing the halls, holding Tommy in my arms, with no diaper, because I was trying to let his diaper rash heal. Unfortunately, he had my sensitive skin. Even that stuff wasn't really hard. I just didn't love those parts all the time, but the love I had for Tommy never diminished.

Loving him and caring for him, that was easy and natural. What was already proving to be difficult was the influence other people might have on him. Phil loved his son, but he wasn't the ideal father in my eyes. I wished I could change that.

I wanted a normal family for my son. I wanted him to have a mother and a father who were married and living together, parents who raised him together. He deserved that. It wasn't fair, but it was what it was. I focused on the positive. Phil loved his son, and I loved my Tommy.

3

Waning Security

It was a struggle dealing with Phil and his family. When Tommy got a little older, I worried about his safety during his visits with his father. I wasn't confident that Phil could protect our son. I was afraid that Tommy would be left to care for himself at three years old. I knew he was loved. I tried not to think about the possibilities, but I started to worry more and more often. I worried every time he was out of my care. The older he got, the more time he spent away from me. It wasn't just during the time he spent at his father's house that I worried.

Other than the worry I felt when Tommy was away from me, motherhood was wonderful. Tommy brought happiness into everyone's heart. He made me happier than I had ever been in my life. We had a great time together. His laughter was contagious. I could listen to it all day long and never tire of it.

Tommy was a happy child. He was easy to please. He was easy to love. It was easy for him to love. He would wrap his arms and legs around me as tight as he could. When he kissed me, he would press his tiny lips, hard, against my cheek. He was an incredibly affectionate child. He made me feel loved. He made me feel needed. I owed him a lot.

Tommy was an easy child. He never whined. He only cried when he got hurt. He was never demanding. He only wanted to play and just be with his family, regardless of their flaws. He was content with everyone, and everyone wanted to spend time with him. People actually asked me if they could take him for the weekend all the time. He had this incredible ability to just make people smile.

Tommy loved the beach. He loved to run through the edge of the water. He loved to run on the sand, screaming and laughing at everything. He could find pleasure in anything. We would take long walks, collecting shells and little treasures for his pockets. I got a big kick out of him chasing after the seagulls. He always thought he could really catch one. Of course, he never did, but he was never disappointed. He would just run after them, laughing again the next time.

Tommy was an angel. He was the best thing that ever happened to me. I guess I wanted him to keep that innocence forever. I wanted to keep him pure. I wanted to keep him oblivious to all the bad in the world. He was beautiful. He was precious. I should have known that my beliefs could hurt him in the end. Life didn't work that way. I couldn't control what Tommy was exposed to for the rest of his life. The bad stuff started right in his own family. It started before he was born, and it continued soon after he entered the world.

The security I felt, my security and Tommy's security, started to slip away even further when he started preschool. It was a proud time, but his independence started to show, as it should have. As problems arose, my need to protect Tommy intensified. I was a good parent. I was there for him, even when I couldn't be a physical presence. He was always my number one priority. My world revolved around him. He always felt protected.

Tommy wasn't a shy child. He was actually very social. His elementary school teachers felt that he was too social because he had a hard time getting his work done at times. They loved him, though. Everyone did. They just felt that he was having too much fun when he was supposed to be learning. His grades were always excellent, so they didn't make a big deal out of it. They were just concerned that it might become a problem in the future. It was something to watch.

Even though Tommy wasn't shy, he wouldn't speak up for himself when he should have. It seemed he wouldn't ask for things out of concern that he may be putting someone out. Tommy wouldn't defend himself when accused of something he didn't do. He felt that it would be disrespectful, whether he was right or wrong. Tommy couldn't say no to his friends, even when he knew they wanted him to do the wrong thing. I didn't see him as lacking in self-esteem, but I wondered why else he would do that. I never considered the possibility that it was just his mild demeanor. He was okay with the world as it was. It was more important to him that he, and everyone else around him, was happy, than to address a disagreement. I didn't consider the possibility that Tommy seldom felt the need to be right.

Tommy didn't seem to consider consequences before he did something, which sometimes led to his feeling bad later. He was a smart child. He cared about people. He had perfect behavior most of the time; he just had an occasional lapse in judgment.

I felt that I had to do Tommy's thinking for him. I didn't want to. I wanted him to do it. He just wouldn't, so I defended him, spoke for him, and protected him. As he grew older, my boundaries blurred. Instead of letting him continue to suffer the consequences for making the wrong decision, or doing nothing at all, I would save him. I felt that I had no choice. He never learned. I thought that he would learn by following my lead. He didn't, so I continued to save him from himself because I thought that was what he needed.

Tommy seemed incapable of looking ahead. I couldn't stop my mind from looking ahead of every situation. That was how my brain worked, so I tried to do his thinking for him. I knew better than he did. I thought that his ability to look ahead was something that would develop as Tommy matured.

The lack of thinking ahead wasn't the only thing bothered me. Tommy seemed oblivious, sometimes, to what was going on around him. It didn't cause much of a problem when he was little. His obliviousness was cute, and the consequences were small. I lovingly termed the problem "magooism." Magooism was Tommy falling up the stairs; never down. Magooism was Tommy tripping or falling over everything in his path;

or outside his path. I wasn't sure if it was his eyesight that was causing the problem, or just plain not paying attention.

Tommy had been born blind in his right eye. He was given the diagnosis, Optic Nerve Hypoplasia soon after birth. His optic nerve never developed, leaving it unattached to his eyeball. The doctors told me not to worry about it. The only thing that he wouldn't be able to do is fly a plane. He had no depth perception, but he seemed to have compensated for that. It was apparent in his athletic ability. His magooism seemed to be caused by inattention. There were other indications to support my theory.

Tommy wasn't hyperactive. He listened well and followed directions perfectly, but he was very messy and disorganized. My neighbor, Joanne, would smile and say, "oh, Tommy. He is so funny." It wasn't anything he was saying really. It was his actions. He just plowed through life sometimes without noticing anything that was going on around him. I found it endearing.

It wasn't that Tommy was clumsy, really. He was very coordinated. He just didn't pay attention to the mundane. I was forever telling him to watch out. I was forever grabbing him to keep him from falling and hurting himself, but if you put a ball in his hands, he knew exactly what to do with it, and he did it with near perfection.

Tommy started T-ball at four years old. He was the star athlete on the team, if there was such a thing in T-ball. He would walk up to the tee and all the kids would cheer him on. Everyone knew he would hit the ball into the outfield every time he was up. I felt proud every time they chanted his name. I would laugh every time the entire team would run into the outfield chasing after the ball. Both teams, in fact, would run into the outfield. I loved watching the kids play sports. I never missed a game. I was a dedicated cheerleader.

Protecting Tommy was a full-time job. I was developing habits that would become fixed and damaging. Tommy was a good child. Almost perfect, except for his inattention and lack of ability to look ahead or speak up for himself. His minor character flaws, as I perceived them, could cause enough stress to make up for his long good streaks.

When Tommy was six years old, he was allowed to go out by himself if he abided by my strict guidelines. We lived in an apartment building then. Tommy could go behind our building. He had to stay between the telephone pole and the end of the fire lane. The pole was as far as I could see from my living room slider. It wasn't far, but it was freedom. If Tommy went outside the boundary lines, he would lose the privilege until I felt he was responsible enough to follow the rules.

I never had a problem with Tommy following my rules, as long as he was paying attention. That is why it surprised me to find him gone one day. I told him that he could only go out for a little while because his grandmother and my cousin were coming to visit, and we were going out for lunch. Tommy went outside to take advantage of what little time he had to play.

Soon after Tommy went outside to ride his bike, the phone rang. It was my cousin. She just called to let me know that she was running late. She was stopping off at the house of a friend who lived in the same town. She wanted to take the rare opportunity to visit her.

I wanted to get Tommy into the apartment. I wanted to make sure he was clean and ready to go. I looked out the sliding glass door. He wasn't there. It took me by surprise. I walked out onto the balcony and leaned over the railing so that I could see as far as possible. I could see past the telephone pole. There was no Tommy. I could see past the end of the fire lane, out into the parking lot. There was no Tommy. My heart dropped into my stomach.

"Tooommmmyyyy!" I waited a few seconds. There was no response. I yelled once more, "Tooooommmmyyyy!" No response again. I ran down the two, short flights of stairs and out the back door to the fire lane. I took a moment to scan the parking lot before I took off in the opposite direction. I jogged the entire length of the fire lane, passing all three buildings. There was no sight of my little boy. Panic was setting in.

I ran, as fast as I could, back to my apartment. My mother was at the back door. "See if he's at Joanne's. I'm going to check his friends' houses." My mother headed back upstairs. I took off running again. I couldn't imagine Tommy just taking off and going to a friend's house without asking me. He had never done anything like that before, but it was an easier thought.

I ran door to door, knocking on any apartment where I knew a child lived. Tommy knew all the kids in the neighborhood who spanned in age from five to pre-teen. It wasn't the time to be picky. I didn't want to miss one possible place. I didn't care what type of relationship they had or how old the child was. I knocked. I asked if Tommy was there, or if he had been seen. I was not getting the answer that I so desperately needed to hear.

I quickly moved through the apartment complex, scanning my surroundings as I went. Nobody had seen him. As I made my way back to my apartment, I had a trail of kids behind me. They wanted to help. Some adults also joined in on the mission. I had one more place to check before calling the police.

Just outside my front door, sat the Abandoned Building. It was the place that all the kids were warned to stay away from. It could be dangerous. There were *No Trespassing* signs on every boarded-up doorway and possible entrance. My neighbors, thankfully, were right there to help.

I couldn't stop the flashes in my head of finding Tommy lying motionless on the floor inside of the Abandoned Building. The inside of the three-story building was never finished. The builder, it was said, had gone bankrupt and left the job unfinished, dangerous to young, curious children.

I climbed through the window where some older kids had ripped off the plywood that had been put there to keep them out. I stepped on the board that was spray-painted bright orange with the words KEEP OUT, on my way into the building. The plywood that had once guarded the empty, dark building no longer stood in my way. I ordered the helpful younger children to wait outside. I didn't want anyone to get hurt. I didn't know what I would find, once inside. The Abandoned

Building looked like a place that would also be attractive to the homeless. I tried to fight back the flashes of finding Tommy lying lifeless, on the ground, with a creepy, dirty man lurking nearby.

My legs were trembling as I cautiously made my way through section after section of debris-ridden, almost-built rooms. I searched as quickly as I could, making sure my older helpers were behind me. My heart was racing. My palms were sweaty. As badly as I needed to see my little boy, the Abandoned Building was not the place where I wanted to find him. Unless, of course, I found him playing and unharmed.

We combed the entire partially-built, three-story apartment building area for what felt to me to be hours. It was more like ten minutes. Everyone exited the building safely. There was still no sign of Tommy. None of his friends had seen him. My mother came up with nothing. It was time to call the police.

I was struggling very hard to keep it together while waiting for the police to show up. I didn't know what to do next. The waiting was driving me crazy. I paced around my apartment thinking of what I could possibly do. I had to call Phil. I didn't want to. I kept thinking it would all just end before things got too far. It didn't end. I was forced to keep taking the next step. I called Phil. I kept my voice as calm as I could, but he sensed my panic. He was leaving work immediately.

I couldn't stay in the apartment. I needed to get outside. I was suffocating. I was trapped. I had no control. I needed to run, but I didn't know where. When I got outside, it started to rain. It was a light rain, but it felt heavy on my heart. It meant there was definitely something wrong. It meant there was something wrong with Tommy. He never would have stayed outside in the rain. It was the last straw. My heart began to beat out of control. My head began to spin. I tried to walk it off. I tried to think of a way to distract myself from my panic.

As I paced up the walkway toward my mother, who was standing outside the front door with a look of deep concern on her face, a couple of young children were running toward me. I didn't really know who they were. I knew they lived in the complex because I had seen them around. I just didn't know their names. They weren't any of the many children who had been in our apartment at one time or another.

For a moment, it was the distraction I needed to keep my body from failing. They started talking before they reached me. It was two little girls. I had to tell them to slow down. I couldn't hear them. My hope faded quickly as I listened to their report. One of the little girls decided to do all the talking. "We saw a strange car earlier over by the dumpsters out front. There were two men in the car. They were driving real slow. We never saw the car before."

The other little girl nodded her head in agreement. "It was a big, old, ugly car."

I couldn't take anymore. I couldn't bear the thought of what was becoming a real possibility. I had no strength left. I had no more control over my emotions. My tears let loose in a flood of grief. My legs let go, refusing to hold my weight any longer. I put my hands to the ground to keep from falling all the way down. "Mom, I can't take this. I can't do this. Someone took him. Someone took my little boy. He would have come home when it started raining."

My mother's face told me that I was overreacting. That it was too soon for such a show.

The reality was, my mother's look was a look of feeling completely lost. It was a blank look. My mind filled in the blanks. I could only see that I was overreacting and I needed to regain my composure, immediately. My mother really just didn't know what to say. She didn't know what to do. "You don't know that, Susan. You have to keep it together. He's okay. We'll find him."

The first police cruiser pulled into my parking lot. I walked toward the officer to save time. Some of my strength quickly returned. I needed to work with the police. I needed to do everything I could to find my son.

I gave all the details that I had to the officer. I told him about my rule and how the rule had somehow been broken. I told him everywhere that I had searched. I told him about the strange car with the two strange men. As we talked, more police cars passed us on the main road through the apartment complex. "We have every police officer on this, Ma'am. We have more units at Cold Spring School. There was a report of a young boy, fitting the description of your son, spotted at the school. The rest are here. We're going to form a human chain and walk through the woods over there. I want you to go back in the house in case he calls you."

I didn't want to go into the house. I wanted to be part of the chain. I needed to keep busy. I knew that I would just pace if I went back in the house, but I knew the officer was right. I had to wait by the phone. My mother came with me. I couldn't be alone.

Twenty minutes was all I could stand. I was losing my breath again. I needed air. My mind had too much freedom to wander to dark places I could not bear to go. I wanted Phil to get there. I needed him to trade off with me. It had only been about twenty-five minutes since I had called him. I knew it would be about another five before he could get there. I couldn't wait. "Mom, I need to get some air. I need space. I have to go outside for just a minute. Can you wait here for the phone?"

Just as I reached the walkway outside my apartment building, a police cruiser was approaching the tarred turn-off next to the Abandoned Building. The turn-off was closer to me than the parking lot. There was just an old foundation and debris from halted construction to cross before getting to me.

As I strained my eyes to get a look inside the car, I saw a little blonde head in the back seat. It was my little boy! He had been found. I was never so relieved in all my life. When the officer opened the door for Tommy to get out, I could see his tears falling from his precious little face. He looked scared. I finally, did not.

I couldn't wait to hold him in my arms. I wanted to squeeze him hard and never let him go. I thanked God for giving my Tommy back to me as I ran toward the police car. The officer was taking Tommy's bike out of the trunk.

"I found him way down in the woods pushing his bike. He was afraid to come near me. He said he didn't know if I was a real police officer. I know he's in trouble, but you should be proud of him for that. I had to convince him to come with me. I had to show him my badge. He said he was just riding his bike down a path when his chain fell off. He stopped to try and fix it. When he turned around, there were two paths and he couldn't remember which one he came from. He took the wrong one and got lost. He's okay. Just a little scared." Tommy knew what to do to protect himself. I was proud of him for questioning his safety in trusting a stranger.

"I'm so sorry we caused all this commotion." I grabbed Tommy and held him tight. I wiped his tears from his face and kissed his forehead. I felt like the luckiest mother in the world.

"It's okay. That's what we're here for. I'm just glad it turned out the way it did." Then, to my son: "You mind your mother from now on. Ya hear me?"

"Yes, sir." Tommy shook his head up and down with the rhythm of his words to make doubly sure we knew he had learned his lesson.

"Your father's gonna be happy to see you, but he's gonna kill you for making him leave work."

"Dad's here?"

"He'll be here any minute. We were out of our minds worried about you."

"I'm sorry. Joey showed me this path they ride their bikes down. I wanted to try it. I'll never do it again."

Phil arrived shortly after we had gone back into the apartment. The tremor in his hands had become visible as he grabbed Tommy to hold him for a moment before delivering his first fatherly lecture. Phil loved his son. He couldn't bear the thought of something bad happening to him. I wanted my turn to hold Tommy again. I never wanted to let him out of my sight.

4

IMPRESSIONS

I had no choice but to let Tommy out of my sight. It wasn't possible to keep my eye on him every second. I adjusted to him going out to play without me and going to school. I struggled with Tommy going to his father's house for weekends. The struggle never ended.

I had gotten myself into parenthood before I was mature enough to make responsible decisions. I didn't realize, at the time, that who I associated myself with would help to dictate what kind of a parent I would become. Not that I ever regretted having a child, not for a moment. I just had my work cut out for me. I had a lot of protecting to do. Tommy couldn't protect himself. There were so many influential people around him, and the influences weren't always good.

Besides all the strangers in the world that I had to worry about, I had most of Phil's family to contend with. Most people who knew me felt I was overprotective and sometimes overbearing. They were wrong. I had plenty of reasons to worry.

Nonie was Tommy's great-grandmother. He loved his Nonie. He wasn't aware of how crazy she could be. He mostly knew the good parts. I was grateful for that. I was glad he called her Nonie. Most everyone else called her Ma, including me. To Phil's younger siblings, the siblings who didn't live in the house, she was Nonie also. Knowing who his relatives really were was important to me. Phil's family was chaotic enough without knowing who was who in relation to each other.

Nonie was crazier than a bed bug, as she would say. She was a happy crazy most of the time. Everyone thought of her as harmless, except for the time she threatened us with a gun. Tommy wasn't afraid of her. He loved spending time with her. She loved telling him her stories of childhood. I'm not sure whose childhood it actually was, but I don't think it was hers. She grew up in North Plymouth, although her stories told a different account. She came from a very rich family with a full staff of servants. Not that she couldn't have been rich living in North Plymouth. That part of town was once a very affluent area, but I don't think there were any large animal farms. I don't think North Plymouth is where she got her southern accent. The kids loved her stories anyway. They were animated. They were fun. They were told with love.

Nonie had this one story that she loved to tell over and over again. Tommy never tired of it. Neither did she. Nonie's farm had geese that were always chasing after her when she was trying to get her chores done. With all those servants, I wouldn't think she had chores, but in this story, she did.

Tommy would sit on the couch next to Nonie. He would sit as close as he could get, intently listening. In her story, Nonie didn't see one of the geese coming up behind her. Just when she least expected it, the goose bit her on the bum. She would press her fingers together in the shape of a goose beak and pinch Tommy on the thighs and belly. He would giggle every time he heard it, like it was the first time. He would say, "again Nonie, again." But Nonie wouldn't tell it again right away. She would save it for another time. The story never wore out.

My favorite memory of Tommy and his great-grandfather involved the Crazy Chicken. This was a yellow, plastic, ride-on push toy Tommy had as a little boy. He loved to bring his chicken to the top of the hill in the back yard and ride down to the bottom into the fence that surrounded the pool. Papa wouldn't let him do it. He was afraid Tommy would hurt himself.

When Papa wasn't looking, Tommy would drag that chicken out from under the porch and hop on quick before Papa could tell him no. He would be half way down the hill, bouncing all over the place when Papa would start yelling, "Goddamn it, Arlene, he's on that Crazy Chicken again! He's gonna kill himself!" Tommy paid no attention to the yelling. He was having a great time. The faster, the better. He would get only one ride, and the Crazy Chicken would have to go back under the porch until his next opportunity. Tommy loved hearing that story long after Papa died.

Tommy wasn't afraid of his Nonie, but she did make him afraid of his Papa. Fright was not her intention. Anxiety was not her intention. She was just trying to ease a sad, confused little heart. Papa died when Tommy was four years old. He had loved his Papa. He tagged along behind him every time he had the chance.

When Papa died, Nonie thought she would ease Tommy's loneliness and confusion. She told him a story. She told him that Papa was sitting on the moon, watching over him. That he was not really gone. That Tommy could talk to him anytime he wanted. Comforting words from a great-grandmother, she thought.

One night, not long after Nonie's story, I awoke to Tommy's sobbing, tremulous voice in the middle of the night. He was calling for his Mama. He came running to my bedside, "Mama, there's a man standing in my room. He's whispering my name." I picked Tommy up and held him on my lap to calm him. I could feel his little heart pounding through his red and blue racecar pajamas.

"There's nobody there, honey. It was just a bad dream."

"No, there is. He's standing by my closet." After a few moments, he was starting to settle, but he didn't believe my words.

Tommy reluctantly walked back to his bedroom, clutching my hand with a force older than his own. I could feel the weight of his body falling back behind me as I led the way.

When we reached his bedroom door, I could see the moonlight streaming through the blinds and landing exactly where Tommy's man was standing. It was his dead great-grandfather. Nonie's words were not comforting after all. Tommy no longer had just happy thoughts of his great-grandfather. Papa became a monster in his bedroom when the lights were out.

Tommy finally calmed down enough to get him to go back to sleep in his own bed, as long as I left a light on. My job was done for the night, I hoped. After I fell asleep, Tommy snuck back into my bed. He was so quiet; I didn't know he was there until the next morning.

It took some convincing after that night, but I thought Tommy finally believed that it was just a pretend story. He never had another nightmare about his Papa. None that he told me about, anyway. He only talked about happy memories, but for a while I found him in my bed, in the morning, more often than not.

I didn't consider Nonie's moonbeam story to be harmful. It was just a mistake. It was intended to make Tommy feel better. Nonie never did anything harmful to him, but that didn't mean she was always harmless to everyone else.

She loved me. She always stuck up for me when Phil was off with other women, running around while I was left home alone. Nonie always welcomed me into her home; she just didn't think right all the time. Sometimes, all rational thought would escape her mind, like the time she chased us out of the house with the shotgun.

Other than causing Tommy to have a nightmare, Nonie was good to him. They loved each other. I loved her, but I didn't want her to baby-sit. I had no choice. Even after the judge heard the shotgun story, he ordered that Tommy could be left in the care of Phil or his Nonie while visiting his father. Nobody else could be given the responsibility. She never did anything to hurt him and I came to trust her. Not because I wanted to; because I had to. It was the other family members who I couldn't trust.

I felt that Danny loved Tommy. He tried to be conscientious; as much as he was able. I asked him not to swear around Tommy. He seldom did. For someone so focused on getting as drunk as he could, as often as he could, he did pay attention to Tommy.

Danny liked to make him laugh as much as he liked to make his friends laugh. He started making up funny songs to sing to Tommy when he was just a toddler. "Tommy, Tommy goosester, kissed-a-kissed a rooster. Then he kissed-a-kissed a hen." Tommy would laugh as his uncle Danny sang and danced around the room, snapping his fingers and moving his legs to his own beat. Danny looked like a chicken, flapping his arms and knocking his knees together with every step he took. Most of the time he was good with Tommy, but sometimes he did have a lapse in judgment.

One of our neighborhood friends, Kevin, also had a

baby about one year after Tommy was born. The mother lived on the same street as Phil. Kevin lived closer to me. He wasn't exactly father material. He was one of the bad boys of the neighborhood. He was a thief. He was crazy. He liked to torture animals. I couldn't imagine him being a father.

Kevin had actually shot at my brother one day, thinking he was funny. After a game of Russian Roulette at Kevin's house, my brother got up to leave, thankful that he was still alive; realizing that he had just done the most stupid thing he had ever done in his life. As he was exiting the rear sliding glass door, Kevin told him to run. Connor looked back and saw Kevin standing there with the gun pointing at his head. "I said run!" Connor hesitated for a second, and then realized he had better take Kevin seriously. He wasn't sure if Kevin would shoot, but he knew it was possible, given his torturous tendencies. Connor knew he was crazy. He knew he couldn't chance it, so he took off running. Kevin did shoot. The bullet grazed the side of Connor's head just as he was getting around the stockade fence, and out of Kevin's sight.

Kevin seemed to settle down a bit after his daughter was born. He didn't suddenly turn into a good person. He was still immature and sadistic. I didn't think he was a good parent, but he was protective of his daughter. I thought it was his only positive attribute.

While Tommy was at his father's house one weekend, Kevin was there with his girlfriend and daughter. I went to pick Tommy up at the end of his visit. When I arrived at Phil's house, I noticed that his throat was marked on both sides with abrasions. I looked at Danny. "What happened?"

"Kevin lifted him up by the throat because Tommy hit Adrian."

"He's only seven years old."

"I know, and he didn't even do anything wrong. Kevin kept telling Adrian to hit Tommy. Then he told him to sit there and take it. He told him not to hit her back. Tommy got sick of it and he hit her back. Kevin got pissed off and grabbed Tommy by the throat. He picked him right up of the floor by the throat and held him in the air."

"Where is he?"

"I don't know. He took off."

"Why didn't you do anything?"

"I didn't know what to do. The kids were here." Asshole, I thought. I was almost as pissed at Danny for letting it happen. He could have, at the very least, done something about it afterwards.

Tommy seemed okay. He wasn't crying, but I imagined he must have been scared to death when it happened. I put Tommy in the car and drove right to the police station. I wanted Kevin arrested for assault and battery. I was told to go to the courthouse and file a complaint. The police officer at the desk told me that it was a domestic case. I told him that I didn't live with Kevin. I really didn't have any relationship with Kevin. I just knew him, so it wasn't really domestic. They took a picture of Tommy's throat and sent me to the courthouse anyway.

I filed my complaint. I filled out the paperwork for a restraining order. I didn't want Kevin anywhere near my child. I was so angry, I wanted to beat the hell out of him. I wanted to do to him what he had done to Tommy, or worse. I wanted to do to him what I had seen him do to a kitten years earlier. I wanted to stick Kevin in a microwave to see what happened. I knew I couldn't. I would have to go through the proper channels to get my payback. I would have to settle for a restraining order, then I would alienate Kevin from his friends.

Shortly before the restraining order expired, Kevin showed up at Phil's house for a cook-out. Danny invited him. I was shocked. I was angry. I told Phil to ask him to leave. Phil told me to let it go, and said that I really knew how to hold a grudge. I was baffled and feeling alone in my beliefs among over twenty friends and family. I knew I was right so I left with my son. Kevin stayed. Danny had one more drinking buddy to hang out with.

I had thought Danny was fairly harmless, as long as I minimized his influence over my son. I started to realize, over time, that I was wrong. I had expected too much out of him. I had assumed that Danny would always look out for his nephew. I guess my intuition wasn't quite sharp enough in my younger years. As it turned out, Danny was just a good-time buddy. You couldn't count on him for anything but a good drunk.

Anita turned out to be a little less influential than Danny. She was present less often than the other family members. She was busy dating or getting married most of the time. Anita did love Tommy, but she had other interests. Small children weren't on the top of her priority list. She loved to have a good time, but her good times were mostly with men. Anita loved to have sex more than anything else in the world, and she didn't care who knew it.

Money was also always on her mind and she was never able to keep it in her pocket for very long. There was never enough. If she didn't have any, she would find it. Anita was generous with her money, or whoever's money it actually was. She spoiled Tommy. The sky was the limit. When she was around, she showered him with gifts. I was just afraid her gifts would be confiscated as stolen property. Her intentions were good, but her lifestyle was questionable.

Anita was oblivious to most things concerning the well-being of a child. She ignored my requests to watch her mouth and her actions when Tommy was around. I was constantly reminding her not to swear. Feeling frustrated and tired of asking, I tried the swear-jar method. That didn't work. She got tired of listening to me, so she stuck twenty dollars in the jar and decided that gave her permission to swear as much as she wanted for the night. She missed the point.

I realized it was becoming a real problem when Tommy swore at my father, thinking it was just a courteous response. Tommy wandered into the kitchen. He was hungry and heard my father milling around in the next room.

"Can I have an apple, Bampy?"

"Sure honey, go back in the living room and I'll cut it up

and bring it to you."

"Okay, fuck you, Bampy." My father took off running down the hall. He couldn't let Tommy see him laugh. It had taken him by surprise. He knew Tommy was confused about his newly learned language. It did sound a little like thank you. The bad words would have to be carefully corrected, but preventing Tommy from learning them in the first place seemed hopeless.

I tried to pick my battles with Anita. There were so many to choose from. I knew all would be ignored if I found fault with everything. It was more important to prevent Tommy from learning how to steal or from seeing his aunty jump from guy to guy.

I just had to keep Tommy away from Anita while she was in her manic phase. That was when the most damage could be done. It took a while, but she eventually settled down with one man. Anita wasn't always around, so she wasn't involved in Tommy's life enough to make a big difference.

Aunty-Sister Sarah and her family were good to Tommy. She was one of two people in Phil's family who I allowed to baby-sit. From time to time, Tommy would spend the night at her house. The first couple of times that Tommy spent the night, Phil and I stayed with him. We wanted him to feel comfortable, and I wanted to make sure it was safe. I felt as comfortable as I could in a family like Phil's. I felt pressured to compromise. I couldn't have a problem with every one of Phil's relatives, but I was never completely comfortable. I always had a fear in the back of my mind that something would happen to my son. Most people would probably say that the fear was in the front of my mind.

Aunty-Sister Sarah and her family loved Tommy, and he liked to spend time with them. I was thankful that she didn't go completely crazy until Tommy was older and stopped going to their house. Her craziness started somewhat subtly and slowly grew out of control.

The first tip that something wasn't right with Aunty-Sister Sarah came when Tommy was about ten years old. She accused Nonie of murdering her own two year old son. She said she had memories of her mother throwing her brother Christopher against the cellar wall. Then she remembered her mother burying Christopher out in a cornfield near their Connecticut home.

Aunty-Sister Sarah went so far as to involve the Connecticut State Police Department. There seemed to be an investigation going on because she was always on the phone with them and always had reports to give the family. The police even interviewed Nonie over the phone. Nothing ever came of it, though. I don't know how true any of the story was. It just all went away one day. Nonie did say she had lost a son in utero. She had delivered a stillborn child. That was the only child she had lost. It certainly made me wonder, but I doubted a murder had ever happened. I knew the family was crazy, but I didn't believe any of them were capable of murder. If I had, I wouldn't have stuck around.

Aunty-Sister Sarah was always on a crusade. She loved to fight for a cause. My favorite crusade was fought against the town of Abington, where she lived at the time. She had Chronic Obstructive Pulmonary Disease. She was convinced that her illness was caused by the trucks that continuously drove past her house, emitting exhaust, while they sat at the stop sign in front of her house. She draped a huge sign across the front of her house, made of a bed sheet with giant letters written on it. The sheet said something about the president being involved with a conspiracy. Aunty-Sister Sarah won her crusade. The trucks had to take an alternate route, avoiding her house. I'm not sure if her C.O.P.D. ever progressed after the exposure to the exhaust was diverted. I never saw her again after that.

I could never leave my child alone with Aunty-Sister Linda and her family. There was no compromising with me. I was adamant. I would do anything to keep that from happening. Phil knew it, so he chose not to fight me on that issue.

I found out, after the fact, that Phil had left Tommy alone with them on a couple of occasions. The thought sent fear straight to my soul. I believed that Harry was a pedophile. I knew, in my heart, that he hurt young children. I desperately hoped that Harry didn't like little boys. Tommy seemed okay. He never acted strange around them, so I was pretty sure that nothing had happened, but I laid down the law with Phil. No compromising. No discussion. Phil knew I was serious. He agreed to my demands. I know he felt that I was being over protective, but I didn't care what he thought. I felt Phil had very poor judgment. He didn't care what I thought, but I don't think Phil ever brought Tommy to their house again. He knew, if he did, we were going straight back to court. That was the only way I could stop him.

The only time when Tommy would see Aunty-Sister Linda and her family was at the occasional wedding or holiday party. I was grateful for that. I was grateful that I had one less huge battle to fight.

Phil's biological mother proved my need to protect my son the most. There was nothing funny about her. I had a hard time calling Tommy's biological grandmother, grandmother. So I didn't. I called her Karen, when I chose to speak to her at all. There was nothing lovable about her. She was a bad seed. Mama-Sister Karen was mean spirited. She was sick. I could barely tolerate having Tommy around her at family functions.

Surprisingly, nobody ever called me overprotective for never allowing Mama-Sister Karen near my son. If she had to be present, I was there. It was enough for me that she didn't raise any one of her five children. She didn't deserve to be a grandmother. I did my job. I kept her away. As bad as her judgment was, she knew not to push me.

Most of the people in Phil's family who were involved in Tommy's life grew up a little and had settled by the time Tommy came along. Those who didn't, weren't around for me to care about. I didn't allow them to be around, but I didn't always have control over who was influencing my son. It drove me crazy sometimes. When Tommy was at his father's house for the weekend, I had no way of knowing what was going on. I didn't like not having control over my own child.

I tried everything with Phil to make him see what was best for Tommy. I tried rationalizing, pleading. I tried laying down the law. My efforts were mostly to no avail. Phil would yes me to death, then he would do exactly what he wanted to do. He usually completely disregarded my wishes. He disrespected my ability to make good parenting decisions. Phil could only see that I was overprotective and overbearing, that I sheltered Tommy too much. He was right to a point, but doing the complete opposite of what I did was not creating a balance.

It was bad enough that Phil would expose Tommy to things he never should have seen. To make matters worse, Phil would agree with me, then later lie about it. When Tommy was old enough, Phil would have him lie to me so that he could take his son wherever he wanted. So he could do whatever he wanted. When I caught Phil lying, he would say, "Tom needs to experience those kinds of things. If you completely shelter him, he won't know how to handle anything when he gets older."

There was no breaking through. We both held our ground. It never got better. It got worse. Phil felt that I was a good mother. I knew he loved his son. We should have found a way to compromise, but we never did. Our different lifestyles, along with our different parenting styles, eventually put an end to our romantic relationship.

Phil thought nothing of bringing random girls into Tommy's life. Some of the girls felt it their duty to act as part-time mom. Tommy didn't need a part-time mom. He had a full-time one who didn't need any help from them. I wasn't worried about anyone lasting too long. Long-term relationships weren't Phil's style. I was just worried about the collective effect it might have on my child. The constant change. The treatment they gave him. There was nothing good about it.

It wasn't all bad times at Phil's house. I wanted my son to know his father. Considering where Phil had come from, he was a good guy. I could be intense and unmoving when I needed to protect my son, but I would always forgive and forget because of the way Phil had grown up. I felt bad for him. I understood that he was doing the best he could. It just wasn't good enough a lot of the time.

Even though Tommy was subject to all the chaos at Phil's house, Phil remained sober when he had his son over for a visit. He might have one or two beers once in a while, but that was it. Even without alcohol, his judgment could be poor, so I was grateful that he was smart enough to stay sober and drug-free when his son was around.

Tommy had a good time with his father. They did boy things together. They played sports, rode the go-cart, went to dirt bike races. They hung out together. Tommy loved his dad. They were buddies. It was better than not having a father around at all. The male influence was good for him. I was grateful for that. Those were the good parenting qualities that kept us wanting a civil relationship after we broke up. It was best for Tommy, with the options we had.

Phil's attention to Tommy dwindled a bit when he found another interest. It was easy for Phil because Tommy would never say anything to his father that he thought his father might not like. Phil took advantage of Tommy's good nature. Most people did. I had to look out for him when I could. I had to speak up when something wasn't right, when something affected my son. Something that might hurt my son.

Phil got married when Tommy was seven years old. I could never bring myself to speak the word *stepmother*. Mother should never have been an adjective used to describe Pam. Pam had four children of her own. Three of them lived with their father. Rightfully so. I didn't know their father, but I knew their mother. The more I got to know her, the more afraid I became of her influence over my son, and the angrier I became with Phil for allowing our son to be exposed to her.

Pam and Phil had a volatile relationship. They cheated on each other. She was an alcoholic. He was a drug abuser.

They got into knock-down, drag-out fights. Tommy witnessed some of the battles. Some of the battles turned on Tommy.

Even though Pam was Phil's wife, I guess she didn't feel as though she had enough quality time with him. One evening, while Tommy was visiting his father, Pam wanted to go out drinking. Phil told her no. He had Tommy for the weekend and he wasn't going anywhere. Pam didn't like that and she became enraged. She started screaming at Phil while Tommy was sitting on the couch next to him. Pam turned her attention to Tommy. She screamed, "You're gonna let that little fucking brat run your life?" Eventually, Pam left for the day and the situation diffused. I was grateful for that, but I didn't want to send Tommy back there again. I had no choice. I couldn't keep him from his father, and Pam was part of the package. I wanted to make Phil change his decisions, but I couldn't. I had no control.

Keeping Tommy away from Pam was an ongoing losing battle. She was there to stay. There was nothing I could do about it but continue to try to prove my point. It shouldn't have been so difficult. There were plenty of signs.

Phil called me one evening after Tommy had spent the night at his house. Tommy was eight years old at the time. Phil said he wanted to talk to me about something before I heard it from someone else. It had something to do with Tommy. I didn't want to hear it. I needed to hear it.

"What is it?" My tone was cold. I knew he had done something stupid. It wouldn't be the first time, but I didn't know why he was telling me. He never told me about anything he did with Tommy. I always heard it from someone else.

"Tommy was lying on the end of our bed while Pam was watching TV. She caught him looking up her nightgown. She's concerned about it."

"What is she concerned about? Tell her to stop exposing herself to my little boy! The concern should be about her, not Tommy!" I couldn't believe it. I couldn't believe Pam had done what she did. I was even more amazed that Phil couldn't see it for what it was. As far as I was concerned, there were only two ways of looking at it and both were Pam's fault. Either Pam was making it up so that Phil wouldn't want Tommy around anymore, or she was giving him access to look. In my mind, any boy would look up a woman's nightgown, given the opportunity. It was natural. It was indecent exposure to a child.

Whether or not the peeking happened, the situation cemented my feelings about not wanting Tommy around Pam. Again, instead of having my warnings taken seriously, I was called over-reactive and overprotective.

My brain was shocked into permanent protection mode. It became a way of life. I was consumed with trying to shelter my child from all the chaos. All the damage. All the sickness. I didn't really look at myself as being overprotective. I didn't feel that way. It was just my job because of the way our life was. I loved my job. I loved being a mother more than anything else in my life. It was a good thing because I needed to be two parents much of the time. Tommy had one parent and one buddy. I had to do the protecting for two.

I didn't always know exactly what went on at Phil's

house. I couldn't. I didn't live there, but I had a good idea because I had lived there at one time. The judgment was not always good in that house. I would hear about things that went on after the fact. Things were not disclosed to me because someone felt that what Tommy was exposed to was wrong. Things were usually told to me because someone felt that what Tommy was involved in was cute, or they just wanted to cause trouble.

Tommy pumping a keg of beer during a party at four years old was not cute. My getting upset about it was not being overprotective. Having Tommy included in a game of quarters was not cute, even though he was given water instead of beer. My getting angry about it was not being overprotective. Constantly worrying about what Tommy was being exposed to did contribute to my overprotectiveness. There were many situations in which protection was needed. I just carried my instinct into every minute of every day. I felt that Tommy could turn into one of the people that he was exposed to, so I tried to shelter him as much as I could, while trying to change them.

I was not a perfect parent. I always knew that. I made my share of mistakes. Most of my mistakes were made with good intentions. Most were made out of love. Most of Phil's mistakes were made with an irresponsible, selfish mind. Phil had poor judgment when it came to kids. He just wanted to be a buddy. He wanted to be the good guy during the little time he had to spend with his son. His intentions were also good.

5

Good Enough

A wise man once told me that I only needed to be a good enough mother. It would be years later when I realized what that meant. It would be years later when I realized it was too late to heed my friend's advice. I don't know that I put much thought into Mr. Vitti's words. I thought he was giving me a compliment. I thought he was telling me that I was too good a mother. I guess I was in some ways, but I didn't analyze his words any further. I didn't know, at the time, that I could be causing damage to Tommy. How could being too good be bad? I couldn't comprehend that. There was no way of knowing the end result before we got to the end. I didn't have the foresight.

Tommy had a good life when he was a little boy. It remained near-perfect for many years. Life could have turned out differently if I had been a little more wise when I was younger, a little more insightful. I would have realized that Mr. Vitti's words were not a compliment. His words had been a warning. I perceived every situation as a life-or-death threat, or a potentially serious assault to Tommy's well-being. I misinterpreted his easy-going character, seeing it as an inability to ask for help, or to react significantly enough.

I proceeded to be a better than necessary mother, regardless of Mr. Vitti's warning. I continued to overprotect and coddle Tommy. I continued to believe that my son and I were one and the same. That I should speak for him. That my world should revolve around him. I was wrong.

I learned and experienced many wonderful things after becoming a mother. Parenting instantly forced me to grow up. I was young when I gave birth. I was still a bit egocentric. Having a child changed that. It was no longer about me, or what I wanted. Life suddenly became all about this precious, defenseless, dependent little being that I was responsible for. How wonderful it was to completely give myself to someone in need.

I learned what true love was all about. I learned how good love was supposed to feel. This was the ultimate love, love for a child to whom I would be bound forever. A love that could never be conditional on either side, that never fades. It would hold strong forever, no matter how difficult things could get, no matter how much stress or enjoyment I had raising Tommy. I was just a little too intense sometimes.

While I was in nursing school and working, I did trust my neighbor Joanne to watch Tommy after school. One day, when I got home, I knocked on Joanne's door. She answered the door with a look of concern on her face. As I looked past her, I could see Tommy standing behind her couch. His head was hung low. What I could see of his face, was red. He walked across the hall in silence. Something was wrong. He wouldn't tell me until we were in our apartment, but I had an idea before we got there. Tommy had on light colored jeans. When he stepped out from behind Joanne's couch, the front of his pants was all wet. It was very obvious what the problem was.

As soon as we had privacy, Tommy told me what had happened. He said that he had asked the lunch aide if he could go to the bathroom. Nobody was allowed to leave the cafeteria during lunch, so she said no. The children were given the opportunity to use the lavatory before and after lunch. Tommy did not take that opportunity, and was denied it when he really needed it.

It was not the first time Tommy had had that kind of accident. I had an appointment set up with his pediatrician to find out if there was a medical problem that was causing his incontinence. I thought that it was behavioral, but nothing I tried seemed to help. It was the first time he had wet his pants in school. The teachers were always good about letting Tommy go to the bathroom when he needed to. It was always urgent by the time he asked, and they knew what the potential outcome would be if they didn't let him go. The lunch aide apparently did not feel the same way.

When Tommy told me the story, I was irate. I couldn't wait until the next day to speak to the principal. It was not going to happen to my little boy again. He would not be embarrassed like that again. I made the call first thing in the morning. I told the principal that I would be coming down to meet with him. He cleared some time in his morning to speak to me, as he should have.

I was still angry when I arrived at the school. I paced around the waiting room, waiting to be called. They had treated my son like he was an animal. They weren't going to get away with it again. The principal was going to get a piece of my mind.

I entered the principal's office. Mr. Johnson sat behind his desk. He was a young, pleasant-looking man. His pleasant appearance didn't deter my anger. It was still boiling over after I entered his office. There was no way to settle it except to release it on the man who was sitting in front of me.

"Do you have a dog?"

"Yes."

"Do you let it out to pee when it scratches at the door?"

"Of course. I'm very sorry that this happened."

"I would like my son to be treated with at least the same amount of respect that you would give to your animal." I glared at him as I spoke through gritted teeth.

"I'm very sorry this happened. It won't happen again. I already spoke to the lunch aides. I told them to let Tommy go to the bathroom when he asks."

"I'm more angry that he was left to sit in his own waste. That is inexcusable. Why wouldn't he be allowed to change? He was made to sit in his own urine for half the day." I rose to my feet. I had to pace. I needed to release some of my pent up energy.

"I didn't know that. You're right. That is inexcusable. I'm very sorry. I will speak to his teacher. It won't happen again. Maybe the nurse didn't have anything for him to change into, but if that were the case, then you should have been called. I'll take care of this."

"I would appreciate that." I was surprisingly calm five minutes into our meeting. I didn't expect so much agreement. I didn't know what I had expected. I had figured he would be defensive. I had figured he would make excuses. The principal did none of that. He agreed with me. I felt better. I felt a little embarrassed for having acted crazy. For having been so angry. I was relieved that it wouldn't happen again.

I guess I went a little overboard in the principal's office. I needed to protect my son. I didn't realize at the time that embarrassment and minor injustices lent an opportunity for Tommy to learn how to cope on his own. Situations like that would prepare him for adolescence and adulthood. He didn't need his mother taking care of everything that happened to him. I didn't regret meeting with the principal, but I did regret how I spoke to him, how I handled the situation. I could have asked for Tommy's input. I could have tried to find out what his needs were. I should have been a little less intense.

Tommy never wet his pants again. I'm sure it was because he didn't want to feel embarrassed. It wasn't because I made sure he would never be treated like an animal again. And I'm sure Tommy didn't want me going to the school to fight his battles; not with the intensity that I displayed.

I didn't want Tommy feeling unprotected. I wanted him to know someone was there for him. I knew how it felt not to have anyone there to help. It was scary sometimes. When I was a child, I would get angry at my parents for not helping me. I can remember crying, praying that they would do something to help me out of some pretty embarrassing or stressful situations. They didn't, and I was forced to figure it out on my own. I was a much better person for it. I became independent early on in my life. I learned to overcome adversity, and I was now appreciative of my mother and father's parenting style. I wish I had realized that there was a middle ground, but it was all black and white to me. I never even considered that there may have been other options.

Not long after the incontinence episode, Tommy came home from school visibly agitated. His mouth was going a mile a minute before he got through the front door. I could tell from the dirt that was embedded into the knees of his jeans that Tommy's day didn't go well. I could tell from his torn shirt and the reddened area on his cheek.

I took his school bag from him and told him to calm down and tell me what happened. "There's this big kid, Billy, on the bus. He kept hitting me and saying stuff to me. I got sick of it, so I punched him when we got off the bus. We ended up getting in a fight and he ripped my shirt. He kept sitting right behind me and hitting me." Tommy's words were rapid and pressured. He was excited.

"Does he live here?"

"Yeah, he lives in this building. The next section down.

He's in fourth grade. He keeps bugging me. I hate him, so I hit him back."

"Just try to stay away from him. Maybe he won't bother you anymore now." I was a little concerned because Billy was older than Tommy. I didn't know how many friends he had. I didn't know what it would turn into, if anything. I didn't want Tommy fighting on the bus or at the bus stop. I was concerned that the school might consider the bus stop to be school grounds. I didn't want him getting in trouble because of this bully. I decided to let it go for the time being. Except my thoughts did not let go.

I was afraid for Tommy. I could only see his torn shirt and dirty knees. I only heard, "big", and, "fifth grade". I ignored, "so I hit him back". I could only see anxiety in place of excitement or mild agitation. Tommy just wanted to tell me about his day. I wanted to save him.

Tommy came home from school the next day upset again. Billy had hit him and taunted him all the way home from school, so Tommy punched him in the face again, leaving a bruise. It didn't look like the problem was going away.

I decided to get Tommy off the bus the next day. As the two boys exited the bus, they were calling each other names. Tommy stopped when he saw me. Billy continued to taunt. He was a very large boy. Twice the size of Tommy. My worry grew, even though Tommy seemed to be defending himself just fine without my interference. I just needed to have a talk with Billy's mother.

After dinner that night, I took a walk over to Billy's apartment. I could see a large woman through the sliding glass doors. I hoped that I hadn't just gotten myself into the same mess that I thought my son was in. My heart rate quickened. She was twice my size. She looked tough. She didn't look like the diplomatic type. I was suddenly wondering if I would be able to defend myself as well as Tommy had.

Billy's mother didn't introduce herself when she came to the door. She listened to me, but she didn't look particularly pleased to see me standing there. She looked bothered. She looked disinterested. I tried to be as diplomatic and as non-accusatory as I could. I just asked her to have a talk with Billy. She glared at me. I told her that I would have a talk with Tommy and see if the boys could either work out their differences or just stay away from each other. The large lady gruffly agreed to my request. I was hopeful that that would be the end of it.

There was fear in Tommy's eyes as he walked through the door with his friend the next day. Tommy and Mark were talking over each other. I couldn't understand a word they were saying. Mark finally shut his mouth so I could hear what Tommy was saying. "Mom, Billy's uncle threatened to beat me up!"

"What are you talking about? Uncle? How old is he?"

"Old. Like you." I didn't think I was old, but they had my attention.

"What happened?"

"When I got off the bus, Billy's uncle was waiting there. He said if I say another word to Billy, he's gonna beat me up!"

Obviously, my talk with Billy's mother didn't help.

"He's not going to beat you up. He's not going to do anything to you." I was irate. I was fed up. No adult was going to hurt my child. No adult was going to threaten my child. They didn't know who they were messing with. I was no wimp. They may have looked scary and tough, but when it came to protecting my child, I could take on anything. I needed to put an end to it. I just didn't know how yet. I needed to think about it.

Later that evening, a heavy knock pounded against my door, rattling the hinges. My mother and I were sitting on the couch talking. The banging made us both jump to our feet. I walked to the door as my mother stood far behind me. When I opened the door, my toughness instantly abandoned me. I was looking at this crazy woman, yelling and pushing a jumbo Lego toward my face. My brain could only interpret her words as static. I tried to take in the information that my eyes were reading, but my brain couldn't keep up. I was afraid for my safety. That was all I could focus on.

It was Billy's mother. Her wavy, black hair was unkempt and had a wet sheen to it. My eyes were level with the biker logo on the front her tight, black shirt. As my eyes scanned upward, they fell on a cloth covered neck brace. No doubt from the last person she beat up. I backed up quickly and leapt over the back of the couch in two steps. The angry woman continued stepping toward me, threatening me with her Lego. I had left my mother right in her line of fire. I had to get my guts back. "Get out of my house or I'm gonna call the cops! Ma, get the phone!" My mother just looked at me. She was frozen. She looked like a deer stuck in headlights. I had thrown my own mother to the wolves. I didn't feel so tough. I rushed around the couch and cautiously slipped by the woman on my way to the kitchen to grab the phone. My eyes never left Billy's mother.

The woman left my apartment as I dialed 911. My moxie was back. My words were impressive. I told the dispatcher the quick version. They said they would send a car. I was relieved she was gone, but my trembling remained for a while.

Officer House wasn't much help. He needed to rest for a few minutes after climbing the twelve steps to my apartment. He was out of breath and needed a drink of water before he could speak. When Officer House got his breath back, he took the report. He said there was nothing he could really do. The woman didn't assault me. She hadn't done anything yet. He felt that if he went to have a talk with her, she might retaliate toward me. I was thinking that she already was. There was nothing to lose. I knew that he just didn't want to be bothered with a petty neighborhood dispute. It was doubtful that he had the physical stamina to make it to her apartment, especially if he was to make it back to his cruiser afterwards. Officer House left with his little notebook miniaturized against his large trunk, as it sat in his left front pocket. I wasn't going to give up so easily. I couldn't. I wouldn't be bullied. I wouldn't allow my son to be bullied.

I called the school the next day to let them know what was going on. I thought someone at the school might be able to help somehow. I wanted the school to know as much as I knew, in case they got into a fight on school grounds. I didn't want Tommy to get in trouble.

The school counselor set up weekly meetings with the two boys to see if they could resolve their conflict. Tommy hated it. He thought it was stupid. I didn't make him go after a couple of sessions because of the direction the counseling took. Tommy left a bruise on Billy's face, so he was considered the aggressor. The counselor decided to meet with Tommy separately a couple of times a week to work on his anger issues. Tommy tried to explain that he was just trying to defend himself. He was just hitting back and he happened to leave bruises every time he did. He didn't have any anger issues. He gave up when the counselor suggested punching a pillow to let his anger out. I agreed that it was stupid and that he shouldn't go anymore. The counselor had missed the point completely. The boys still hated each other, but there were no more fights. I didn't have any further interaction with Billy's mother.

It might have been better if I hadn't involved myself in the first place. I seemed to have made matters worse. I almost got myself beat up; and I almost got Tommy beat up by Billy's uncle. The conflict between Tommy and Billy could have been a good opportunity for Tommy to independently learn how to cope with peer conflict. My interference didn't produce a resolution. Tommy resolved the conflict by defending himself. I'm sure there were many situations that could have been good opportunities for Tommy to learn how to grow independent from me. Instead, he became dependent on me. He came to expect me to answer for him, to protect him. He didn't always want my help, but he never said anything either way. He just went along with it, as he did with everything. My intensity was a minor frustration in his life.

Tommy was a happy, mild-mannered child, until adolescence. Other than having a crazy paternal extended family, and an overprotective mother, everything came easily to him. Schoolwork was easy. Friends came easily and plentifully. He had a natural athletic ability. He loved to play sports. Besides being born with so many natural attributes, other things came easily to Tommy, wonderful things. He was a lucky child. He seldom had any stress in his life. What occasional stressors he did have, I took on as my own. He was okay with life. I overreacted and needed to fix every unpleasant situation he was faced with.

I took Tommy on a trip to Florida when he was nine years old. We went to Disney World, Sea World, Typhoon Lagoon. We had a blast. The best part of our trip came while we were at Universal Studios.

While walking through the park, we noticed a long line of people and a sign. The sign read, "Do you want to be part of the 'What Would You Do?' studio audience?" It was Tommy's favorite TV show. We were excited to join the herd. We couldn't believe our luck. What were the odds of being at the park during the taping of Tommy's favorite show?

While we were standing in line, staff from the show were walking along, stopping to talk to the waiting people. There was a woman holding a clipboard and a man holding a television camera. There was a couple more staff just talking to random future audience members.

The crew stopped when they reached Tommy. The woman said he looked adorable with his blonde, spiky hair and farmer jean shorts. She loved the way one strap hung at his side. They asked him where he was from. They all laughed when Tommy replied, "Bawstin". They asked him to say Boston again. When he repeated the word, they all laughed again. Then they asked him to say the name of the man who hosted "What Would You Do?" They all laughed again and quickly asked if I was his mother. They wanted my permission to allow Tommy to co-host the show that day, if he wanted to.

Tommy walked with the crew as they escorted him back stage to prepare for the show. I couldn't wait to see him on stage. They gave us seats near the front. We were positioned perfectly in order to get the best view. Tommy ran pies out onto the stage, after introducing the host in his cutest "Bawstin" accent.

Tommy was an instant star when we got back home. The phone didn't stop ringing. He was a celebrity, and it would start all over again every time they would repeat that episode, which was pretty often.

Tommy's luck didn't stop there. Just after the fourth grade school year began, I received a call from a large department store. They said Tommy had won a contest. He must have filled out an entry form while we were shopping for school clothes. I wondered what the catch was. The woman on the phone said Tommy had won a college scholarship for one thousand dollars, a football package that included a New England Patriots jacket and four tickets to a game, and he was to bring one of the Patriots' football players to school for the day. She assured me there was no catch.

I couldn't wait to tell Tommy the good news. His celebrity status was still going strong, thanks to repeats and the popularity of the show, "What Would You Do?", and his status would climb even further when he walked into his school with a New England Patriots player.

Tommy wasn't the only one who got excited about his good fortune. His fourth grade teacher, Mr. Sampson, made the upcoming event school-wide. He scheduled an assembly, in the gymnasium, for the day Tommy was to bring his professional football player to school. He set it up so that Tommy would get his football package in front of the entire school. It would be presented to him by the football player.

Not only did Mr. Sampson turn Tommy's good fortune into a school-wide event, he turned it into a town-wide event. He called for a press conference to be held at the school one week before Tommy's visitor was to arrive. All the local newspapers were there. The excitement in the school was boiling over. Tommy was the most popular child in the school. Everyone wanted to sit next to him. Everyone wanted to go to the game with him. Tommy was a happy boy.

I received a phone call from Mr. Sampson one afternoon after the press conference was held. He told me that Tommy had gotten himself into a little bit of a jam. He told four kids that he was going to bring them to the game with him. Then he asked Mr. Sampson if he wanted to go with him. Mr. Sampson assumed his invitation came because Tommy needed a way out of the other promises that he had made to his friends. He felt that Tommy had just gotten swept away in all the excitement and might need a little help getting out of his quandary, and that maybe I should step in and make the decision for him so that Tommy could blame me. It would make it easier on him when he told his friends that they wouldn't be able to come after all. If I didn't step in, Mr. Sampson was concerned that Tommy would get overwhelmed and his great experience would turn into a negative, stressful event.

I agreed with Mr. Sampson. I had a discussion with Tommy about it that night. He agreed that it would be easier on him if I made the decision. I told him to pick one friend. The other two tickets would be for me and his father. I told him to choose the friend he spent the most time with. He chose his neighborhood friend, Mark. His other friends could blame me.

Tommy felt instant relief. He could enjoy the rest of his experience without anyone getting mad at him, without feeling any pressure. I fixed his problem. I did what a mother was supposed to do. I made things better.

Tommy and I stood in the front parking lot of the school on his special day. We were waiting for the football player to arrive. The teachers were having a hard time keeping the rest of the children inside the school. They were too excited to sit still. It was a good thing our football player arrived in a regular car, instead of the limousine Tommy and I were anticipating. The staff wouldn't have been able to hold back the crowd. Nobody knew he was there until we were almost to the entrance of the building.

The excitement exploded as we reached the side door. The children's cheers were deafening. Their spirit was contagious. Tommy and I walked in with the massive football player. The rest of the school trailed behind. The children's laughter was music to my ears. Mr. Sampson had done a great thing by including everyone.

The newspaper press came for the ceremony. Tommy would be in the paper for the second time. The gymnasium was packed with children and teachers. Tommy had his picture taken with the representative from the department store as he was presented with his college scholarship. He had his picture taken with his football player, as he was presented with a trophy, four tickets to a game, and a box of New England Patriots clothing.

Tommy sat in the front row after he had received all of his gifts. All the children tried to crowd around him on the floor as the football player talked to the children about the importance of school. He talked about staying away from drugs and listening to their parents. It was all surreal for Tommy. I was so happy for him. I was proud of him. He was a good boy.

On the day of the game, we were taken on a tour of the football field and the facilities. We didn't get to meet any more football players. We thought the players might come out onto the field while we were there, but they didn't. It was still a fun day.

We went to our seats before the start of the game. We

were seated two rows from the top of the nosebleed section; too far away to make out who the players were. We couldn't see where the football was. The man behind us was kind enough to lend us his binoculars once in a while so that we could see what was going on.

The highlight of the game came at halftime. It was the most visible event of the day. Tommy's face was easy to see, displayed on the Jumbotron, at the end of the field. It was a surprise to us. Nobody told us they were going to put his picture up for the entire stadium to see. The announcer told all the fans what Tommy had won. The people sitting around us recognized the little boy sitting among them and the cheers rang out. It was exciting. I felt proud of my son. The entire stadium clapped for him. There was something about Tommy that brought happiness all around him. His luck was something that everyone wanted a piece of. I would later wonder why that had changed.

I didn't want adversity interfering with Tommy's good life. I wanted to get him out of the projects. Our neighborhood had started out as a middle-class condominium association. As the housing market boomed, the condo values dropped. Autumn Hill was quickly heading toward government-subsidized rentals. I didn't want that for my son, so I decided to move.

The apartment I found wasn't in a great neighborhood either. It was only a couple of streets away from one of the toughest sections of Plymouth. The apartment itself was nice. It was in a building of four units. It had once housed the families of the workers of the Rope Company. After the Rope Company closed, many years later, the buildings were sold off and rented out.

Our landlord lived in the end apartment. Tommy's baseball coach and Boy Scout leader lived in the apartment next to them. I rented the one next to the coach. It was perfect. Tommy was friends with the coach's son. There were plenty of things to keep him busy and away from the bad section of Plymouth.

I wasn't worried about Tommy's safety until he came home one day with his friend Mark. He told me that he and Mark were jumped for his bike. Tommy wouldn't let go of his bike. He took a beating for it, but he came home with it. Mark said the kids threatened to shoot them the next time they saw them. Mark couldn't believe how tough Tommy was. He would not let go of his bike for anything. He had handled himself the best he could. I was surprised by Tommy's minimal reaction to Mark's words.

I panicked. I believed it was possible for Tommy to get shot. There was a history of shootings not far from where we lived. There were drug dealers and break-ins. There were drive-by shootings. I was afraid Tommy had come across some younger brothers of some bad people. I felt that moving to that neighborhood had been a big mistake.

I reacted immediately and drastically, without asking for Tommy's input. I only saw it one way. I had to move again. I didn't know there were other options. If I had, I'm sure I would have made the same decision, but I didn't even consider the possibility that what the kids were saying to Tommy and

Mark was just bravado. I didn't consider the possibility that Tommy and Mark were embellishing their story. I only heard the threat to their lives, so I removed Tommy from harm's way. I moved myself and Tommy into my friend Joanne's extra bedroom until I could find a better place to live. I couldn't take any chances.

6

Found Passion

Tom had always been a well-adjusted child, until he experienced a couple of major, unfortunate, and unfair crises. He had learned how to adjust to difficult situations early on. He had adjusted to a broken home and to the craziness in his father's family. He had even adjusted to the move away from his friends. He just didn't seem to have the ambition to change things when life became extremely difficult. Maybe he didn't know he could. He wasn't old enough to have lived through any truly major crisis, and to have come out the other end. He couldn't know it was possible until after he somehow made it happen.

Tom and I moved to Rockland when he was in fifth grade. I needed to move us out of Joanne's guest room as soon as I could. We had only been there for a couple of weeks when I found the apartment in Rockland. I didn't want to move fifty minutes away from family, but I wanted to finish my last year of nursing school and not have to commute an hour in each direction. I needed more time at home. Tom was getting older and had more freedom, which meant that he needed more supervision. I needed to be around as much as I could, especially after moving to a new town.

The center of Rockland looked like a ghost town compared to Plymouth. There wasn't much there, only a few stores and a bar where a well known bikers' club hung out. It was a small town. The buildings were painted in drab colors, and were long past needing a new coat. They were old and mostly run down. There was no ocean. I felt so far away from everything. I had always felt that way when I wasn't near the sea. It was a strange feeling. I missed my home as soon as I left it.

I didn't know anything about Rockland. Some areas looked like a typical, middle class, suburban town. Some areas looked poor. I didn't see any affluent neighborhoods. I'm sure they were there, just hidden from the unsightly part of town. It seemed like a quiet town. We lived about a half mile from the center. It didn't take long to find out that it wasn't the plain, quiet suburb I had thought it was.

Tom and I moved into a small, second-floor apartment in an old house. It was a nice house. Our space was small. There was only one bedroom. I gave the bedroom to Tom, and I used the living room as my bedroom after Tom went to bed. I had a pull-out couch that was uncomfortable. I had to pile my bed up with egg crate padding to make it bearable enough to sleep on.

Tom's room was enormous. I gave him my full-size bed.

He loved it. There was no room for the computer desk in the living room, so that went in the bedroom also. I found out later that it wasn't a great idea for him to have easy access to the computer. I didn't think he would be able to gain access to the internet without me allowing it, but he did.

The landlords were nice, but strange. They lived in the rest of the house. Their space consisted of the entire downstairs and half of the upstairs. There was a door that led from their bedrooms to Tom's bedroom. I didn't like that, so I put a deadbolt on the door. There was no sense in taking any chances.

Our first meeting with the landlords was a little bizarre. The mother and father felt the need to tell me all about the father's alcohol problem. He had been sober for some time. The Lord was their strength. They had two children; a boy and a girl. The son was introduced to me and Tom by name. There was a girl playing in the living room while we were there for the first time. She was not introduced to us right away. On our way out the door, the mother said, "That's girl." Tom and I just looked at each other before exiting through the front door. We didn't say a word.

Before we left, the landlords wanted to show us their above-ground pool that was in the backyard. We all walked around to the back of the house together, except Girl. What we saw next should have made me think twice about taking the apartment. I'm not sure why I went through with it. I guess I was desperate for a place of my own. I had usually had better judgment.

We reached the back yard, but there was no pool. There was a large round area in the dirt that looked like something was once there. There was definitely no pool. The family talked about the pool as if it were there. I didn't know what to say, so I said nothing. Tom and I just looked at each other again.

Off to the side of the "pool" were three water toys shaped like giant noodles. The mother said she had gone out and bought one for Tom after speaking to me on the phone and finding out I had a son the same age as hers. She wanted Tom to have a toy for the "pool". I said thank you. Tom said nothing. I thought maybe I had misunderstood something, but Tom looked as puzzled as I did. Girl and her family were bizarre, but they were very sweet. I took the apartment. I didn't have any choice anyway, because there was nothing else available.

Rockland bordered the city of Brockton, which I didn't know when I moved there. Brockton was a pretty tough city. I suppose every city can be. It wasn't Dorchester or Roxbury, but it was tough enough to worry about. The gangs, along with the drugs, spilled over from Brockton into Rockland. The fights also spilled over into our new town. It was all the more reason for Tom to keep busy. I only had one more year of school left, then we could move to a better place. We would both need to keep busy for the next year.

I noticed the announcement for basketball sign-ups in the local paper. Tom needed a healthy outlet. He loved sports and I had to do my best to keep him involved in good things.

Tom had never played basketball, but it was the only winter sport I thought he might be interested in. He didn't like skiing. I had taken him a couple of times when he was little. He had sprained his ankle and consequently lost interest. Skiing was too expensive anyway and it wasn't something that would keep him busy after school.

I suggested trying basketball to Tom. He wasn't crazy about signing up. I had to talk him into it. He didn't like to skate, so hockey was out of the question. He was only interested in sports, so basketball was the only choice left in the town we lived in. I strongly encouraged it, but I didn't want to force him. I wanted it to be something he would like to try. I needed him off the streets. Tom didn't argue, but he wasn't excited about it either.

The night that the sign-ups were held was the same night the coaches began the process of assembling the teams. It was sort of a try-out. They had to see how everyone played so they could make the teams as even as possible. A couple of coaches were mostly watching for talent. They were looking for the tallest, the fastest, the most talented. They wanted to know who to pick for the All-Star team.

Tom had never played a game of basketball in his life, but it was apparent right away that he was better than most of the kids on the court. He may have been better than all of the kids. He was tall, athletic, and competitive. He moved right for the game. He immediately felt completely at home. Tom just needed to learn technique and rules. One of the statements I kept hearing from the coaches was that Tom listened. He was easy to teach. They only had to show him something once and he did it right. They knew he would learn the game fast.

I had coaches and fathers coming up to talk to me that night about Tom's talent. They couldn't believe how natural he was, having never played a game before. I felt so proud. I was happy for him. They were telling me about the All-Star team. They thought he would make it with no problem. That would mean traveling to different towns to play. Tom was excited, and I was excited for him. Tom was an immediate celebrity. He always stood out in everything he did. He always came out on top without even having to apply much effort. Everything always came so easily to him.

I was so excited to watch Tom's first basketball game. He took off to the sideline to stand with his team as we entered the gym. I headed for the bleachers. I was feeling a little awkward being the only mother, but I wasn't going to let that ruin my excitement. The fathers were all nice to me. They liked Tom. They liked what they saw at try-outs. The guys were interested in how he would play in a real game.

Tom did not disappoint. He surpassed everyone's expectations. Watching him run up and down the court with such confidence filled me with pride. Tom was the tallest player on the court. He won his first jump ball to start the game. He won almost every rebound. Between Tom and one of his teammates, they scored almost all of the points. I was amazed at how well Tom compensated for his lack of depth perception. The doctors told me it was easier for a person to adjust when they were born blind than for someone who loses their sight later in life.

My heart was racing from the start of the game. My hands were sweating. My knees followed Tom as he passed by me on his way to the basket. As the ball dropped through the hoop, my body left the seat quickly, with my hands raised in fists of victory. I was his biggest cheerleader. Tom scored thirty-two points in his first game. He had found his passion. I loved every second of it. There was no place else I would rather have been. I didn't think about missing my home while I watched Tom play basketball. It was an exciting escape.

7

Stolen Innocence

Uncle Danny decided to have a cookout and wanted Tom and me to come. He suggested that we bring a tent for me to sleep in so that we wouldn't have to make the hour-long drive home later. Tom could sleep in his cousin's bedroom. The girls had one room and the boys had another. Everyone else had to set up a tent in the backyard. I hadn't slept in a tent in years. I didn't remember how horrible it could be, but it was better than driving home after a few drinks, so I packed the tent.

I awoke early on the morning of June 23, 1997 with an uneasy feeling. The sun was up and penetrating the boundaries of the tent with its warmth. I wondered if my neighbors were feeling as uneasy as I was. Stew, my childhood friend, left the tent to go into the house to use the bathroom.

I lay there thinking that it had been a nice family party. I had grown up with Phil's family and couldn't shake their company long after we had split up. I loved Danny's children. They were the only cousins Tom had that were close to his age. I thought it was important for Tom to have a relationship with them.

We had managed to keep most of the troublemakers in the family away for the night. Aunty-Sister Linda had shown up for a little while. She came with her two daughters and left Harry at home. If she had come with Harry, I would have gone home. She didn't cause any trouble. She just announced that she had a new ailment, one that nobody was aware of until that night. She now had Insulin Dependent Diabetes. Of course, she needed to give herself a shot while she had everyone around her. She asked me if I could help her out by administering her insulin. I welcomed the practice, even though I had a strong feeling that the syringe was filled with saline and not insulin. I was only a nursing student, but as far as I knew, the syringes weren't pre-filled with insulin, bearing no label. I didn't care. It would be good practice. I had none of the anxiety that I once had, as a nursing student, when giving a patient a shot. I gladly gave the shot to Aunty-Sister Linda. As soon as the attention was off her, she went home. That was fine with me.

The barbeque had been a success. The food was plentiful and the music was nostalgic. The drinks were kept manageable and fun. The camping was not as accommodating as I remembered from childhood, but it was safe. Nobody had to drive home if they didn't want to, or shouldn't. There was plenty of room on the acre of land for two tents. There was plenty of room in the house for all the children to sleep comfortably. There were plenty of woods for the children to explore in the daylight hours. It was worth roughing it for a night.

Stew came back to the tent, where I was lying awake. I could see that he was visibly shaken when he opened the front zipper. He told me to get up. His tone was low and serious. My uneasiness grew. I jumped to my feet and stepped outside into the warm, comforting, morning sun. I had never seen Stew panicked before. He was tense. He was trembling. There was an urgency invading his voice.

"Something happened to Tom. He's okay right now."

"Where is he? What happened?" I started for the back door, not sure if I was heading in the right direction. I could tell from the look on Stew's face that it was an emergency. I could sense his fear by the trembling in his voice. I was sure it was bad. I had only had that feeling of complete and utter panic once before. It was when Tom was six years old and went missing.

I was feeling it again. The fear was overwhelming. It consumed my entire body. I felt that familiar feeling as I headed for the back door. I prayed to God that whatever it was, things would turn out as well as they had after my first parental panicked experience. Stew put his hand on my shoulder to slow me as he tried to keep up with my pace.

"That guy Eugene came back last night after everyone was asleep. He went into the kids' room and did something to Tom." There was a moment of hesitation as I let this information make its way into my brain. I couldn't believe my ears. I wanted him to take it back immediately. I wanted it to be a sick joke. I would rather hate my friend forever than have this new information be real. Stew was not taking it back.

"Tom's in Johanna's room. I told him to stay there and wait for you." I shook his hand from my shoulder and ran to my child, telling myself to remain calm. I had to remain calm for him. Had to. Had to. Had to. He didn't need any more drama; whatever had occurred. I still didn't know what had happened. There was no mention of the authorities being called. I had no idea what I would find when I got to Johanna's room.

I will never forget the look on Tom's face when our eyes met. It will be forever etched into my soul. It was a look of deep sadness. It was a look too mature for an eleven-year-old little boy. It was a look that said, *I was just changed forever, mommy.*

I held my handsome, blonde-haired, blue-eyed young man tightly in my arms. He needed a safe place. He needed security. He welcomed my affection. After a few moments, we walked outside. I wanted to get him away from everyone. I wanted to know what had happened so that I would know what to do next. We stood on the side of the house, in the nook of the chimney. I almost couldn't bear to look at his un-innocent face. I had to hold his gaze. I didn't want him to think that he had done something wrong. I knew, instinctively, what had happened. I had an idea, anyway. His eyes gave it away.

Tom wasn't capable of saying very much. I did not push him. I just wanted something concrete to go on. He looked worse than what his words were telling me. I knew it was worse than what he was saying.

What broke my gaze were Tom's last words to me while standing in our private nook. "He's still in the house." I couldn't take the fear in his eyes. I couldn't believe that guy was still in the house. I thought it had happened several hours earlier. I assumed he was long gone.

"Stay right here. Don't move. I'll be back in a few minutes." I calmly walked away. I had to. There was no way my little boy was going to feel unsafe for one more second.

My rage was building as I neared the back door. I entered the kitchen quickly, not caring that I didn't close the door behind me. As I approached the dining room, I could see him standing in the living room, in front of the picture window. Stew must have read my mind because he jumped in front of me as my body lurched forward.

Stew couldn't stop me. Ten men wouldn't have been able to stop me at that moment. I broke through his blockading arms with ease, using the dining room chair behind me as leverage. I felt like I was flying through the air. I don't think I was. I think it was more of an out-of-body experience, a sort of depersonalization. I had no control. I was on him, swinging with both arms, fiercely pounding over and over. Danny and Lisa were holding him there while waiting for the police to arrive. I don't think they had expected me to beat the police to their prisoner.

I heard the crack of his head, smashing the window sill on his way to the floor. That was all I remembered until I was being pulled off of him. I don't remember the sounds of my fists hitting his flesh. I don't remember any sound. I don't remember feeling any pain with the impact of the blows on my knuckles. I don't remember any sights, any sounds, any feelings. Nothing. I don't remember what his face looked like because that would make him human and he was not.

I started to feel present again when I heard a muffled voice repeating, "Susan! Stop. You have to be here for Tom. You have to be here for Tom! Stop!" I stopped short. I did not want to get arrested. I couldn't leave Tommy like that. This monster was not going to take his mother away along with his innocence.

I forced myself back. Every millimeter of space that I allowed him was a struggle. The force of doing what was right for Tom was stronger. He needed me there. Tom won. Eugene broke loose from the arms that bound him. Danny and Lisa let him go and Eugene ran out the front door as I ran for the back. I couldn't allow him to set eyes on my child again. He didn't, and I was with my son once more.

I didn't want to stay in that house another minute. I'm sure Tom did not want to either, but we had to wait for the police. It was long from over. I wanted to take it all away from him. I wanted it to be my pain. All of it, but I couldn't. I had no control, no ability to fix it, no way to take it away. I couldn't accept that. It was tearing me apart.

The special victim's police officer was the best person they could have sent in such a horrible situation. He was pleasant and non-threatening in appearance. He had a young face and soft voice. There was something trustworthy about him. I don't think I could have talked to him if there wasn't.

Tom looked so small, sitting on that couch with the police officer. He looked younger than his years. He looked fragile. He looked broken. I just wanted to hold him and wipe away his tears. I wanted to wipe it all away. I wanted to put the innocence back in his face. I wanted to take the vacancy, with flashes of fear, out of his eyes. For the first time in my life, I wanted to take another human being's life. That man did not deserve to live. I wanted to be judge, jury, and executioner. There was no need for a trial. I knew what he had done. It was written all over my little boy's face, the face that had once smiled, the face that had once brought smiles to everyone around him.

I had an intense desire to turn back the clock. I wanted, with all of my being, to have the chance to prevent what had happened. Just one more chance to protect him, one more chance not to fail my child. One more chance to protect him from what I had vowed to never let happen, one more chance not to let my guard down. I had done it for eleven years. I was only pleading for one night back. Six hours? Three hours? Whatever it was. I would give anything for the time.

I had known there was something about that guy that I just didn't trust. He was the only person there that night that wasn't family. He had just shown up, uninvited by the hosts. I had asked who he was, because I wasn't comfortable with him. He was apparently the friend of a cousin. I still had not liked him.

There was nothing that really stood out. It was just my

instincts. He was quiet and pleasant enough. He didn't show the children an obvious, inappropriate amount of attention. I still didn't like him. He had left the party early, and I thought it was over. I was wrong. He had come back after everyone had fallen asleep. Eugene had invaded the home, making it no longer a safe place for children. It was now dark and ugly, a place to which we no longer ever wanted to go. I shouldn't have let my guard down.

I had seen this man one time before. It had been another strange encounter. He had shown up, months earlier, to Anita's wedding reception, uninvited. Anita's younger brother, Robbie, asked me who he was. I told him I had never seen the man in my life. Robbie said he didn't like him. I agreed. There was nothing either one of us could put a finger on. We just didn't trust him. Robbie asked him to leave the reception. He left without incident and I hadn't seen him again until the cookout.

My initial instinct should have been enough. It was so clear to me later. I racked my brain for an image of him playing with the children. There was none. I searched my memory for an image of him watching the children. There was none. I didn't connect my distaste for him to the children. I should have. My intuition was yelling at me to pay attention. I didn't do it long enough. I didn't listen intently enough. I failed.

If I couldn't have time back, I just wanted some normalcy for Tom. I wanted to get him to a place with no reminders, except for what was in his head. I wanted him to be around people who didn't know, so that he would feel more comfortable, so he could feel a little more normal. I could not do that either. We were trapped in a horrible nightmare.

After meeting with all the children individually, the officer met with the parents while the kids were in another room. I felt myself unraveling while he was talking to Tom. I was thinking that he was talking to him for too long, longer than anyone else. Something was wrong. I felt it in my bones.

When the police officer came to talk to me, he said that what happened to Tom was worse than Tom could say, worse than he could bring himself to talk about. He wasn't just touched. The police officer's voice became muffled in my head. He told me that he had been a special victim's officer for a long time and knew it was more traumatic than Tom was capable of admitting to.

My legs started to tremble and burn. I didn't think I had the strength left to hold myself up. The officer brought me back. He told me I had to keep it together as he watched my tears flow down across my cheeks. My knees began to buckle. I forced my mind into thinking, what next? What do I need to do for Tom? I needed a plan to focus on. I struggled to pull myself together for Tom. It wasn't about me or my failures. It wasn't about the pain I was feeling for my child. It was about Tom.

I called Phil and asked him to meet us at Jordan Hospital. I would be waiting by the emergency room, at the ambulance entrance. Tom didn't go to the hospital by ambulance, but the police wanted him to go through a private entrance without having to wait in line for hours. They wanted him to have some privacy.

The sexual abuse examiners team was on their way to meet us. The doctor was already there working his regular shift. Life was moving too fast. Staying out of my own head was a battle that I was constantly on the verge of losing. There were unpleasant thoughts there. There was rage there. There were feelings of complete failure about the part of my life that meant the most to me. It was not a good place to be. I needed to stay present. I needed to do what Tom needed me to do.

Phil was not yet aware of the events. I just told him that he needed to come to the hospital right away. Tom was okay, but he wanted his father to come. I didn't want to tell Phil over the phone and risk his getting in a car accident on the way. I wanted to tell him face-to-face.

Phil arrived all the way from Middleboro in record time, only a few short minutes after we arrived. It had taken a long time for us to leave the house. The police had had to collect the evidence. They hadn't wanted to miss anything, so we had stayed to point things out. I stood in the kitchen and watched the men in latex gloves pile belongings into large brown paper bags. Belongings that became the property of the state. Belongings that were no longer welcome in that house. We left for the hospital.

When Phil arrived, I gave him the short version. I preceded the story by saying that Tom needed him to keep it together. He needed him to remain calm. It sounded funny in my head. It sounded hypocritical because I was barely holding onto my own sanity. Somehow, saying it to someone else, saying it out loud, made it feel concrete in my body. In my brain. I was saying it to myself as much as I was saying it to Phil.

Logically, I knew the steps that were being taken inside the exam room, but it felt new to me. I had read about it in nursing books. I had held the evidence collection packages in my hand. I had even looked into becoming a Sexual Abuse Nurse Examiner myself. This was different. This was personal. It was cold, routine, scientific. It was necessary. I no longer aspired to be a SANE nurse.

I was drained of every bit of energy in my body. I felt heavy. I felt weak. The only part of me that couldn't stop was my brain. I needed drugs to quiet my mind. I hated drugs. I didn't even like to take Tylenol when I had a headache, but I wanted drugs. I just didn't have the energy to find them. I didn't have the energy to ask for them. I just wanted to sleep. I wanted it to all go away.

When we got home, I stood in front of the bathroom mirror brushing my teeth. I looked awful. Blackness was invading the fair skin around my eyes. There was no shine to my blonde hair. It just hung, limp and lifeless, from my head. I couldn't remember a time when I had looked so bad. I needed sleep.

The first of my recurring nightmares came that restless night. It was fresh in my mind when my eyes opened to start the day the next morning. There was no escaping the crisis. It had really happened. My nightmare assured me of that. It was unsettling, but my role in it was strangely satisfying.

The prison bus was headed down the long dirt driveway toward the prison. The prisoners were lined up, seated along the inside of the bus facing each other. They were shackled to the floor of the old school bus. My prisoner was among them.

I could see the big, brick building approaching quickly. The spiraled barbed-wire that topped the electrified fence was becoming clear in my vision. I was running out of time. I had to act fast.

I was crouched behind the seat that my prisoner was assigned to. The prisoner that stole my child's innocence. The punishment would be death. I rose to my feet, holding my butcher knife above Eugene's head. I wanted him to see it coming. I couldn't linger too long. I didn't want to be stopped. I swung my arms down across Eugene's orange, prison-garb covered chest and slashed his crotch wide open before plunging the knife deep into his chest.

I awoke in a panic. Blood clouded my vision. My heart was racing. I was afraid, but relieved at the same time. I was afraid because I had just murdered someone. I was relieved because it was my demon that I had murdered. It was the only relief that I would find for a while. I looked forward to sleep. I looked forward to my nightmare. I didn't look forward to the mornings. Every time I woke up, I knew what I had to face. I was reminded of the nightmare that I had to live every day. I preferred my nighttime nightmare. It felt so good to kill him. It scared me that it felt so good.

I lay in bed that first morning, not wanting to face the day. An overwhelming feeling of failure had crept into my brain. I was a complete and utter failure as a mother. Everything I had worked for in the preceding eleven years was all for nothing. All the time and effort I had spent protecting Tom was a waste. When it came right down to it, I hadn't been there. When he had really needed me, he couldn't count on his mother. I had blown my one chance at the most important thing in my life, being a mother to my child. It was the most important role that I would ever have. Being a mother was who I was. I could never get that chance back. It was over. I had promised myself I would never let that happen to him. I had let myself down. I had let my son down. I had let my family down. Everything good I thought about myself was ripped away in one night. I had failed my son in the worst possible way.

I got Tom ready for basketball camp the next morning. I didn't tell him what his options were, even though he did have a few. He could go to camp. He could stay at home. He could come home early. Whatever Tom had needed to do, I would have been there to support him, immediately. He didn't ask. I felt that he needed to live in the present. He would be thinking of the past enough. He needed his friends. He needed the distraction. He needed basketball, if he was capable.

While Tom was at camp, Phil and I headed to the courthouse for Eugene's arraignment. The old, dirty halls were filled with family and strangers. People were shuffling along the cracked linoleum floor. The walls were lined with local reporters. The story had gotten out. I threatened the reporters with the biggest lawsuit they would ever see if they even insinuated who the child was.

The guards walked Eugene by us. He was dressed in an orange jumpsuit. Shackles bound his arms and legs. People began to yell at him. They spit on him. Strangers joined in when they heard what he was. I could only faintly hear what they were saying because I was waiting for my opportunity as he passed me by. I didn't waste it. I got him right in the face. It felt good. I didn't feel disgusted with myself for spitting in someone's face. I felt a little relief watching it cling to his cheek. I didn't feel bad because he wasn't human. He deserved worse, but that was all I was allowed at the time.

Phil was surprisingly calm. He was preoccupied. His behavior was nagging at the back of my brain. If I hadn't been so focused on not missing my opportunity, I may have been worried. There was definitely something different going on in Phil's head. He was acting strange. He was quiet as he sat in the courtroom while everyone else was jamming the halls. Security had to bring Eugene back to lock-up so they could calm the crowd and clear the corridor. They needed a plan before someone got hurt. Phil remained in the courtroom while they formulated their plan.

They opened the courtroom again, but only to friends and family of Tom and his cousins. We entered through the double doors at the end of the short corridor, leaving the reporters behind. Phil rose to his feet and began directing everyone to where they were to sit. He said he just needed to be able to see and hear the judge. It was unlike him, but he was the father and everyone respected that. We gave him his space.

As they brought Eugene through the doors, I turned to look at Phil. He was sitting funny. One foot was on the bench, crunched under him. It was only a few, short steps to where the prisoners were seated, but Eugene did not make it there. As he passed by us, Phil leapt high in the air, diving straight back down with his fists leading the way, pilling Eugene's body into the bench that was beside him.

Everyone watched in shock as Phil's fists drove into Eugene's face, over and over again. Nobody tried to stop him. We watched with pleasure. The courtroom erupted in chaos. The judge was ushered into his chambers. All the court officers rushed the scene, but not before Phil did some serious damage. The three officers who were Eugene's escorts were not strong enough to stop Phil's fury.

Phil was dragged from the courthouse and put into the back of a cruiser that was waiting by the side door. Eugene, once again, was rushed back to lock-up. The courtroom was cleared until they could safely bring Eugene and the judge back in. The arraignment took place without Phil. He didn't care. He had accomplished what he had come for.

Phil was later charged with disorderly conduct. He was given a tongue-lashing by the judge for making his courtroom unsafe. He was fined two hundred dollars, with two years to pay off the fine. He was then released with an invisible pat on the back.

We later saw a picture of the damage that Phil inflicted on Eugene's face. The picture was taken by a reporter. I'm not sure how or when the reporter had gained access to him because the court officers had rushed Eugene out of the courtroom in a shield of bodies. The pictures were powerful. Eugene's face was completely black and blue. He was unrecognizable with all the swelling and hue in his flesh. The picture was displayed in the newspaper for all to see. I felt a little satisfaction.

8

TROUBLE

Life had drastically changed for Tom. He was a different person. I understood that he had been through a lot. I understood why he felt life had turned its back on him. He had reasons for being angry, reasons to give up on life. But I didn't want that to happen. I knew there was another way. I knew life for Tom would be full of disappointments, just like it was for everyone else, but he couldn't give up. He had to fight. I knew he could make it, despite the disappointments.

I noticed that Tom wasn't taking care of himself like he always had in the past. He had always kept his hair short, in a fade-style cut. He knew the numbers that the hairdresser needed to use to make his hair perfect. He had always dressed nicely, with matching pants, layered shirts, and sneakers or Doc Martens. He had always looked neat and well-dressed. He had always cared about the way he looked. Watching Tom let himself go was upsetting to me.

Tom never had time to get his hair cut. Suddenly, I was after him to get it done. Before, he had always been the one to ask me to make an appointment for him. Suddenly, I was asking him if he wanted me to iron his clothes. He was always the one to put his clothes together and decide what he was going to wear. When I asked him why he wasn't taking care of himself anymore, he would just tell me that it was the style.

Life went on despite the trauma Tom had experienced. He didn't want to see a therapist, but he went because I asked him to. No matter how many therapists I brought him to, it never worked. Tom denied anything was wrong. He refused to talk about his issues because, he said, he had none. He would talk about sports. He would talk about anything pleasant. He would say that he didn't need to be there, and the therapist would agree with him. I didn't want to force him to continue. He didn't need to be angry about anything else. He would have to figure out how to deal with what had happened in his own way. All I could do was try to show him options and be as supportive as I could. I needed to do what Tom needed me to do. He just never told me what he needed from me.

Tom found his therapy in basketball. He loved it. He was a fierce competitor, but always a nice person. The game took him away from everything bad. The court was where he needed to be. I was grateful when he joined the summer league.

Finding basketball also made living so far from home a little easier. It kept us busy doing something we both loved. We visited our friends and family in Plymouth often. In the summer, we spent almost every weekend there. We needed loved ones around us.

Tom never missed a basketball game. Nothing could keep him away. He was obsessed with the game. It kept him busy and happy, securing the smile back on his face. I never missed a game either. I went to every town game, All-Star game, and summer league game, cheering every point. It may have been Tom's therapy, but it still wasn't enough. Trouble began to find him.

Tom looked concerned when he told me that he needed to talk to me about something. He had my undivided attention. "What's wrong?"

"There's a gang here in Rockland. They have a junior gang too. The juniors are the kids that are too young to be in the real gang. The older kids want to prepare the younger ones to join them when they're old enough. They tried to recruit me today."

Initially, I was thinking that it probably wasn't serious. We had had a gang in Plymouth when I was growing up. I figured every town did. They were just a bunch of tough kids that hung out together. The Bandana Boys hadn't really been much of a gang. They had gotten in a lot of fights, but I don't think that qualified them as a gang. "What did they do to try to recruit you?"

"A couple of older kids from the real gang came up to me after school. They had weapons. One had a pipe down the leg of his pants. The other one had a gun. They told me I had to join and that I would have to carry a weapon." It sounded more serious than I originally thought, more serious than the Bandana Boys. I kept Tom home from school the next day so that I could investigate and keep him safe at the same time.

I went to the school first thing in the morning. I asked to speak to the principal. I was shocked by what he had to say. He told me that gangs were on the rise. The school was aware of the problem and he wanted us to stay in town. He didn't want decent people being run out. After hearing his words, the decision was easy and immediate. We were leaving. It wasn't our fight. We already had a tough enough fight on our hands. We were facing Eugene's upcoming trial.

I told my landlord that night that we would be leaving the next day. I explained what had happened and that I couldn't take a chance on sticking around. I was a tenant-at-will, so I paid the following month's rent, giving them time to find a new tenant.

Tom was not upset about the sudden move. He was relieved. He was excited. He couldn't wait to be back with his old friends, in his old school. He needed the move. I knew he couldn't handle a gang problem after what he had already been through.

I knew it was the right move when I brought Tom into his old school to register him. He was instantly happy when we walked through the doors. He saw some of his old friends and teachers. He looked like the old Tom. He looked carefree again. He didn't like having to live in my friend's parents' finished basement, but it was the best I could do in one night. It was temporary. Tom knew that I would find a place of our own. He adjusted okay.

We moved down to South Plymouth shortly after the conclusion of sixth grade. Tom liked the basketball team in that school. I wasn't so sure I wanted to live in that part of town because it seemed so far away from everything. It felt like a different town. There were different schools. Everything would be different. South Plymouth was a quiet, more rural area of Plymouth. Maybe that would be good, I thought. There were no housing projects in that part of town. There were no trouble areas. I thought it might be good for Tom. He really wanted to go, so I figured I would give it a shot.

I remember one evening, after moving to South Plymouth, when Tom and I had a talk. He was twelve years old at the time. It was the calm before the storm. I didn't see the storm coming. He said he was happy. He loved living back in his old town, spending time with friends during organized events. He was having a great time at his basketball tournaments.

Tom had always been too social. It was a statement that had described his behavior his whole life, but lately, unless he was at an organized event, he chose to stay in the house. I was always after him to get out and play, but he never would. I didn't know why he was being like that. I thought that kids just didn't know how to play outside anymore. They were so programmed to watch TV or play video games that they didn't want to go outside. That was part of it. The other part, I was about to find out about.

Tom looked stressed one night when I pressed him

about why he wouldn't go outside to play. He was obviously struggling with something. He said, "Mom, I don't want to leave you alone. What are you going to do?" I couldn't believe he was asking me that. I was shocked that he had put that much thought into the way I might be feeling. I was shocked that he worried about me that much. He should have been worrying about himself.

I told Tom that he didn't have to worry about me. I did not need him to keep me company. I was fine and it would make me happy for him to do his own thing. He needed to spend time with his friends, making his own life. I told him that I would be there when he came home. He was supposed to do those things. It was okay. I didn't realize that my words were saying something different from my actions.

My actions, for the previous twelve years, had been telling him something different. I was teaching him to be too dependent on me, teaching him that our lives were one and the same. In retrospect, staying at home was the best thing Tom could have done. I couldn't leave well enough alone. I could have begun my separation without pushing him out the door.

I needed to keep Tom close, but he was confused about why I needed to keep him close. It wasn't for me. It wasn't to ward off my loneliness. It was so that he would be safe. We both worried too much about each other. I thought by pushing him out the door, I was giving Tom his freedom. I released him from his feeling of responsibility for my loneliness, and he was off and running.

Most of Tom's friends were on his basketball teams. He

was very involved in his sports, so he saw them often. I thought that by keeping Tom involved in sports, it would be enough to keep him out of trouble. I happily spent most of my free time taking him to all of his sporting events. There were more mothers involved in Plymouth basketball than there had been in Rockland, so I felt more comfortable there. Tom settled into his new routine nicely.

The South Plymouth basketball try-outs were like the Rockland sign-ups all over again. Everyone was in awe of how talented Tom was. It was even better because he actually knew how to play at that point. He was the best in town. He was immediately picked for the All-Star team at the regular season try-outs.

Tom also tried out and made the Amateur Athletic Union team out of Marshfield. He was on three teams by the time he was in seventh grade. I was worried it would be too much, but it never was. His grades were always good and he was never too tired. The more basketball Tom played, the happier he was. He was picked to play first string on every team he played for, so he didn't see the bench much. We traveled around the state a lot with his All-Star and AAU team. He still never got tired. He would just get more excited, and he was exciting to watch.

I loved going to Tom's games. He usually led in points and rebounds. He wasn't a leader in assists because everyone else was assisting him. All his friends looked up to him. He was the tallest boy on the team. He had a slight beard at twelve years old. He wasn't full of himself. He was still a team player, even with all of his talent. The younger kids looked up to him and aspired to be just like him.

Tom loved his hometown team. His best friends were the All-Star kids. They had so much fun at their tournaments. Tom would lead the pack into the gym, wearing his leather jacket, and sporting what little beard he had. They felt on top of the world. They would have the stands wild with cheers and boos.

Tom's All-Star team was superstitious. They had funny little rituals they had to do for every game. They had to eat a Snickers bar before the game. They had to wear one sock up and one sock down, and they had to be green. Tom and another boy had to have a bowel movement at the school they were playing in before the game. They said that they felt better afterwards. It wasn't planned. They just got the urge every time they entered the gym. Weird.

Tom's All-Star team was undefeated in seventh grade. They were flying high on adrenaline. The high school coaches couldn't wait for them to reach ninth grade. They were the talk of the town, especially with Tom being in the local newspaper almost every week, sometimes on the front page.

Tom had a great group of friends. They started to hang out together a lot. I loved having them over the house. Sometimes the whole first string would spend the night after a tournament. Tom was happy. I knew he would be okay.

Tom also liked living closer to his father. Moving back to Plymouth was easier on all of us. It was easy for Phil to stop by to see his son. It was easy for us to visit him. The room Phil rented in his friend's house was only twenty minutes away. Everything seemed to be working out.

9

TRUE CHEMISTRY

One hot, Saturday afternoon, Tom and I went to visit his father. We were sitting by the side of the house, on the beautiful two-acre grassy lawn, chatting. The sun was shining in the clear blue sky. I was distracted by Phil's landlord, Dave. His shirtless image was more interesting to me than Tom and Phil talking about sports.

I couldn't stop my eyes from watching Dave work on his house. I was thinking that it would be wonderful to meet a man just like him. I had known Dave long enough to know what kind of person he was. He was a good, hard-working, responsible man. And he was a great father.

Dave was pleasant to look at. My eyes traced the hard lines of his biceps and triceps as he held the weight of a section of his front porch. His soft blue eyes wouldn't allow me to look away. They were comforting to me. I could tell they were filled with security in himself, and for anyone he cared about. It was too bad he was Phil's friend. Phil was married, but it still wouldn't feel right. I saw no signs that he was interested, but I felt a strong chemistry whenever we were together. I thought it was one-sided.

Dave came to my college graduation party. I invited him, but I wasn't sure if he was going to come. I was glad to see him walk through my front door. We had always had a good time together. He was a little shy, but completely comfortable with who he was. I understood that. It was a nice quality to see in such a good-looking guy. It was a rare quality. We were comfortable with each other.

After having a few celebratory drinks, my inhibitions started to fade. I couldn't stand having the feeling I had any longer without saying something. We had known each other for fourteen years. I had had a crush on him for twelve. I didn't want any more years to pass, so I decided to speak my mind.

We found ourselves standing in my garage alone. "I know you're a friend of Phil's, but he's been married for quite a few years now. Why don't we go out to dinner and see if this chemistry I'm feeling is mutual?" Dave grabbed me and pulled me in close to his body. He kissed me without saying a word. My legs went weak. I didn't expect his response.

"I didn't think you'd be interested in an old guy like me."

"Old? You're only twelve years older than me. That's not old, but what about Phil?"

"Like you said, he's married. He'll just have to get over it. We should get back to your party, though. You might be missed."

"I suppose you're right, but I like it better down here." I didn't want to go anywhere. I was perfectly happy right where I was, but I knew he was right. I couldn't neglect my guests.

As we reached the top of the stairs, Dave pulled me across the hall and into the bathroom. He backed me into the wall as he kissed me again. His shyness was gone. "I just had to do that one more time before I go. I'll talk to Phil to see how he feels about this. I'm going to tell him that I want to take you out on a date. I'll call you tomorrow and let you know how it goes."

The next morning, my phone rang. The caller ID displayed Dave's number across the screen. I felt like a kid. My heart began to race. My hands began to sweat. I was nervous. It was the first time I had felt that good about a man.

"I talked to Phil on the way home last night. He doesn't have a problem with us going on a date, so how about lunch? Are you busy today?"

"No. Today is good."

"Do you know a place near you?" I couldn't think, but I said yes anyway. There were plenty of restaurants to choose from. I just had to slow my brain and decide which one would be good for us.

"I'll be there at twelve. Is that okay?"

"Twelve is perfect. I'll see you then." I couldn't wait to see him again. I had never looked forward to spending my day with a man as much as I did with Dave. I had no fear of things turning out badly. I felt no self-consciousness. I just wanted to be with him. I had fun with him. There was never a lack of conversation because we had a lot in common to talk about. We both understood what it was like to be a single parent. We could both be ourselves.

Lunch was perfect. It was easy. Dave didn't talk about any of his baggage. I knew he had some because he was divorced, and it hadn't been civil, either. He never mentioned it. He didn't talk about himself, unless I asked him a question, then he told me whatever I wanted to know. Dave was focused on me. He wanted to know what I liked. What I was interested in. What I didn't like. I told him that I was a fan of the blues. He liked that. I told him that my priority was my child. He liked that. I told him that I loved boating. He loved that. We were a good match. We had a good time together.

The hardest thing about lunch was saying goodbye. We had such a good time, we didn't want it to end. We both had our kids to get back to. We both had other lives to tend to. I couldn't wait to see Dave again before the date was even over. I would have to wait until the following weekend, when I planned to cook dinner for him.

Dave wouldn't tell me what he wanted me to cook. He wanted it to be a surprise. I wasn't worried because I loved to cook, and he wasn't picky. When I brought out the sea scallops wrapped in bacon, he said it was his favorite appetizer. When I brought out the main course, Dave was pleasantly surprised. It was his favorite meal: stuffed Cornish game hens and asparagus with hollandaise sauce. I thought it was strange that I had picked all the right foods. I felt that it was a sign of how right things were between us.

Being with Dave was easy. It was fun and exciting. There was nothing to deter my growing love for him. There was no other shoe to drop. The hardest thing about our relationship was waiting out the week until we could be together again.

I loved Dave right from the beginning. The only thing that was still a mystery was whether I was correct about him. Time was telling me I was right. He was the man I thought he was. I loved everything about him. I loved the way his head shook slightly, and his voice quickened when he spoke on the phone because it made him a little nervous. I loved watching him play softball. The way his knee slightly bowed out as he ran was sexy to me. Every imperfection was perfection. I adored him.

I knew there was nobody more right for me. Dave was my one in a million. He made me feel like he felt the same way. He held me up on a pedestal. He made me feel loved, always putting me first. One year after we started dating, he made me the happiest woman in the world. Dave asked me to marry him.

We went for a walk one cool Saturday afternoon in May. We went to our favorite romantic place, the bluff at Quissett Harbor. I loved Quissett Harbor. The tiny bay was quaint with sailboats dotting the water. The sandy beach was secluded. I loved to stop at my favorite old tree which towered above the rest in the center of the wooded peninsula. Its outstretched limbs were inviting and reminiscent of my carefree childhood days. I chose to just look, in fear of tiring the massive old branches by climbing them. I wanted it to stay forever.

When we got out to the bluff, we were alone. We were standing, holding each other, as we looked out across the green-blue Cape Cod ocean. Unexpectedly, Dave dropped to one knee. He took my hand in his. He asked me to marry him. In his other hand, he held his mother's wedding band as he waited for my response.

I couldn't believe he had saved the ring for me. His gesture meant so much to me. I loved and respected his mother immensely, even though I had never had the chance to meet her before she died. Everything I heard about her was respectable. She was strong. She was smart. She was loving in ways that made differences in people's lives. She kept a good home. She had raised a perfect son. She had given me my husband. I would feel proud to wear her ring forever.

Dave didn't have to wait long for my response. I was never so sure about anything in my life. The only question was what date to choose for our big day. It wouldn't be a difficult decision because we both loved summer. We both loved the beach. It would be just as easy as everything else was with us.

I could handle anything knowing I had Dave's love on my side. No matter how bad things got, I knew I had him. I thanked God every day for putting him in my path. There were days when I didn't think I would have made it through without him. He made everything better.

I worried that my marriage would be hard for Tom to accept. He said he was okay with it. He was happy for me. He never had a bad word to say about Dave. It wasn't just him and me anymore, but he denied that it bothered him. It was hard for anyone to find fault with Dave. Even if Tom didn't like it, he knew Dave was good for me. If it did bother him, he would adjust. There was no reason not to make it work. Dave was a good man.

I think Tom was grateful that Dave was there for me. He had his family to support him through the court process and all of the after-effects of what Eugene had done to him. I had Dave. Tom must have known that I needed him because he accepted him so easily.

Any concern that I had had that Tom wouldn't be able to accept Dave disappeared on the day of my wedding. We were married in the Florida Keys on a tiny island at sunset. Our reception was a luau on the beach. Tom entered the reception in true form, donning a grass skirt and a coconut bra. The hula dancers loved it. They grabbed Tom and pulled him up to the stage, putting maraca-like instruments in his hands. The maracas were attached to their handles by a rope. Tom was to follow the MC's instructions as he swung the maracas wildly in the air. He had everyone roaring with laughter as he clocked himself, repeatedly, on the back of his head. We laughed harder every time he stopped what he was doing to modestly re-adjust his bra.

After the luau show had ended, Tom decided to show off his dancing skills to Dave's niece, who had had several years of dance lessons. He dove to the ground, sliding into his best Worm performance, to the beat of the calypso music. When he jumped to his feet, he stood confidently as everyone laughed at his sand-covered body. Every inch of bare skin was coated with sand. Everyone laughed harder after Dave's niece followed suit, but ended her performance without a speck of sand on her. Tom had made our reception more memorable. He had a great time. He was truly happy for me. Tom's attitude toward Dave didn't change after we returned home.

I would need Dave's support after the call I received from the district attorney's office. They had decided to allow Eugene to take a plea. The evidence had somehow been contaminated at the lab. None of it was any good. All we had was Tom's word against Eugene's. We still had a pretty good chance of winning the case, but there was no physical evidence. I felt like we were getting a rotten deal. I was angry. It wasn't fair. It wasn't fair to Tom. The only positive aspect that I could find was that the hearing would be a lot easier on Tom. He wouldn't have to testify. He could give a victim witness statement if chose to, but he didn't have to do anything if he didn't want to. The statement wasn't a testimony. It would have no bearing on the judge's decisions. There was no pressure.

Eugene pled guilty and accepted a sentence of nine to thirteen years, to be served concurrently with the sentence he had already received for raping his mentally impaired nephew. The sentence was much shorter than if the case had gone to trial. We had been seeking twenty-five years at trial, but we had no choice or input. We had to accept what the court decided, no matter how difficult it was. The thought of that monster ever being free again to destroy more little lives was unbearable.

Tom decided to write a statement. The judge allowed him to go up to the witness stand and speak directly to her.

Tom was relieved, but he would have done it any way they dictated. He wanted to be heard. I was proud of him. He did a great job.

When it was my turn, I had to read from the first bench. I didn't feel so strong. My hands were trembling. My voice was cracking. I felt dizzy. My head was spinning. I could see the back of Eugene's head. I hated him. I wanted him dead. I didn't want him to have the chance to look at my little boy ever again. Thirteen years wasn't long enough. Twenty-five years wouldn't have been long enough. No sentence would have been long enough.

I wanted to make a statement, but not for the reason they offered. I didn't want to vent. I didn't want to be heard so that everyone would know what that animal did to my child, what he did to me, what he did to my family. I wanted to make a statement in hopes that it would influence the judge's decision on the sentencing. I wanted her not to accept the deal he had made with the district attorney. I wanted her to give him the twenty-five years we were told he would get. The twenty-five years we had been pretty much promised because we had such an air-tight case. The judge had the power to do that. Sentencing wasn't supposed to be based on my statement, but I thought if it were powerful enough, she would have to respond without admitting that it was because of my words. It was something I needed to do for my son.

I tried to concentrate on getting through my statement. I wasn't sure I would be able to get through the whole thing without losing my composure, without fainting, without attacking the pedophile that I hated so much. I thought of Tom. I had to be okay for him. I thought of Dave. I knew he was just a couple of benches behind me. I took strength from him, from his support. I needed to keep it together.

Eugene had a chance to speak also. My desire to kill him became stronger. He wouldn't admit to anything. When the judge read the charges, instead of agreeing, he said, "Whatever you say. I guess so." He had no remorse. He didn't even admit that he had done anything wrong. He made me angry, angrier than I had ever been in my life. I was angry at his words. His cold, unremorseful, disrespectful attitude gnawed at every fragile string that was holding my sanity together.

The judge didn't see it the same way. She accepted the plea. She gave him nine to thirteen years, to be served concurrently with his previous conviction. It felt like a kick in the gut. It felt like he was getting away with one of the crimes, getting a free ride. My child didn't count. To me, it felt like nothing but a conviction without an admittance, a conviction without a punishment. My words didn't make a difference. My emotional state didn't matter. I felt like a fool for being such a mess, for displaying my emotions in front of the monster who had hurt my child in such an evil way. He had won again. He had hurt my little boy's mother and had made me put that hurt on display. I wanted to take it back. I wanted to take back the control, but it was too late.

I couldn't understand why the judge was so easy on Eugene. I wondered if it was because Tom seemed like he came through his trauma okay. Maybe she thought it wasn't really all that traumatic for him anyway. He looked fine. He looked handsome in his suit. He was polite and well-behaved. He didn't show any signs of being traumatized. He was a sweet, well-adjusted boy. She had no idea what he was going through. No idea that it hadn't even begun. I wondered what she knew about the after-effects of sexual assault on a young child. She knew nothing. For a judge, she was ignorant.

I wondered if the judge went so easy on him because Eugene was related to a judge. It was just conjecture on my part. I knew there was a judge with the same last name, but I had no idea if he was actually related. I assumed he was somewhere along the line, because the spelling was the same. There had to be a reason she did what she did, but I would never know what that reason was.

I had to find a way to accept the circumstance. There was nothing I could do to change it. I had to focus on the positive things in my life. The hearing was good for Tom. He didn't go into it with the intention of changing the judge's mind. He went into it with the intention of being heard, being visible. To confront the situation head-on. He did what he had come to do and he had done a great job. I was proud of him. I still had my son. I had Dave. Tom had basketball. We had our family. We would find a way to move past this.

10

Dislocated

Tom wanted to put the court case behind him. He only wanted to focus on basketball. As soon as one season ended, he was looking for the next one to begin. When there wasn't basketball, he would play any other sport.

Sports weren't Tom's only talent. He was smart. He was registered for advanced placement classes in high school. His grades were always excellent. When Tom was in second grade, he was placed in third grade math. His teachers thought he was struggling to keep up with his second grade classmates. I told them he was bored. Tom was doing simple addition at two years old. I knew he wasn't having difficulty, he just needed more of a challenge. As soon as they moved him, Tom excelled. When Tom was in fifth grade, he created a formula for a particular type of word problem. He placed second and third in a few of his science fairs. His academic and athletic accomplishments continued into high school.

Tom was a nice kid. He always thought of other people's feelings. Once, during a basketball game, he jumped for a rebound and came down on top of his opponent's ankle. Tom stopped in the middle of the game to help the boy off the court. He continued to walk the boy to his mother as the coach was screaming at him to get to the other end of the court. The boy's mother came up to me after the game to tell me what a nice kid my son was. I was so proud of him. I felt blessed with such a near-perfect child.

He was interested in wrestling. He talked to the high school coach who told him about an open tournament in late summer, before ninth grade started. The tournament was held to scout the upcoming talent for the high school wrestling team.

We walked into the South Plymouth junior high school gymnasium. It was packed. There were kids who had traveled from Cape Cod and Boston to participate in the tournament. Many of them were from high school wrestling teams. There were boys from eighth grade through twelfth. There were three mats set up for three matches to take place at the same time. The youngest boys had their matches on the mat in front of where I was sitting.

The eighth-graders wrestled each other according to weight. The winner would advance to the next division. Tom won match after match. The top wrestler from eighth grade advanced to the ninth grade matches. Tom was the top wrestler from eighth grade. He was amazing in everything that he did. He was a great athlete. I always felt so proud of him, not just for his athletic ability, but for everything. For who he was.

Tom's match against the ninth-grader was set to happen at the far end of the gym on the mat furthest from where I was sitting. I had a good view, even though I was pretty far away. Tom's opponent had wrestled before. It was obvious by the wrestling uniform he wore. I didn't think Tom would win this time. He was strong and athletic. He was competitive, but he had no experience wrestling. I was proud enough. He didn't need to win.

Tom was holding his own. It actually looked like he might win a couple of times, but in the end, he lost more than the match. Tom's opponent was about to pin him. Tom wouldn't give up. He would not allow his left shoulder to touch the mat. I could see the space from where I was sitting. I couldn't understand how he could hold out as long as he did, until I looked at his feet. I knew there was something wrong.

When Tom was in pain, he would curl his toes and move his legs a certain way. I couldn't see his toes, but the tops of his sneakers were bent upward. His legs were moving up and down. I looked at his face when it turned in my direction. It didn't look right. He was in agony.

The match went on. I couldn't stop thinking, *Tom, just let your shoulder fall.* He wouldn't. Every second felt like an eternity. I rose to my feet. I wanted to rush down onto the court and stop the match myself. I should have listened to my instincts, but I didn't want to embarrass him by having his mommy run out in front of everyone to help him. I stood my ground and waited.

Finally, the match was called. Tom didn't get to his feet. He was curled up on the mat, holding his left arm. He started writhing around on the mat as they raised his opponent's arm to show the winner. They left him lying there, ignored and in pain.

I couldn't take it anymore. I abandoned the bleachers. I had to. Nobody was doing anything. It may have been ten seconds of Tom being neglected, but it was ten seconds too long. I jogged across the blue, sweat-covered wrestling mats. I was consciously trying not to move too fast. I had to keep his embarrassment to a minimum.

What I saw, when I reached my son, was gruesome. Tom was in sheer agony. He bit down hard on his lip while the blood rushed from his face. I thought maybe his arm was broken as I approached, but realized quickly that it was something else. It was worse than I first thought.

Tom's shoulder was not sitting where it once had. His arm was torn from its joint. It was forced down into the side of his body, beneath the area that was once his arm pit. When I brushed his shirt sleeve upward to get a better look, I could see the skin stretching down from his collarbone, way farther than it ever should have stretched. It looked like his skin was about to tear apart. There were indentations in his skin that ran downward from the bony protrusion that was left in place of his shoulder, to where his arm finally came to a halt.

I didn't know what to do. I wanted to fix it. I wanted to stop his pain. There was nothing I could do but assure him that we would get him to the hospital and they would stop the pain.

Tom was thrashing back and forth in pain. He was past words. His face was as white as a ghost. He was twisting and sliding his feet back and forth. He could barely form a word. I yelled out for someone to call for an ambulance. That was all I could do for him at that point.

It took far too long for the ambulance to arrive. I had waited twenty minutes when I wanted to make the second call. I couldn't stand it. I had no control over anything. I just wanted to stop his pain.

The EMTs finally arrived. No paramedics were present. The female EMT asked if she could use my watch because it had a second hand. It annoyed me. I figured that a second hand watch should be a requirement for the job. When we got in the ambulance, the male EMT asked me the quickest way to get to Jordan Hospital. I was astounded. I couldn't believe they were asking me for directions. I was trying to comfort my son. They were increasing his anxiety. They were supposed to be there to help. I could have done better on my own. I regretted not taking Tom to the hospital myself. We would have already been there.

It was a long, painful ride for Tom. They couldn't do anything for him, except give him a ride. A ride that I had to direct. I figured maybe it was worth it just to have him taken right into an exam room instead of having to sign in and wait to be called from the waiting room.

When we finally got to the hospital, I asked that someone medicate him right away. It was going on forty-five minutes of agonizing pain. I knew Tom needed some relief as quickly as possible. He couldn't take it any longer. When the doctor came in to examine him, she couldn't believe how bad the dislocation was. She said it was the worst she had ever seen. She would have to get an orthopedic team in to help her reduce his arm. She gave him a shot, herself, right away. There was no question that he needed immediate relief.

I had to walk away when the reduction process started. I couldn't bear to watch. The team didn't want me to watch. There was one orthopedic doctor standing on top of the hospital bed, straddling Tom with his feet. There was another orthopedic doctor, and a nurse holding his left arm. There was another person at his head, able to reach the place where Tom's shoulder should have been. I walked away just as the brutal pushing, pulling and twisting began.

I could still hear what was happening. I could hear the grunting and groaning coming from the doctors. My toes curled at the thought of what was going on behind the curtain. Butterflies soared through my belly and up into my throat. I couldn't stand it. I wanted it to be over for him. I could hear that the crew was having a very difficult time trying to get his arm back where it belonged. I was just grateful that Tom couldn't feel much at that point. His pain was already gone. The doctor had given him morphine to prepare him for the procedure.

I could hear talk of possible surgery because they were having such a hard time meeting their goal. After trying a few different scenarios, they finally got Tom's arm back where it belonged. I was relieved that there would be no surgery that day.

When the doctors came out from behind the curtain, they were drenched in sweat. Their hair was a mess. They didn't look like they just completed a medical procedure. They looked like they had just gotten off the basketball court.

The ER doctor needed to check for any vessel or nerve damage before sending Tom back for more x-rays. The second set of x-rays was to make sure there were no fractures, and that the reduction had been successful. Tom was put in a sling that bound his arm to his chest. He had no movement in his left arm. He was given a prescription for pain medication and sent home to follow-up with an orthopedic surgeon. There was a lot of damage to his shoulder that required surgical repair, in their opinion. Tom would be out of basketball for awhile.

The next day, we were off to see the orthopedic surgeon who Tom's pediatrician had highly recommended. Tom was getting bored sitting in the exam room. We had waited a couple of hours to get into the room. I couldn't thumb through any more magazines. I was bored myself.

Tom started touching everything, trying to relieve his boredom. I tried to distract him with conversation. It was to no avail. He wanted to play doctor. He paid no attention to my requests to leave everything alone, until I could muster up enough seriousness in my flat mood.

I could see Tom's mind working as he sat impatiently, wearing only his SpongeBob SquarePants boxer shorts. He decided it would be funny to start showing off his muscles by flexing. I told him to stop. The doctor would be walking through the door at any moment. He ignored my request and put one leg up on the table where he was sitting. He rested his right elbow on his knee and jutted his chin forward, resting it on his fist. The hand of his injured arm was balled into a fist and rested against his bare waist. He looked like *The Thinker*, only much less serious.

I started to laugh. I couldn't stop myself. That was all Tom needed to hear. Things got more out of control. Suddenly, he noticed the large window behind him that overlooked the busy hospital district from six stories above. He stood on top of the exam table, facing the window, and jumped into his best muscle man pose, leaving one arm out of it. I laughed harder. Tom looked more like Charles Assless than Charles Atlas. His body was long and lean, but his muscles hadn't had the chance to fully develop.

Tom stretched his leg out to the side so that I could see him make his thigh muscle ripple for the unnoticing audience below. One arm went up into a flexed position. The other helped to display his "massive" thigh muscle. I laughed so hard, tears stung my eyes as I watched his drooping behind and thin limbs posed with such confidence.

There was no stopping him. I pleaded with him to get down, but there was no seriousness in my laughter. I really was afraid that the doctor would walk in on him while in that position. I just couldn't control myself. I didn't know if it was my boredom or Tom's knack for making me laugh. His facial expressions were too much. His carefree attitude was fun to be around.

I was grateful that Tom jumped down off the table as the

doctor entered the room, putting a stop to his show. It was time to be serious. My giddiness quickly faded. I needed to focus on Tom's health.

The doctors in the emergency room were right; he needed surgery. There was no question about it. There was too much damage to fix with physical therapy. Tom had little use of his left arm, so the surgery needed to be scheduled right away.

On the day of Tom's surgery, Dave and Phil came along. They wanted to be there for him. Dave wanted to be there for me. Everyone at the hospital was so nice. The staff paid attention to every detail. The surgeon came in and wrote the word *yes* on one of Tom's arms, and *no* on the other. He used thick black marker so he wouldn't get confused about which arm needed repairing.

The nurse came in to start the IV. She rubbed some numbing cream on the back of Tom's hand. He was excited and fascinated with the magic cream. He couldn't believe the attention he was getting. I loved the freedom Tom's mind allowed him as he found pleasure in things typically not experienced by his peer group.

They wheeled Tom off to the operating room. I was left with only my worry. I knew the odds were good that everything would go okay. I also knew there was a chance that they wouldn't. I tried to focus on the positive. He was a healthy kid. He would be all right.

I had a hard time leaving the waiting room while Tom was in surgery. I didn't want to miss an update. Someone from the operating room would periodically call out to the receptionist and give an update on how the surgery was going, another great service they provided for the families. Every update was good. They had found more damage than what had been shown on the MRI, but Tom was doing great. There were no complications. When the surgery was over, the doctor came out to talk to us and show us pictures of the operation. I wanted to know every detail, but even more, I needed to see my son.

Six hours after they had wheeled him away, we were escorted to the recovery room. Tom looked so fragile. The anesthesia still possessed his body. The machines were monitoring his internal workings. A shroud of ice packs and bandages blanketed his left shoulder, while a warming blanket enveloped the rest of him. I found his hand under the blanket. I gently laid my hand over his, careful not to disturb his recovery sleep.

"We had to put a warming blanket on him. He started to shiver. He has had a bit of a shock to his system, but he's okay. Everything looks fine."

Shock said more to me than it did to my two companions. Shock was a common word for Dave and Phil. It was more than common to me. It was a frightening word to me. He could have a pulmonary embolism or a hemorrhage. He could have an infection. I tried to redirect my mind as I sat there looking at Tom's pale, young face. He was okay. He wasn't actually in shock. The nurse had meant it in the common sense of the word. I had liked it better when I was ignorant about medicine. There was so much less to worry about. People didn't realize how freeing it was not to know what was happening to them or their loved ones. I wanted to be in that position again. I would never be able to return to that time. I was a nurse. I would be a nurse forever.

I tried just to be a mother, as I sat there monitoring his body temperature with my hand. I kept my eye on all the machines. I took mental note of Tom's pulse, his blood pressure, his oxygen saturation. I wasn't going to miss a thing.

Tom's eyes weakly opened with an uncertain gaze. He didn't know where he was for a moment. The condition of his body quickly reminded him. The beeping of the machinery helped to bring him into the present.

"Do you have any pain?" The nurse was right there to meet any need that Tom might have.

"A little." Tom was already attached to a morphine pump that the nurse would control until he had the mental status to do it on his own. She pushed the button, releasing the first dose of post-op comfort.

Tom was released from the hospital two days after his surgery. He would be home for two weeks before he was well enough to go back to school and start his physical therapy. It would be a long road to a full recovery. Daily bandage changes and cryogenic treatments would progress to three days a week of physical therapy and daily exercises. Tom just wanted to recover quickly enough to play the next season. It would be a big season. It was his first year in high school.

11
The Replacement

When Tom did get back on the court, it wasn't the same. He was playing again as soon as his body allowed. He needed the therapy and passion back in his life. All the games he had organized at the park in the off-season gave him the practice needed after being incapacitated for so long, but he didn't have his magic back yet. I figured it would take a while for Tom to feel comfortable. I'm sure the fear of his arm coming out again held him back, but he stuck with it and improved over time. Tom's talent had ebbed a bit, but he was still a stand-out player. I could just see there was something different.

Tom knew there was something different also, but he didn't want to talk about it. He didn't want to admit it. He couldn't face it. I tried to talk to him about it, but he denied anything was wrong, as usual. I was sure there was a problem. There were signs telling me something was different.

Tom's grades began to decline when he got back to

school. In one semester, he went from an A/B, advanced placement student, to a C student in the classes he was least interested in. He would ace all his tests and his papers, but the lack of completed homework brought down his grades.

I tried to work with the school. I tried to come up with a plan to make sure Tom completed his work. He would lie to me. He would tell me he had already done it. He would show me something that he said was his completed homework, but it wasn't. I fell for it. I trusted him. Every time I trusted him, it was more time bought to continue his decline.

I trusted the school. I didn't have any reason not to. I believed they would notify me if there was a problem. They didn't. I wouldn't find out until his report card came. The school didn't have the time to dedicate more attention to Tom than to all the other students in the school. I didn't have the time to dedicate my entire life to keeping Tom on track. I had to work. I had to sleep. I couldn't read his mind. I couldn't tell when he was lying to me. The school never gave me any suggestions. The therapists never gave me any suggestions. They would tell me that he didn't need therapy. I guess he wasn't bad enough yet. He was a nice kid. Everyone said so.

I wanted to use basketball against Tom. I wanted to tell him that if his grades didn't improve, he couldn't play the next season. I had a hard time taking basketball away as a punishment, though. It was his only healthy release. I was afraid it would make him even angrier. I decided it wasn't the right tactic to use. I had tried taking things away and I had tried reward systems, but nothing had worked. I needed to come up with something that was really important to him.

Tom's pubescent facial hair was important to him. His beard and mustache began to show at eleven years old. As long as he didn't shave it off, it became thicker and thicker. By the time he was fourteen, it had grown in fully. He loved it. His friends loved it. It made him appear larger, older. It made him look more intimidating on the court. It was something I could use. It was a better tactic than taking basketball away, so I told him that if he didn't keep his grades up, the beard and mustache would have to go.

Tom decided to test my rules. His grades continued to decline. The time came when I would have to follow through on my word. I told him to shave, but he flat-out refused. I told him that it wasn't an option. He continued to refuse and became angry. He told me that his beard and mustache were who he was, part of his identity. I couldn't take that away from him. He couldn't see that it was him who had taken it away. He thought I was a bitch. He hated me for it. He still refused. It was unlike him to be that defiant.

I called Phil for back-up. I could tell he didn't want to do it. He hated to discipline his son. He hated to back me. Dave convinced him that it was the right thing to do. He had to stand with us. Eventually, Phil came around to seeing things our way, or he just went along with us. Either way, he came to back us up. He told Tom that if he didn't go shave, he and Dave would have to hold him down while his mother shaved his face. Tom was pissed, but he resentfully shaved on his own. He became more angry. His grades didn't improve; they continued to get worse. Tom decided to take it to the next level. He started skipping school.

I didn't find out about Tom's absences for a long time. The school didn't notify me right away, and it didn't show in his grades until it was too late. Tom was able to show up for tests and ace them, so it took time for his grades to decline. Friends in his calculus class would get frustrated because Tom didn't need to be there to do well on the tests. I was frustrated with Tom for wasting his good brain.

I felt like I was fighting a losing battle, and it was only the beginning. I didn't seem to have any positive impact with anything I tried. I asked the school to call me if Tom didn't show up. They didn't call until he had missed so many days that he was in danger of failing. I asked again. They still didn't call. My punishments didn't work. My talks didn't work. Therapy didn't work. I didn't know what else to do. I couldn't get a handle on it.

I didn't have Phil's support most of the time. Tom would manipulate him. He told him that I was always yelling at him. That we just fought constantly. Tom considered being told what to do as fighting. He didn't respect my authority. His view of my role in his life was distorted.

Phil believed his son. He would say things to Tom, like "You know how your mother is. She'll get over it." Phil couldn't see what was going on. He couldn't see that Tom was manipulating him, that Tom was going down the wrong path. He couldn't see that we needed to do something to stop it. To Phil, Tom was a nice kid with a bitchy mother. Nobody believed me. Tom was a nice kid as far as everyone was concerned and they thought that I was just overreacting. I knew there was something very wrong. I knew his health was bothering him. I knew there were old demons bothering him, demons that he had never dealt with. Demons that he refused to talk about. Demons that he denied were ever there. I knew better. I just didn't know what to do to fix it, so I panicked. I was losing my son and nobody could help me.

A couple of months into ninth grade, I realized Tom's dreams might be coming to an end. His shoulder surgery hadn't worked. He had a couple more dislocations after he started fully using his arm again. They weren't as traumatic as the first one, but it meant that he hadn't healed well. The pain of that realization cut much deeper than the physical pain. It was a huge disappointment.

We had felt confident that Tom would be fine. His surgeon had come highly recommended. He had two anchors holding his shoulder in place and the tear had been sewn together. The odds had been good. We were told that the surgery had an eighty-five percent success rate. It would take four months of healing and physical rehabilitation, but he would be back on the court, good as new.

That didn't happen. The pins didn't do their job. Tom didn't do his job. He didn't continue with the weight training program that was necessary to completely overcome his injury. When he finished his physical therapy, he figured he had done enough. He didn't. It wasn't going to be that easy.

Tom needed another surgery; a different type of procedure; a different surgeon. The second surgeon wanted to do a capsular shift. He said that the shift would repair both tears in Tom's shoulder capsule. One tear hadn't been noticed or sewn up the first time. That gave me hope. If there was something missed the first time, than the odds felt better the second time. This time Tom would really be fixed.

Tom decided to put off the surgery until after the basketball season was over. If he had his second surgery right away, he would have to miss his first year of high school ball. He didn't want to do that. He couldn't do that. He decided to do everything he could, other than surgery, to make sure he could play. He went back to physical therapy three to four times a week. He did his assigned exercises every day. He was going to make it work.

Basketball season was approaching and Tom was really following through on what he needed to do to be able to play. He spent his gym periods in the weight room. He was doing his exercises at home. He was really looking forward to tryouts. Everyone was looking forward to the season. They had a great team that had played together for years. Tom's talent was still just as good, if not better, than anyone else's on the team. He had just gone from outstanding to great. He was working on it.

The excitement around the school was palpable, until the school put an end to Tom's basketball aspirations. They took away his dream, all because of a misunderstanding. All because of a wannabe cop. Things turned sour fast.

I received a call from the head of guidance one day. The woman told me that Tom had been suspended and possibly expelled for holding, and possibly lighting and sniffing a glue stick. I was dumbfounded. I knew it was a mistake. A misunderstanding. I asked what led to the accusations.

The head of guidance told me that the school security officer had observed Tom hand his peer a glue stick. One of the boys lit the glue stick and possibly sniffed the vapors. Possibly? What did that mean? Everything had been observed except the sniffing. Was it an assumption? Was it an illusion? What did he mean by "possibly?" I couldn't say much until I spoke to Tom, but I knew it was an extreme overreaction on the part of the school.

When Tom got home, I asked him to tell me what happened. I knew he didn't do anything wrong because he didn't have that guilty look on his face. He didn't hesitate to tell me the story, and his story made sense. There was nothing sketchy about his words like there always was when he was lying to me. Tom repeated the same story as the guidance counselor, but with a little more detail.

Tom told me that while he was sitting in the cafeteria for study, the kid next to him dropped something. He was talking to his friend at the time when saw something fall. He reached down next to his foot, where the glue stick had landed, picked it up, handed it to the kid that was sitting on the other side of him, then turned back to continue his conversation. He saw the kid light the glue stick, but didn't mention the sniffing. When I asked him about it, he just said he didn't see that. He thought the kid was stupid for lighting it, but figured he had nothing to do with it. The next thing he knew, he was being brought to the guidance department for disciplinary action. He was informed that he was being suspended and possibly expelled. The expulsion would be determined by the principal when he returned the following week.

Tom asked if he could attend basketball tryouts while he waited to sort the problem out. He denied any responsibility or wrong doing. He admitted to picking up the glue stick, but didn't feel that it was a criminal act or even bad behavior. He just wanted to go to tryouts later that day. He was denied his request.

I went in to meet with the head of guidance and the security officer the next day. Tom came with me. They just repeated the same story. The security officer was uptight. He was accusatory and insistent that he had busted Tom doing something terrible. Tom stared right back at the officer and denied that he did anything wrong; another sign that told me Tom was telling the truth. He never would have faced the man if he had done something wrong. He would have been quiet. He wouldn't have made eye contact. He would have just rolled with the outcome and kept his mouth shut. This guy was out to get him.

I asked how they could consider the charges of possession of an illegal substance when they provided the substance. The glue stick was taken from art class. I asked if the art teacher should be charged with distributing. They thought my question was as ridiculous as I thought their accusations were. They still didn't get my point. They were taking this all the way. They were considering bringing in the police.

I didn't wait for the principal to return. I decided to talk to a lawyer. I went to see Peter Sherwood, who told me not to worry about it. The school could try to press charges and expel Tom, but Peter could clear it up if they wanted to bring it any further than they already had. He wanted me to go to the meeting with the principal the following week. He knew the principal. He said he was a nice man, a logical man. If the principal decided to continue with the disciplinary actions, I was to call Peter and he would take it from there.

Tom was more concerned with missing basketball than he was anything else. He was afraid the coach hated him for no reason. He was afraid his reputation was destroyed. We went to the meeting the following week to try to clear Tom's name. While we were sitting outside the principal's office, the basketball coach walked by. He looked at Tom without saying a word. I knew Tom's fear was a reality. I could tell by the look in the coach's eyes. To him, Tom was just a drug addict, trouble-maker. It would take some work to change his mind.

The meeting didn't take long. The lawyer was correct. The principal was a sensible man. He wiped the entire incident from Tom's record. He took back the suspension and gave his permission for Tom to play basketball. He didn't see any grounds for disciplinary action. I was so relieved by the principal's actions that I wasn't concerned with what the coach might still think of Tom. I guess I assumed that he would just forgive and forget as the principal had.

That wasn't the case. Tom had missed tryouts. They had already picked their starting lineup. Tom wasn't on it. There was not even a chance of replacing a less talented player with

Tom, once he was allowed on the team. He would have to find a way to prove the coach wrong.

As poorly as the team was doing, the coach seldom gave Tom any playing time. It was painful watching from the bleachers. His legs were constantly jumping. He would bite his nails. He would look to the coach, with pleading eyes, to let him on the court. He was ready at any given moment to hop up off the bench and be where he needed to be. His behind barely touched the seat. Tom felt frustrated watching his team lose because he knew he could turn things around if he were given the chance.

What made it even harder was the brief amount of time Tom was given to play. When he got out on the court, he would catch the team up in points. Then the coach would bench him. The team would start to lose again, and Tom would have to endure the stress of having to watch. It felt like intentional punishment. Like the coach hated him so much, he let the team lose just to rub it in Tom's face.

The love and excitement I had once had about watching Tom's games turned into stress and frustration. I couldn't stand it. I tried to talk to the assistant coach, but my words fell on deaf ears. He didn't say much. He acted like he had no input and no opinion about the matter. The head coach never even made eye contact with me. He wouldn't give me the time of day. I wanted Tom to fix it, to do something. He played hard when he was given the chance, but that was all he did. I guess that was all he could do.

About halfway into the season, Tom dislocated his shoulder again. Any slim chance of changing the coach's mind was gone. Any hope of fixing his shoulder without surgery was gone. He couldn't continue to prove himself on the court anymore. All hope was taken away from him. It was back to the sling, back to the doctors' appointments, back to the knife, back to the couch.

There was no denying that Tom needed surgery again. I had to accept that. I tried to convince Tom that everything would be okay, that it would all be worth it in the end, but he didn't seem convinced. He didn't say much at all. I don't think he accepted his situation. He just went along with the plan because he was told that it was what he needed to do.

The new doctor had an even better reputation than the first. He was the Chief of Surgery at Children's Hospital. So it was back to Boston. Tom promised to follow the treatment plan. He would do anything to get back to normal. He would do anything to get back on the court. He had no choice. Tom wouldn't accept the end of his basketball career yet. We still had hope.

The second surgery went well. The prep was different. There was no numbing cream for the back of Tom's hand. He was older and the cream wasn't age-appropriate. Tom would have found pleasure and comfort in it again. I would have found peace of mind in Tom's comfort. He wasn't a little boy anymore, so he was no longer treated like a little boy.

It was just Tom and me the second time around. His shoulder problems had become routine. I still worried as much as I had the first time. I didn't get as many updates as I had that time. That didn't help my anxiety. I wondered if the hospital had had to make budget cuts. The receptionist was unnecessary. It was a way to save money. I kept in contact with everyone by phone whenever I did learn something. It gave me something to do, something to distract my mind from all the possibilities.

The surgeon was confident that the procedure was successful. It would be a long recovery again, but the prognosis was good. Even though they had to open his shoulder again, they wanted to send Tom home on the day of his surgery. They told me that he would only go home the same day if they did the repair arthroscopically. I was hesitant, but trusted the opinion of a world-renowned surgeon, so I brought Tom home. I could take care of him. I was a nurse. I was also his mother. He was in safe hands.

I settled Tom onto the couch when we got home. I didn't want him going up and down stairs during the first twenty-four hours or so. I gave him his pain meds right away. I knew he would need them after moving around so much. There was no morphine pump this time. Just pills. Pills that I needed to track so that his pain wouldn't start to break through before I gave the next dose.

After the sun went down, Tom spiked a fever. He was in terrible pain, even though I tried to stay ahead of it with his medication. The suture line was bright red. I was worried that he had an infection. I called the surgeon who was on call, but I didn't find much comfort in that. He told me to give Tom acetaminophen to bring down his 102-degree temperature. I knew how to bring down his temperature. I was worried about infection. I was worried about controlling his pain. I was worried about being an hour away from the hospital where his surgeon was. I had no choice. I was on my own. I wouldn't show my concern to Tom. He needed to feel as comfortable as possible. He needed to feel confidence in me.

I made Tom as comfortable as possible. I spent the night sleeping on the matching, over-stuffed loveseat next to him. I didn't get much sleep because I was too worried. I listened to Tom groan in pain all night. I watched his head swing from side to side. I watched his toes curl in his typical display of extreme pain as I wiped the sweat from his clammy, blotchy forehead. I held his head so that he could swallow his pills, and I prayed that he would get through the night all right. He never complained. He just left it to me to care for him.

Tom woke up the next morning feeling a little better. His pain had subsided a bit. I could tell by the calmness of his feet. His fever had broken, and his wound was no more red than it had been during the night. The drainage showed no liquid signs of infection. There were no visible signs of infection at all. I felt relieved as Tom's condition gradually improved. We both regretted coming home that first night, but he survived. He was on his way to a full recovery.

Sitting on the sidelines, donning his fancy sling, and watching his teammates play was killing Tom. He wanted to be out on the court more than anything in the world. He had a lot of work to do before he could try to reach his dream. He had physical therapy three days a week again. He had isometrics to do three times a day. He had a full program of rehabilitation. It would take a certain amount of commitment on Tom's part to make a full recovery.

I was seeing signs early on that Tom wasn't doing everything he could to make a full recovery. There was no way of knowing if he was doing the isometrics, but I had a feeling that he wasn't doing them as often as the surgeon had told him to. I knew he wasn't doing the at-home physical therapy exercises every day. He did them on most days, but there was a reason, once or twice a week, why he couldn't get them done. He wasn't making it a priority. In his condition, he had plenty of time. I knew how badly he wanted to play basketball. That's why I couldn't understand why he was being lazy about it. It seemed like he was giving up.

I think Tom just wanted to wish it all away. He didn't want to do the work to make it happen. He wanted to depend on the surgery alone. He was angry about it. It had been a long road. It had been almost two years and two surgeries, and he still wasn't back to normal yet.

Eventually, Tom was given the okay to play again, but he wasn't a hundred percent. The older he got, the more the competition was catching up to him. He wasn't able to overcome his injury completely. Tom was losing hope for a full recovery. He was losing hope of the coach ever believing in him again.

After ninth grade ended, Tom's shoulder dislocated again. It became more unstable than ever. It would just fall out of place when he fell asleep. I had the feeling that no matter how much of a workout he did, his shoulder would still be too unstable to continue playing competitive sports.

The end of Tom's basketball aspirations was a real turning point in his life. Basketball had been everything to him. It was who he was. He loved all sports, but basketball was his passion. The moment Tom had stepped onto the court for the first time, he had known that that was where he belonged. He had realized as quickly as everyone else that he had a natural talent for the game. His passion was being taken away from him. His release was being taken away from him. His identity was being taken away from him. I would have done anything to give it back, but I had no control over it. The only thing I could do was encourage him to do his part.

I tried to get him interested in other things. I paid for theater lessons. Tom tried it for a while. He liked it. He was pretty good at it, but he wasn't passionate about it. I paid for modeling classes and photo shoots. He went to the classes. He posed for the camera, but he didn't take it any further than that. There was no passion. We went through one thing after the other trying to find a replacement for basketball. Tom decided to throw his life into something else. It became his only focus. It became my nightmare.

Instead of trying to overcome his injury, Tom decided to be angry at the world, angry in a secretive way. His attitude didn't drastically change overnight, but his actions did start to transform into something new, something different, something not-so-healthy. He gave up on basketball. He gave up on himself.

The first sign came shortly after I was married. Out of

the corner of my eye, I saw a funny looking soda bottle in Tom's room while on my way to do laundry. The bottle was partially filled with dark water. I stopped to pick it up. It had a melted hole near the neck. The reek of pot floated up through the neck of the bottle and into my nostrils. My heart sank. I had had no idea. I didn't want to believe it. I didn't want to admit that Tom was doing drugs. I was scared to death. It wasn't just a roach. It was a homemade bong. It must have meant that he knew what he was doing. That it wasn't his first time. I really didn't want to go down that road. I had worked so hard to avoid it. It wasn't fair. I had had different plans for my son. This was never in my plans.

I tried talking to Tom about the choices he was making. I tried telling him where drugs would lead him. He seemed disinterested in my lectures, shut down by my intensity. He had spent the last couple of years building a wall. I had seen the construction going on, but it was being built more rapidly than I thought. I didn't know what it would take to bring it down, but I knew I had to work fast.

I didn't want to overreact. I didn't know if it was normal teenage experimentation, or an escape. I needed to figure it out before it was too late. My heart was telling me that Tom needed help. My brain was telling me that there was a major problem developing.

I tried to piece all the signs together. Tom wasn't taking care of himself the way he once had. He refused to go to counseling to deal with the trauma in his past. He continued to deny that it even bothered him. He said he never even thought about it. I knew that his denial was because he couldn't think about it. He had to bury it until he was strong enough to handle it. It had to bother him. He couldn't be the only one in the world to come through something like that unscathed. I knew that he would have to deal with things in his own time. I just didn't want him to bury it so deep with drugs that he wouldn't be able to find his way out.

Tom refused to work out in order to play the game he loved. He turned his back on the only passion in his life: his release, his confidence, who he was. Instead, he was angry. He was apathetic. He gave up too easily. Life had turned its back on Tom and he was out to get even.

I couldn't stop thinking about the soda bottle. I didn't know how serious it was. I didn't know how much he was using. I didn't know if there were any other drugs involved. I didn't think so, but I was missing a lot of changes that were going on in Tom's life. I had to act fast. I needed to put a stop to his downward spiral. I just didn't know how. I obsessed over it. I prayed. I bargained. I begged.

I couldn't talk to him. When I did, I did all the talking. He continued to deny that anything bothered him. He had only tried pot *one time*. He *just didn't like to work out*. He was *fine*. I was *overreacting*. I got nowhere. His attitude was changing. He wasn't as pleasant as he had once been. He wasn't easy to talk to anymore. He had a new edge to him that I had never seen before.

I brought Tom to a new therapist. I asked him to please just give it another try. I told him that if he really hated it, I wouldn't force him to go back after a few sessions. I was told the same thing. *He's fine. He doesn't need to come back. He's just a normal teenager. He's a nice kid.* Everyone kept telling me that Tom was a nice kid. I knew he was a nice kid. That wasn't my question. My question was: there is a problem, what do we need to do to fix it? What could I do after being told there was no problem? I brought Tom to the best. I worked in the field. I was given referrals to top-notch therapists and psychiatrists. They told me nothing was wrong. I tried to accept their advice, which was to do nothing, but I couldn't ignore my instincts.

Every one of my overreactions was another brick in Tom's wall. Every one of Phil's under-reactions was another opportunity for Tom to master his manipulation skills. I struggled to get ahead of the game. I took all of Tom's possessions away: his TV, his computer, his video games. He continued to do what he wanted. I sentenced him to his room for two weeks. He snuck out while I was at work or sleeping. I extended his sentence, but he continued to do what he wanted. Tom's sentence reached four months before I abandoned my approach.

I was out of options. I wanted to send Tom to a boarding school, but Phil was firmly against it. He thought he was just doing normal teenage stuff. Sending him away was an overreaction. My mind needed a break. I couldn't think. I was running out of time. I knew it was about to get worse. I felt that Dave and I were alone in our battle to save my child. Tom was slipping away, and nobody could convince me otherwise. I knew my son and I was not about to abandon him.

12

STRIKE ONE

It was a day like any other day. I arrived at the Cape Cod Psychiatric Center at a quarter to seven in the morning. After listening to the report recorded by the night shift, I received my usual assignment. It was my turn to pass meds, run the education group and do the first admission, if there was to be one. It was a typical assignment for a per diem nurse. It was a busy assignment, but that was the way I liked it.

After I finished the eight am med pass, I was sitting behind the nurses' station getting some information off the computer for a pending admission. It was always busy in the morning. Patients were asking for toiletries to take a shower. Most discharges from the hospital took place by eleven am. There were family meetings and a lot of paperwork to do. There were patient belongings to collect. The phone seemed to ring more often in the early hours of the day. The twenty-bed unit was full of life.

While I was waiting for the printer to spit out the information I had requested, the unit secretary told me I had a call waiting for me on line one. I wasn't expecting a call from anyone. I had already gotten a report on the admission from the sending nurse. I picked up the phone and pressed line one. "Hello?"

"Hi, Susan?" It was my mother. Instantly, I knew something was wrong. She would never call me at work unless it was an emergency. Before she could tell me why she was calling, I thought that maybe something was wrong with her. It couldn't be too serious or she wouldn't be the one to call. I thought, maybe something was wrong with Tom. I thought all of this during my mother's hesitation. My heart rate quickly advanced from its usual slow pace. My body temperature seemed to rise instantly. I was feeling a little clammy. My hands were no longer cold, as they usually were.

"Hi. What's up?"

"I'm sorry for calling you at work, but I thought you should know right away."

"That's okay. What is it?" My mother sounded panicked, but I was hoping it was her usual overreaction. She often sounded panicked when there was nothing to be panicked about.

"Tom was arrested at school today for marijuana possession." I didn't know what to say. There wasn't much I could say. My co-workers were standing all around me. There were patients standing at the nurses' station counter a few feet to my right. They were close enough to hear any words that might slip past my cautious lips.

"Where is he now?" I said with as much emotional control as I could possibly muster up.

"He's home now. His father picked him up and brought him home. He has to be in court in the morning. I'm sorry, honey. Is there anything you want me to do?" *Yeah, make this go away,* I thought. *Bring back the son I had once had.* That would be nice. It was an unrealistic request. A request she would gladly deliver if she could.

"No. I'm not sure when I can get home."

"Don't worry about it. I'll make sure he stays in the house until you get home."

I still had the receiver in my right hand while I was holding the button down with the index finger of my left. I was thinking about what to do next. I was trying to keep my composure. I was frozen in place. I was shocked. I was trying not to think about the content of the phone call. I was trying not to think of all the consequences Tom was about to face. I needed to get to a place that was safe. I didn't know what to say. I didn't know if I should leave work. Should I just say I have a family emergency? Should I try to finish out my shift? It probably shouldn't have been a difficult decision. It's amazing how inept you become when under extreme stress.

My manager's voice broke through my noiseless self-dialogue. I couldn't imagine what I looked like, but Michelle knew something was wrong. I'm sure the blood had drained from my face. I felt embarrassed, but there was no blood to show it on my cheeks. "Is everything okay?"

"Not really." I had to keep it short for fear of losing my

composure.

"Do you need to leave?"

"I think I should." A couple of tears triumphantly slid through the ducts that had once held them restrained. They rolled down my cheeks and landed on my chest, making an obvious splat stain. My boss didn't ask any more questions. She instinctively knew she shouldn't. I grabbed my bag and headed for the thick, beige, locked door at the end of the hallway leading away from the nurses' station.

It was a relief to get out of work, but only because I didn't think I could prevent myself from unraveling much longer. Otherwise, work would have been a good distraction. I had to go home and face the situation.

I couldn't believe Tom was ruining his future. He was starting to cause irreparable damage that I wasn't aware of until the drug charges. He already had a record of driving an unregistered and uninsured vehicle. He already had a charge of minor transport of alcohol. Now he was facing possession of a class D substance and he didn't seem to care. I was the only one getting upset.

I turned into the driveway and pulled my car up to the top of the hill. The sliding glass door on the side of the house was unlocked. I walked through the door reluctantly. I wasn't ready to face everything. I had to try to get control of my emotions, so I walked past Tom and my mother and went upstairs to figure out a plan for keeping myself together. I needed to be alone for a few minutes. I needed to figure out a plan about what to do with Tom. I needed to stop thinking of him as a little kid, the kid he used to be. I had to start facing reality.

So there I sat, on the edge of Tom's bed, trying to figure out where I had gone wrong.

The harder I thought, the heavier the pounding became in my head. I couldn't come up with an answer. I couldn't figure out why this intelligent, good-looking, well-liked boy was throwing away his life. Nothing I was doing was putting a stop to it. I couldn't even slow him down. Things were getting worse instead of better. It was happening too fast.

No matter how bad things became, I was still hopeful. I still had time to try and change things. Tom was still a minor and would have his record sealed at eighteen years old. I had almost two years to work with. I would do whatever it took to help him. I just wished I knew what it would take. I wished I knew what the next step was. First, I needed to get the whole story, or as much of it as Tom would give me.

Tom was sitting on the couch watching television. My mother was sitting on the loveseat next to him. She looked uncomfortable. You could feel the tension in the air. I wished she weren't there. I loved having her around, but it was just a terrible visit for her. There was nothing that she could do, but that didn't stop her from trying. I could tell they had been talking before I got there. At least she was. Tom wasn't a boy of many words, especially when he was in trouble.

I was looking for the answer in the wrong place. The signs were all there. I saw them. I just hadn't known what they meant. I didn't know how to stop it. I couldn't understand him. He was getting into trouble all the time, and he was blatant about it, as if he wanted me to see it. I saw it, wide-eyed. I just didn't know how to fix it, or why it was happening. Tom wasn't a punk. He wasn't disrespectful. At least his words were not, but his actions were. He showed remorse when he did something wrong, but he kept on going down this terrible path, regardless of the consequences. He was telling me something. Something I didn't understand at the time.

I couldn't figure out if Tom was intentionally getting in trouble. I couldn't help but wonder if he was trying to make me angry. I couldn't imagine that he was so egocentric that he couldn't think outside of his own needs long enough to stay out of trouble. I knew that all teenagers are selfish to a point, but it was constant with Tom. He never learned from his mistakes. It was as if he didn't get enough of a reaction. Maybe he was getting too much of a reaction. He just kept upping the ante. I wished I could read his mind. It would bring an end to all of it.

I couldn't help but think Tom had set out to make me angry. I would find marijuana remnants just lying on the kitchen counter. I would find baggies reeking of pot in the pockets of his jeans when I did the laundry. I was losing the battle, and the harder I fought, the more ground I lost.

Dave and I finally presented the "three strikes" rule. I was prepared to follow through, no matter how painful it might become. We had to put a stop to Tom's illegal, self-destructive, disrespectful behavior. If it didn't work, at least we wouldn't have drugs in our home. We couldn't condone that. We had to stand behind our convictions.

We called a family meeting. The three of us sat at the formal dining room table to discuss the situation. Tom reluctantly dragged himself to the table with his eyes studying the wide-planked oak floor, as if he was seeing it for the first time.

It was almost impossible to get Tom to be in the house at the same time we were, except when we were eating or sleeping. He was supposedly in school all day. He would come home before we did and supposedly get his homework done. He wasn't even in school most days, unbeknownst to us. After his homework was done, he would go out with his friends for about an hour before he had to be home for dinner. I would have dinner ready at five-thirty every night and Tom had to be there. He would go out with his friends as soon as he was finished eating.

Tom had every excuse in the book to get out of eating dinner with us. He wasn't hungry. He wanted to eat at his friend's house. He didn't feel well. It was never the truth. It was never, *I don't want to sit around the table with my family and pretend that I want to be there. I want to sit around with my friends and smoke pot.* Every day was a constant battle, with Tom trying to manipulate every rule or request that we made. It was utterly exhausting.

Tom's curfew was ten, the same time that Dave and I went to bed. It was amazing that Tom always had something to do until ten o'clock at night, every night. And he was always a few minutes late. He was hoping that we were already upstairs, in our bedroom. He didn't want us to see his eyes. He didn't want us to recognize the person he was with his friends.

Tom had an excuse for everything. He had an excuse for why he couldn't be home for dinner. He had an excuse for why he was going to be late getting home at night. He had an excuse for why he couldn't go to family functions. I was so sick of it.

He never let up. He asked for permission to get out of every obligation, and no matter how many times I said no, he kept on asking. I told him that if he asked me again, he would have to stay home more often, but Tom kept on asking. I didn't know if he was stupid. I didn't know if he was a jerk. I didn't know if he was just the most stubborn person I had ever known. My God, did he have staying power. If only he had put that much effort into something positive, he really could have been something special. But Tom just wanted to get high.

We lay it all out in front of him that night. Simple rules. No variances. No excuses. No discussions. Only actions. Tom's actions would determine our actions. This is how it would go.

Strike one: If any drug or drug paraphernalia was found in our house, Tom would lose all privileges. I explained that we would not allow that kind of behavior in our home. I had a nursing license and a reputation to protect. Dave and I both had reputations to protect. We would not condone Tom's criminal behavior. Dave and I spelled out the consequences. Tom would not be allowed to go out with his friends for a month. Tom would not be allowed to have any friends in the house for a month. Tom would have no phone privileges for a month. Tom would have no internet privileges for a month. All of his social contacts, other than school, would be cut off. We would hit him where it hurt; his social life.

Strike one came. Nothing changed. Tom was not afraid of the "three strikes" rule. I was angry. I was shocked. I was afraid. I was still losing him. I shouldn't have been shocked, but I was. I had hope every time we came up with something new. I had to have hope. Hope is what kept me going. Anxiety is what kept me going. Fear of failure as a mother is what kept me going. My overwhelming need to protect Tom from himself kept me going, but I was always let down.

I panicked when strike one came because I couldn't bear the thought of being a step closer to strike two. Tom had to stop what he was doing. He couldn't let it get any further. I needed him to know that he couldn't take it any further without ruining his life, without forcing me to do something I didn't know if I was capable of doing. Something that would tear me apart. I couldn't let him force me into strike two.

When I thought I was out of options, and nobody but Dave would listen to me, I screamed. When Tom wouldn't hear me, I screamed louder. My words were the same worried, pleading, loving words they had always been. They were just louder. Sometimes, much louder. I needed him to hear me. Through my tears, I screamed loud enough to penetrate Tom's wall, but instead of making a crack, I made the wall stronger and I was left feeling guilty for pushing him even further down his dark and miserable road.

I found the pot in the pocket of Tom's jeans. Surprise, surprise. The laundry, again. Boy, did I hate doing the laundry. It always brought unpleasant surprises. I developed an aversion to Tom's laundry. I would never wash his clothes again. I would never stand in my basement, under the cobwebs that accumulated under the unfinished ceiling, to do his laundry again. I would never stand over the washing machine with my hand innocently searching his pockets for anything that might hurt the machine, only to find things that hurt my heart instead.

Tom didn't put any more energy or effort into hiding his bad behavior than he ever had. It was right there. Right where he knew I would find it. I didn't get it. It wasn't like he wouldn't get in trouble. It wasn't like there was a chance that I wouldn't find it. What could he possibly be thinking? I asked myself that question over and over again. The only thing that I could come up with was that Tom had either wanted me to find it or he really did not care.

Tom seemed to care. He seemed remorseful. At least he acted remorseful sometimes. He was apologetic. He had once been a lovable child, and still was at times. He didn't like being punished, and he didn't seem to blame me after he settled down and accepted his punishment. Tom never showed any anger toward me after he calmed down. Was all this niceness just manipulation? Was it him? Was he really a nice kid? How could I not be able to figure this out? I was a child and adolescent psych nurse. It was tearing me apart.

Tom lacked all common sense. It was ridiculous. Someone that smart could not be that stupid. I thought Tom might have Attention Deficit Disorder, but that didn't make you stupid. He could hyper-focus on anything he was truly interested in. He was interested in drugs. I'm sure he was interested in not getting in trouble, so it had to be intentional. Tom wanted me to find it. But why? What was he trying to tell me?

I had to follow through on the plan. Maybe when Tom realized that we would be unwavering on the consequences, he wouldn't want to get to strike two. Tom's privileges were taken away. There was no way for him to communicate with his friends outside of school. We hit him where it hurt. No more friends in the house, not that he had friends over very often anymore. He preferred to go out, but that would be halted for awhile. No more internet. No more phone. It was all gone.

We had an added bonus from Tom's punishment; the computer would work better in the meantime. There would be no viruses that Tom would deny bringing into the house. Our phone bill would be lower for the month. It would give us a little break from not knowing where he was or what he was doing. Tom wasn't bad to have around. He was only bad when he wasn't around.

Tom seemed to take his punishment well: too well, in fact. He didn't seem bothered at all. He just went with it. He never stayed angry or irritable. He never yelled or cried. Tom was either happy, or he was just existing. He would lie in his bed and read. He would play video games. And, he would ask from time to time if his girlfriend could come over. We did not waver, at first.

Eventually, Tom became frustrated. It took a couple of weeks. He tried not to show it, but it certainly came out. Before we realized what was really going on, we allowed his girlfriend to come over. Tom was being good, and Angie was a good influence on him. She was a good kid who never got in trouble. She did well in school, and when she came over, she pushed Tom to do his homework. It seemed like the right thing to do. It seemed like the best thing to do. I couldn't think of a reason why not to agree, so I did.

A couple of weeks into Tom's punishment, I started to find the evidence. I checked Tom's history on the computer. He had been using the computer all along. He had been online the whole time. I couldn't imagine how. I had deleted his screen name and password so that he couldn't gain access to the internet. I couldn't figure out what this sixteen-year-old kid was doing with my computer without my knowledge.

I called AOL. They said there was no way he could get my password unless he found it or I had given it to him. I explained that I never wrote it down and I never told him what it was. There was no way he could have gained access through me. AOL assured me that Tom could not access my account without my giving it to him. There was something AOL was missing because Tom had access, and I had not given him my password.

The only thing I could do was to take the phones to work with me. I was still connected by land line for a reason. I couldn't trust Tom, and I needed a way to keep control of my electronics. It didn't work. He still gained access. He must have had his own phone line somewhere and hooked it up when I was gone. I still couldn't figure out how he was getting past my password, though.

Every time we confronted Tom about breaking the rules, he would deny it. The proof was sitting right in front of his face, but he still denied it. We extended his punishment. He still denied it. He was going to continue doing what he wanted and I knew it. I didn't know how to stop it. What else could I do?

Just stick to the plan. That's all I had. All he had was the determination to win this battle.

Eventually, I found out how Tom had gained access to the internet. He had downloaded a free internet service. There was no credit card required. Through this free service, Tom could download Instant Messenger from AOL. He had kept the programs hidden somewhere on the computer where I wouldn't look. He had access any time he had a phone line. That is, until he ruined the computer with worms and viruses. I was sick of the silent, disrespectful battle. I got rid of the computer and bought a laptop. I got rid of the phone line and took the computer with me everywhere I went. I put an end to the computer problem.

13

STRIKE TWO

I was sitting at the picnic table one morning, during my coffee break. The sun was baking the back of my neck. Summer was approaching; it was my favorite season. The hotter, the better. I spent every possible moment outside, trying to take advantage of every ray of sunlight that I could. The warmth passed too soon every year.

My cell phone began to ring inside my front pants pocket. When I flipped the phone open, I could see the caller ID on the screen. I knew it was Plymouth South High School. I had the number memorized. It was ten o'clock in the morning, but I had a sudden feeling that my work day was over. I was no longer paying attention to the rays that had been warming and relaxing my body.

It was Tom's guidance counselor. She was a very nice lady. She had a difficult job, always being the bearer of bad news. If I had known her outside of her realm of practice, or at least in a capacity not involved with my son, I probably would have liked to hear from her. If Tom had not been connected to her voice, I probably would have liked to talk with her. She may even have been someone I would go out to lunch with. We were in similar professions. We had a lot in common. The thing that ruined it was Tom. No matter how much I liked her, I hated hearing her voice. I felt like Pavlov's dog. Every time I heard the phone ring at an unusual time, my heart raced and my hands began to sweat. Gloom and doom overtook me. Every time I saw the school number, I winced. Every time I heard the counselor's voice, I cringed. It was a negative reaction to a known action.

Tom had skipped thirty-five days of school and was flunking every class. He hadn't lost any social time with his friends at all. He had gained time. He just needed to rearrange his schedule to suit his needs. School was not one of his needs. I was sure he was hanging out at our house with his friends, smoking pot. The little bastard had gotten me again. The school had never called me. I was so frustrated with him and the school. I had told them to call me every time Tom missed school. Not on the thirty-fifth day, when it was too late to do anything. I was angry at Tom. He was blowing his future and he didn't care. I didn't know how to make him care.

Tom's punishment was extended to three months by the time strike two came, but the three months didn't matter anymore. Strike one didn't matter anymore. We were at strike two. Tom was not afraid. The consequences did not deter him. My heart sank into my stomach, where it sat burning like a hot rock from a campfire. This time it was quite a blow. It was always a shock when Tom was in trouble, but this was different. He knew what was coming. He knew what the consequences were and he didn't care.

Tom didn't put any more effort into hiding his criminal behavior than he ever did. He put no effort into it at all in fact. The evidence was in my face again, screaming, *LOOK AT ME! LOOK AT ME! I'M IN YOUR FACE AGAIN! HA, HA, HA. WHAT ARE YOU GOING TO DO ABOUT IT? I DON'T CARE! I DON'T! ARE YOU HURT? I DON'T CARE!*

I hesitantly walked into Tom's room. I didn't want to go in there, but I knew I had to. The signs were there. He was skipping school and his mood was down. He was apathetic and less talkative. I couldn't ignore the signs any longer. Part of me didn't want to know what was going on with him. The other part had to know. He was my son and he was in trouble. I imagine that was why I continued walking. I stopped after each step. I closed my eyes. I wanted to make it all go away. My need to help my son kept winning after every hesitation. My need to protect him from all things bad was strong. The drugs. The drug addicts. Himself. I had to fix it. I had to protect him.

I was not thinking of protecting Tom at that moment. After nervously scanning his bedroom with my hopeless eyes, I began to pick up clothes from the stained, once darker blue carpet. As I made my way to the end of his bed, my heart began the familiar slide into the pit of my stomach. A little deeper this time, as if that were possible.

My eyes fell upon a scale, barely sitting under the edge of his bed. There it was, just sitting there, teasing me. It was only partly hidden by the sheet and blue and beige comforter of his typically unmade bed. It was just a plain, white, Kitchen Aid scale: an inanimate object, harmless in most situations, but not at that moment. Not sitting in Tom's bedroom. Not placed next to a messy pile of unused sandwich bags. No. It was not innocent anymore. It was just sitting there saying, *look at me. Look at me. Take that! Why don't you just give up? You're not going to win this one. How much more can you take? Because I have a lot left to dish out!* That thought was scary because I didn't know how much more I could take. It didn't feel like I would be able to see this through. He wasn't budging. Tom was getting worse and I was getting weaker. I wished Tom could have realized that I was fighting for him, not against him. To him, this was a knock-down, drag-out battle of wills that he did not intend to lose.

I think I was running on pure adrenaline as I looked further. Every inch of paraphernalia-covered carpet assaulted me harder and harder the further my eyes journeyed. It is amazing how painful it can be just looking at a box of plain old baggies, never made to hurt anyone. But they did. They cut as sharp as any knife. They cut deep into my soul.

I kept going, searching, pleading with God to have every new discovery go away. The pipes. The soda bottle filled a quarter of the way with rotten, stinking, dark brown fluid that had found my nostrils independently. The stench was cruelly burrowing its way into my brain. The smell was intruding. It was not wanted. It refused to leave, long after I left it. It wafted through the melted plastic hole at the upper end of the bottle. I put the stench-filled bottle down on the dresser.

I placed the bottle next to the funny name that was scribbled on the scrap piece of paper. I didn't care about the number that was written below the name. It was the name that kept my eyes prisoner. I knew it had to be a drug dealer. Who else had a nickname like Buzz? Later on, when my mind had room for other things, I thought it funny that a drug dealer didn't mind bringing attention to him by giving himself an identifiable name like that. You would think they would call themselves Bob or Joe. Something common and unsuspecting. Not a name that any ordinary person would take notice of. I imagined it was true, what they say about criminals. They are not very bright. I guess if they were, they would be more successful, and more people would want to try it out.

Exhausted, I slowly lowered myself to the carpet with my arms stretched out behind me, holding my body as steady as I was able. I didn't want to move anymore. I didn't want to think anymore, but the things that I had found wouldn't leave my mind alone. They were taunting me, laughing at me, wearing me down.

I couldn't understand what was happening. I wasn't able to grasp the entire reality of the situation. I could see what was in front of me, maybe better than a lot of parents. I was aware. I cared. I noticed. I just couldn't understand. Tom was a perfect child. He was respectful and intelligent. He was lovable and loved by all. Teachers loved him. Parents loved him. His peers loved him. Why was he doing this to himself? Why was he doing this to me? To the family? He had been so caring at one time. He could have never hurt me like that. Not before. But, before what? What had happened? What had gone wrong? I racked my brain, searching for the answer. I never saw it staring me in the face. Not until it was almost over. Not until it was too late. At least not until it changed his life, possibly forever.

Tom was fighting for his independence. He was fighting for his right, at sixteen years old, to do whatever he felt like doing. He didn't care that there was no such right. Tom was choosing the lifestyle he wanted to live, regardless of what his family wanted. Tom was choosing the friends he wanted to have, regardless of who and what they were. Because of who and what they were. He was in it to win, and he was playing dirty.

I understood that some kids went through a normal stage of partying and experimentation. I was one of those kids. With Tom, it wasn't normal. He didn't care about getting caught. He wasn't afraid of the law. He was reckless and impulsive with no concern for consequences. I was scared to death of ruining my future. I was afraid to get in trouble with my parents. I put more effort into not getting caught than what I was doing wrong. I had respect for my parents and the law.

When I was sixteen, I felt more mature in some ways than many of my friends. I was forced to grow up too early which led me to make poor choices. When I made those choices, I accepted responsibility for my actions and made the best of it.

Financial responsibility was always a part of who I am. I planned for the future, not the moment like Tom. We were different even though we did a lot of the same things. I struggled to understand him. I wasn't perfect by any means, but I was different.

Tom didn't know that I was in the fight for him to win. He didn't see it that way. He was so stubborn. It wasn't a game for me. It was a matter of life and death, and I didn't want anyone to lose. The stakes were too high.

Strike two scared me half to death. It didn't seem to scare Tom. I had to follow through with the plan. I had no choice. I had to stop him. As soon as I could get my legs underneath me and stable enough to walk, I would put the plan in motion.

I called Dave at work and asked him to come home as soon as he could. I needed his support, his strength, his logic. I didn't feel very logical or in control at that moment. I needed to talk out the plan of action, even though it was pretty much laid out already. I just needed to review things. Nothing was clear in my head. I felt awful. What I had to do to my own child was awful. It didn't feel right in my heart. It did feel right in my head. I was having a hard time grasping the reality of it. I just kept telling myself that I was doing it because I loved him.

I paced around the house while I was waiting for Dave to come home. I needed him to walk me through the steps. I would do it, I just needed support. I played it out in my head over and over again. Dave and I would have all the evidence on the island in the kitchen. As soon as Tom came through the door, we would call the police. While waiting for the police, we would confront Tom and tell him what we were doing. It shouldn't be a complete surprise to him since he already knew the steps of the three strikes rule. The police would come and arrest him and take him to jail. That was the end of what I knew would happen.

What we hoped to get out of this plan was putting fear into Tom. We wanted him to feel what it was like to be a criminal, to be embarrassed. To be knocked down a few pegs to where he wouldn't think he was so cool anymore. Tom was a clean-cut, smart kid. At least, he had been at one time. He wouldn't like sitting in the back of a cruiser. He wouldn't like sitting in a tiny, dingy, lonely jail cell with nobody to talk to. We hoped that he would never want to go through that again. I couldn't go through it again. I didn't know how I would get through it the first time.

I could feel the tightness in my face when Dave walked through the door. I wasn't sure if the salt that had dried hard lines down my cheeks was visible. I was sure that Dave couldn't see the whites of my eyes through the busy, vine-like, red design that had invaded their space. I didn't have to look in the mirror; I knew what I looked like. Dave didn't say a word when he finally arrived. He just held me in his strong, protective arms until he thought I could cry no more. My insides were begging for him to say "forget the plan," but we couldn't do that. I would have agreed at that moment, but I would have been wrong. He didn't say it and I forced myself to move forward.

"I think we should go talk to his therapist before we call the police. He has an appointment at two o'clock today. I think we should go without him." Dave just stood in the kitchen, looking at me. He didn't say a word, but I knew what he was thinking.

"I'm not saying we're not calling the police. I'll stick to the plan. I just want to talk to Tom's therapist first." Dave agreed. I'm not sure if he really felt the same way, or if he knew that that was what I needed to do. He always knew what was right for me. He always stood by me, no matter what.

"I wish I could take this pain away from you honey. I am so tired of him hurting my wife. Whatever you need to do, it's fine with me."

Dave and I went to Tom's therapy appointment without him. I'm sure he didn't even remember he had an appointment, or he would pretend he didn't remember because he didn't care to go, even though I never forced him. He still could not be honest. Tom could never just say what he felt or what he wanted. It always had to be a guessing game.

I didn't know what Tom was really like. Nobody did, including Tom. People only knew funny Tom; caring Tom; party Tom. Nobody knew what he really liked or didn't like. Nobody knew what made Tom angry. Nobody knew what hurt Tom's feelings. He always pretended that everything was okay with him. He absolutely could not stand up for what he believed, no matter how much he hated what he was doing. He would not speak up for himself. I realized it was a habit that had developed after sixteen years of someone else doing his thinking for him.

We sat in the crowded waiting room, anticipating two o'clock. As I looked around, I saw tired-looking mothers. Some were trying to keep their children from destroying the waiting area. There were the aged, doomed faces of the chronically ill. There were hard-working men there to meet their wives. I knew most of their stories. Stories that were more painful to them than they ever could be to me. I couldn't get past my own pain, my own fear. I was consumed with my own problems.

We followed Tom's therapist to his tiny office with no windows. We told him our story. Tom's therapist suggested that we take out a Children in Need of Services petition. I knew all about a CHINS. I had suggested it myself to many parents. I wasn't crazy about it in Tom's case, but I listened to what the therapist had to say. Most kids that have a CHINS have parents that can't set up rules and consequences, or they are unable to follow through and be consistent. I was doing that; Tom just didn't care. He would break every rule with complete disregard for the law. He would be taken out of the home and placed in foster care. Then he would, most likely, have even more freedom to break the law, break the rules. He would just get worse and I knew it. I didn't want Tom living in some strange house with less structure and rules than we had. I thought it would be disastrous. We told the therapist that we would go talk to the juvenile probation officer about it on the way home.

Dave and I did stop at the Plymouth County Probate

Court to talk to the probation officer. Dave felt the same way that I did. Nothing changed. It wasn't the way to go for us. I felt a little better knowing that we had checked out another option.

"Why don't we stop by the police station on our way home? I'd just like to talk with an officer first to see what they have to say before we actually go through with this." I was struggling with the idea of having my son arrested and I needed to cover all bases first. I needed to know what would happen in a hypothetical situation, or at least without us giving up the evidence yet. I wanted to know what was going to happen, before it happened. There were too many unknowns for me. I wanted him to be scared and embarrassed. I wanted him to feel like a loser. I just didn't know what the reality of the consequences would be. Would the judge just lecture him because of his age? Would Tom get probation? Would he have to do community service? Would he go to juvenile detention? I needed to know the possibilities.

Dave and I spent forty-five minutes talking with a very nice police officer. We sat in a small glass room to the left of the giant brick lobby in Plymouth's brand-new police station. It was a much larger building than their old residence. It was empty. It was cold. I guess it wasn't the kind of place that needed to be cozy. It was all business, mostly bad business.

The police officer that we spoke to really seemed to care. He listened to us. He wanted to help us. Dave and I told him everything. We told him what our plan was. We told him what I had found earlier that day. The police officer said that it sounded like Tom was basically a good kid who was starting to go down the wrong road. He said that Tom probably just needed some fear of the law put into him. He agreed that we should go home and call the police. He said they would come to the house and probably just scare him. They wouldn't want to arrest him because he was basically a good kid with a very small amount of pot. They would see what kind of family this kid came from. He just needed a little scaring. I felt better. I felt more confident. I was ready.

Tom was home when we got there. We made the call before we talked to him. We didn't want him taking off before the police arrived. I felt like such a traitor making that call. I couldn't believe I was about to have my own son arrested. At least Tom would think he was being arrested. I wasn't sure. He didn't know about the conversation we had had with the police ahead of time. There was still a chance that they weren't coming just to scare him, though. It wasn't as if the police were all in on our plan.

One Plymouth Police cruiser pulled up the driveway about ten minutes after we made the call. He stopped halfway up the driveway. I was worried about what the neighbors were thinking. I didn't want our home to be known as the troubled house. I didn't want a bad reputation. I didn't want anyone thinking badly about my child. There was still time to turn things around. There was a chance that I could feel proud again.

Dave stood guard while I collected the evidence and brought it downstairs to the kitchen. We kept it brief with Tom. We just told him we found drugs and the police were on their way. The police officer came to the front door, instead of the side door like everybody else did. By the time the officer marched up the steps of the porch, Dave and I had all the evidence on the kitchen island.

We called Tom to the kitchen, as we headed in the same direction from the front door. The tension was thick. The fear was even thicker, at least inside me. Tom looked concerned when the police officer started to question him. He asked Tom if he was dealing, while he picked up the scale to take a closer look. The police officer asked me if it was mine, as he continued his intense study of the object. He asked if Tom got it from my kitchen. I told the truth. I said no. Something inside me was telling me that I should have left the scale out of it. I knew Tom wasn't dealing, yet. The police didn't know that. They had to go by the evidence only. But I had told the nice policeman at the station, and he didn't think much of it. He believed Tom was probably just thinking about it. He didn't tell me to exclude any of the evidence. I was having second thoughts, but it was too late. I wondered why some things only made sense after it was too late.

Suddenly, Officer Blake was cuffing Tom. His hands were behind his back. His head hung low. His cheeks were red. Tom looked defeated. The tears began streaming down my face without notice. It was so difficult looking at my son in that way. He looked so innocent to me. He wasn't a criminal. He was just a stupid kid who needed to learn a lesson.

Officer Blake told us that he would be taking Tom down to the police station to book him. He told us to meet him there because Tom was a minor and would be released to us in about an hour, on his own personal recognizance. We followed him to the station, wondering, without speaking, had we done the right thing? I was glad Tom was coming home. He didn't know that yet because he was in the back of the cruiser when the officer told us.

When we arrived at the police station, Tom had already been taken inside to wherever the booking process took place. The officer who arrested him came out to talk to us. He had a tough streak in him. He wasn't looking to help us, to help our troubled child. It didn't feel that way. It felt like he was just getting another criminal off the street.

Officer Blake told us that Tom had been crying on the ride to the station. He felt that Tom was remorseful. I wasn't sure that really meant anything to Officer Blake because he didn't want to hear any excuses. That was something for the courts. The officer didn't question Tom about specifics after we left our kitchen. He wasn't allowed to question a minor without a parent present. I was grateful for that. I felt we were in deep enough already.

It was a quiet ride home that night. I'm sure none of us had a quiet mind, but we were keeping it all to ourselves. We had to be in juvenile court in the morning. We talked about the specifics of that, and that was all. What time, where, what to wear. That was it.

The juvenile court was in the old brick armory building in downtown Plymouth. I had lived there most of my life, but I had never known where the juvenile court was. It was old and dirty, and full of troubled kids. I couldn't believe I was sitting there with my son. I felt different from most, if not all, of the present company. Tom looked different from the rest of the kids. I was wearing a dress. Most other mothers, or foster mothers, were in sweats or jeans. They looked frumpy. They looked annoyed. They looked fed up. I felt uncomfortable. I felt embarrassed. I was worried that Tom was going down the same dead-end road that these kids were going down. The difference was, most of the other kids had reason to seek trouble. Many were in foster homes due to abusive or neglectful parents. Some parents just didn't care what their children were up to. I knew Tom had reasons for getting in trouble. I thought by being a good enough mother he wouldn't go down this terrible road. I thought I had the power to save him.

Tom was dressed in a black suit. Most of the other kids were wearing jeans that were halfway down their asses, which were covered only by their oversized boxer shorts puffing out the top of their pants. The girls were wearing tight pants and had their midriffs showing. They acted tough. They acted like they didn't care what happened. They bragged to each other about what they had done, like it was funny.

The other kids talked about what they were doing later. I thought it was strange that they were allowed to make plans with each other while their parents or guardians sat by looking disinterested. I thought it was strange that they would be allowed to leave the house later. Tom sat quiet. Tom looked concerned. He was not laughing. He was not making plans. Tom was not allowed to make plans. I was not disinterested. I wished I could be. It would be less painful. I would feel less anxious. I wanted to be proud. I wasn't.

We found out in the courtroom that things were not going as we had planned. The situation had gotten completely out of control. Tom was charged with possession with intent to distribute. They wanted to charge him as an adult. He was facing ten years in adult prison for dealing marijuana. My anxiety turned into panic, fast. This was wrong. We had to put a stop to this somehow. I requested to speak to a probation officer about the juvenile diversion program that the useless court-appointed attorney had told us about. He was not fighting for the program. I needed to do whatever I could to slow things down.

The program sounded perfect. It was for kids who had begun going down the wrong path. It gave them a second chance. Tom would get community service, amount and length to be determined by the judge. He would be drug tested for a year. Perfect, I thought. He would be on probation for a year. If Tom got into any trouble while on probation, the juvenile diversion program would end and Tom would have to face the original charges. This was perfect.

The court-appointed attorney was telling us that the new District Attorney would not agree to it. He was tough on drugs and wanted to go all the way with this one. He wanted the distributing charges to stick. The probation officer told us the same thing. I was blown away. I had to do something. I felt like this was all my fault. It wasn't supposed to go this way.

Dave and I decided to talk to Peter Sherwood before going back to court. He was the best defense attorney around. He had had some pretty high-profile cases in the past and had done well. I wanted to hear what he had to say. I figured it would cost us a small fortune to actually hire Sherwood, but I made an appointment for the three of us to talk with him. I wanted to hear what our options were.

We pulled into the parking lot of Attorney Sherwood's two-story, country-red office building, which was once a private residence. The inside smelled of money. The walls of Peter's office were lined with books. Mostly legal journals, I was sure. The rich, brown leather furniture was inviting us to sit and talk in front of Peter's large, almost red, mahogany desk that commanded attention as it took up a quarter of the space of his office.

Peter had us go through the entire story. We told him about our trip to the therapist, then about the probation officer and the police station. We told him everything we said, and everything that had been said to us at the station. Then we told him what actually happened when the police arrived at our house. Peter said our biggest mistake was trusting the police. They had gotten what they could out of us to make an arrest. It fell right into their laps. Stupid us. We had been taken advantage of.

Peter talked to Tom alone, since he would be working for him, if we hired him. We would just be the ones paying the bill. Peter called us back into his office to tell us what he could do for us. He told us that the new D.A. was hard on drugs and we wouldn't be able to do much in the Plymouth court. He would have the case moved to Brockton and have Tom put on the Juvenile Diversion Program. It would cost us six thousand dollars, but we would get what we wanted. We would get what Tom needed. Tom would not go to big-boy prison for ten years. I felt relief already.

Dave and I decided to sleep on it. Actually, Dave decided to sleep on it. The decision was already made in my mind. There was no way my boy was going to prison for ten years because he thought he was cool and might take up a new line of business, and because Dave and I had stupidly trusted the police. We had screwed up big time, and it was going to cost us.

I dropped the retainer off at Peter Sherwood's office the next day. We had to do it. We had no choice. I felt awful about it. This was my son, who kept getting into trouble. My son, who was costing us another six thousand dollars.

I was sick of Tom causing problems with my marriage. The issue was more worry on my part, than actual problems. Dave was surprisingly good about it. He hated to spend money. He hated to just throw money away, but he knew Tom didn't belong in prison. He knew we had made a huge mistake by trusting the police and he knew we had to pay for it. So we did. We paid dearly.

The case was moved to Brockton and Tom was put on the juvenile diversion program. He was assigned his community service at the local dump, and he was ordered to have weekly drug testing for a year. It was a relief to get it over with. It was a relief that my son was not going to prison for ten years.

Tom managed to avoid trouble for the next year. He didn't actually stay out of trouble, he just learned to hide it better. He didn't seem to learn anything from the experience. He never did, no matter what the consequences were.

Just when we thought something might get through to him, the other shoe dropped.

14

Strike Three

Tom didn't realize it, but he got a lot more than three chances. Once he was on probation, and working on his community service, I wanted him to complete his obligations to the court before he ended up in jail for violating his probation. If he could just get through one year, the charges would be continued without a finding. He would have no criminal record. He wouldn't go to jail for ten years. So I let a few incidents go, without his knowledge, in order to get him through his current sentence.

I think I overlooked the evidence mostly for me. I didn't want to continue the battle. I was tired and worn down. I needed a break, so I looked the other way. Not only did I look the other way, but I actually held the evidence that I needed in my hand. I threw it away. I knew I couldn't keep doing that, though. I needed to keep my word and follow through on the plan. It was best for everyone. I just needed the strength to throw my child out of my home. To put him on the street, if his father would agree not to take him in. That is what needed to happen.

The opportunity came again, as soon as I was ready for another round. I didn't need to do laundry or enter Tom's bedroom. Although if I had been looking for opportunity, that is where I would have gone to find the evidence. It would be there. I didn't go into his bedroom, though. I only needed to walk through the back door of my own home to get strike three under way.

There it was, one evening after work. It was just sitting there in the brightest room of the house, as if the evidence wanted to make sure I saw it. As if it had known I had been looking the other way and wanted to make sure it grabbed my attention. It did. I couldn't look away anymore. It was time. I picked up the folded white piece of paper that sat amongst the remnants that were not good enough to make it into the pipe. The pieces that would erupt into angry little explosions if forced. The pieces that would stifle the glowing embers and ruin a good burn. They just lay there, scattered on top of the counter, in plain sight.

I stood, quietly holding the tiny rectangle in my hand. Only for a second did I allow the realization that Tom was doing more than smoking pot. Only for a second did I let my brain hold onto the knowledge that that little rectangle of white paper was holding what I knew to be cocaine. That was my first thought. That was the correct thought. It was not the thought I chose to keep in my mind, though. Somehow, suddenly, in my mind it was there because it had once held pot. Just enough pot to fill a joint. At least enough to fill the bowl of a pipe. I had never seen pot packaged in little, tiny, white, paper rectangles. I unwrapped the paper. Why did I always have to look further? Why did it always hit me so hard? Things always turned out worse than I would allow my brain to acknowledge or anticipate.

I did my best to steady my finger enough to push the buttons on the phone. I only needed one do-over. My safe place was on the other end of the connection. My rock. Boy, would I need his strength this time. I just hated dumping on him again. I was tired of the problems. I felt guilty that it was all because of my son. I hated it, and I wanted it to stop. I wanted to have peace in my life. I wanted to enjoy my husband of only three years. I did not marry Dave to have someone help me deal with my troubled child, but he was always there. He would say, "I told you, as I said in my vows, that I didn't just marry you. You were a package deal. Your son came included. Don't feel guilty. It's not your fault. We will get through this together." God must have sent him to me, I thought. To hold me up, to help me push on. To keep my head out of a bottle. To be my logic.

Dave was a saint for putting up with everything. I don't know if I could do the same in his place. He never wavered from his word. Not once. I'm sure he had thoughts of regret. He would never admit it, but how much could a person take? Dave hated the fact that someone was breaking his wife's heart. I could see that it was eating at him. I could see the restraint he had to force when dealing with Tom sometimes. I couldn't fault him for wanting to protect me. There was no fault there. The only fault there was lay within Tom, and maybe in some of my mothering skills.

There was something that I knew I had done wrong. Something that I needed to change. Something that I still couldn't see. Dave refused to agree that Tom's problems had anything to do with my parenting skills, even though at other times his words were saying something different. He kept telling me to let go of Tom, but I didn't hear him.

Part of me couldn't wait to throw Tom out of the house. I was angry at him. I was fed up and didn't want him around if he was going to continue hurting himself, hurting me, hurting my husband. Of course, I felt guilty about that. I wanted him to go in hopes that he would grow up. I thought that maybe if he had nothing left and lost everyone that mattered to him, he would have to change. I thought that Tom would realize that his so-called friends were not the people he should give his strongest allegiance to.

My second call went to Phil. I had to convince him not to take Tom in. I explained the whole "three strikes" plan. I explained the results Dave and I were hoping to get out of it, and how things would have to go in order to get those results. Phil didn't see things the same way. He never did. He was Tom's buddy. He couldn't leave his buddy out on the streets when he had a perfectly good, dirty black futon for Tom to sleep on. He had a perfectly good, tiny, dark, dingy living room for Tom to take up residence in. Phil had different ideas on how he was going to turn Tom around. He didn't want to take on the full-time responsibility, but now that the situation was presenting itself, it was his chance to make things right. He was going to have a good talk with his son. Maybe clear some of his own guilt for not being there to raise him.

The plan was disintegrating. It would not have the same impact as it would have if Tom had no place to go. I still had to follow through with the plan. Tom would no longer live in Plymouth. He would be a forty-five minute drive from his druggie friends. He would have to go to a different school in the fall. He would not have mommy to hold his hand anymore. He would not have a big, clean house to live in. He would not have a home-cooked meal waiting for him. It would be different. Life would be a lot harder on Tom, not living at home. I had to take what I could get. I had no choice but to let Phil give him "a good talking-to." I guess he thought he could do better than me.

The upside to knowing that Tom had a place to live was that we didn't have to give him time to find a place on his own. We had planned on giving him two weeks' notice, regardless of whether or not he found a place. He was out in two days, off to live with his father. It was something he had threatened to do in the past.

There was another upside to Tom living with his father. I would not have to lie awake worrying about where he was. If Tom was out on the street, it would have been torture to my mind. I didn't know how long I would be able to stand it. I didn't know how long I would be able to hold out, if he asked to come back. I wouldn't have to worry about that if he lived with his father.

When Tom left, I cried. Tom did not. His expression was flat. Mine was too animated. My chest heaved. His lay quietly in his body. Tom didn't care. He probably looked forward to his freedom. I'm sure of it. It didn't feel free to me. I wanted, more than anything, to be free of my worry. Sending Tom away would not take away my fears.

Tom had finished his community service at the local dump before he left. That was all he had completed. He still had weekly drug testing, if his color was named when he made his call to the courthouse. I wasn't too worried about that. Tom knew how to pass a drug test. A quick trip to the closest health food store would ensure a passing test result. Tom still had weekly visits with his probation officer. I wasn't too confident that he would make every appointment, but he only had a couple of weeks left.

The thing that quieted my nerves about his probation meetings was Tom's ability to charm people. Whoever it was, they would forgive him. They always did. Everyone liked Tom. Everyone was always willing to give him another chance.

The thing that really worried me was his inability to keep himself out of legal trouble. If he blew the last two weeks of the juvenile diversion program, he would have to face all those drug charges in addition to whatever he was being arrested for. It was just like Tom to leave me crazed with worry. I would never get used to the sleepless nights, or the squirming in the pit of my stomach. I would never get used to the feeling of urgency when there was no crisis, yet. I would never be okay with the impending doom.

It was a strange feeling, not having Tom in the house anymore. It felt lonely when I thought of the good Tom, the old Tom, the Tom that I wanted to exist again. It felt freeing when I thought of the bad Tom, the Tom that hurt me over and over again, the Tom that was the root of most of my fears. I felt riddled with anxiety when I thought about what could happen with all that new-found freedom. He was functioning as a twelve-year-old, not a seventeen-year-old. Not that there was much difference there, but the court might think so if he violated his probation.

I was filled with guilt for throwing my child out of our home. I felt like I had contributed to ruining what mattered most in my life: my child. I was filled with guilt for not being able to fix him. I was a mother. I was a nurse. I could not fix him. I had failed. Tom's room was empty. My heart felt empty.

15

Letting Go

I couldn't believe my eyes on that sunny, warm, Saturday afternoon. Tom rolled up next to me into the parking lot of Ocean State Job Lot, as I anxiously waited for him. He sat, waiting for a moment, in his junky maroon 1987 Buick Regal; as if it were a question of whose vehicle we were going to talk in. I wouldn't mind sitting in his car, except that what little I could see, was nothing but trash. It was filthy. I wondered how he drove without getting his foot caught on the stuff that littered the floorboards. It looked like Tom was living in his car.

Tom looked awful, the worst I had ever seen him. His blonde, immaculate, fade-style haircut had grown into something unrecognizable to me. He hadn't shaved in days. His five o'clock shadow was long past five o'clock. What was left in its place was mangy and unbecoming. Tom's clothes were worn and dirty. His pants must have been on the fourth or fifth day without seeing a washing machine. This was not my son. My son was always immaculate. He even insisted on a clean bathroom or he would rather go without a shower for fear of touching something dirty while naked. He could be a little obsessive, even. This was someone else who I didn't know.

Tom looked sad, maybe even depressed. This was also unrecognizable to me. No matter how bad things had gotten, Tom always had a smile on his face. He seldom showed anger. He never showed sadness. It was usually only laughs for him. I would get angry at him for not letting his feelings show. His feelings were showing that day. He didn't have to say anything because it was written all over his face. He looked desperate. I wanted to reach out to him, but I knew I couldn't. If Tom wanted my help, he would have to ask for it. It was something he had never done, something I was afraid he never would do.

Tom started our conversation with common chit-chat. He told me everything was going okay, but I didn't believe him. There was something untrusting in his words, something in his eyes. He was a bit shifty. His eyes darted down toward the floor too often. He told me he was working full-time for a painting company and was making decent money. He had to get up every morning at six. It was earlier than he had to get up for school and he didn't like that.

Tom said it was okay living at his father's house. He hadn't made any new friends, but he got to see his friends from Plymouth once in a while. He saw them when he had gas to get to Plymouth, or when they had a ride to Bridgewater. Tom was saying things were okay, but his voice was saying something else. His tone was low. His rhythm was slow.

Eventually, the story began to change. Tom actually admitted that things were not what he had hoped they would be. He wanted to come home. He missed being in school with his friends, and he didn't want to work full-time in a dead-end job for the rest of his life. Tom wanted to graduate high school and go to college. He had the brains. It would be a waste if he didn't go. A glimmer of hope leapt back into my heart, but I had to quickly readjust my thoughts. I couldn't let myself go there again. I had to wait it out.

Once he got going, he couldn't hold back. He was talking. Tom was actually talking about his problems, without having to be forced. He was thinking about things, instead of just blowing everything off. He wasn't just living in the moment without worrying about what consequences his actions would bring in the future. Tom admitted to his mistakes. He apologized for all the trouble he had caused and the pain he had put me through. He missed being home. He wanted to come home. He was tired of sleeping on the futon in his father's living room. I could see his weariness without hearing his words.

Tom needed to be home, but I would not take him back just like that. There would be conditions and rules. If Tom was not willing to go along with all of them, then he would not be allowed to come home. Of course, I needed to talk to Dave first. We needed to work out a plan. I told Tom that I would get back to him. I felt that he needed to sweat it out for a little while.

Dave was okay with Tom coming home, with the condition that he would have to leave again if he brought any drugs into the house. We had other conditions as well. If Tom was serious, he would have to go to Outward Bound for a twenty-eight day troubled youth program. We told him that he could not have any contact with his friends when he moved back home. He needed to be drug-free to get into the program, and I wanted to make sure that happened. Tom was reluctant. He wanted to go to Outward Bound, but he was frustrated with losing his freedom. He agreed to the plan anyway. I knew it would be difficult for him to suddenly lose all his freedom. I knew that if he couldn't follow our rules, he didn't really want the things he said he did, the things that put hope back into my heart. It was a test. I needed to wait for the results. I couldn't just believe in him. Tom needed to prove himself.

Tom came home and followed the rules, as far as we knew. We didn't find any drugs or catch him sneaking out of the house. He was bored. He would ask for things and say that we were treating him like a baby when we said no. We didn't waver. We were determined to stick to our plan. We thought he complied.

Our second huge monetary attempt at fixing things didn't feel like anything had actually been repaired. It cost us close to seven thousand dollars by the time the program, Tom's equipment, our air fare, and the hotel for the parent's seminar were paid for. Dave and I had to fly to El Paso, Texas, the last weekend of the program to meet with staff and the other parents.

This was my last-ditch effort at trying to help my son. It was the first time he had actually asked me for help. I had doubts that it would work. I had doubts that I should even try anymore, but I knew that if I didn't give him one more chance, I would regret it. This was the end of the line. I had tried everything in my power, everything that I knew, everything that was suggested to me. This was it. Nobody could say I didn't try. I would have no regrets. My main goal was to help Tom. I would do anything to turn him around, but if that didn't happen, at least I would have peace of mind with my own fortitude. I would feel comfortable that I had tried my best. We had spent all the money that we could afford. I had exhausted all my emotions. I had used all my connections.

When Tom returned from Outward Bound, he was to go back to school. He would be a year behind because of all of his absences. He had already skipped too many days to advance to the next grade. Going to Outward Bound would add to those absences, but that was the deal. Take it or leave it. Tom decided to take it. We dropped him off at the airport with his luggage and instructions for meeting the Outward Bound staff at the airport in Texas. Tom had one layover. I was a little worried, but I didn't say anything to him. He could find his way. He wasn't nervous; he was excited. I'm sure Tom knew I was nervous for him. I didn't have to say anything.

The night Tom left for Outward Bound was the best sleep I had gotten in years. I slept a solid eight hours. I was comfortable lying in bed the next morning. I couldn't believe how relaxed and refreshed I felt. I hadn't been that awake in a very long time. I was relieved that Tom was in a safe place. He was in a place that had no drugs. He was in a place that had no laws to break, at least none that Tom would break. He was in a southern Texas desert. He was staying clean and learning how to cope with life. He was learning new skills. He was learning how to survive on his own. I wanted him to stay forever, as long as I could visit him. I knew that was not realistic. He would have to come home and deal with life, and the messes that he had created. I was grateful that I would have the time to re-group, time to recover, relief from my anxiety. I needed a break desperately.

All the parents were anxiously waiting in the meeting hall of the Holiday Inn when the stench reached us. It was the worst body odor that I had ever smelled, but when I saw him, he was happy. He was dirty, but he was confident. I could see it in his stride. He looked healthy, despite his initial appearance to everyone else. I was his mother. The dirt was not the first thing that I saw. God, I wanted to savor that moment forever, except for the smell.

The ceremony took place on the twenty-eighth day of Tom's journey through the desert. It was a proud day for me, even with that nagging, always negative, voice in the back of my mind.

The staff announced that Tom had stepped forward to tell them what happened in a situation when nobody else would. One of the children had smoked a cigarette. The staff knew about it, but nobody would own up to it. Tom knew what happened because he was present when it all took place. He told the truth and the staff members were proud of him. That was a good one. Tom never owned up to anything. He had a hard time with honesty. His candor meant something to me.

Tom was the clear leader in this diverse group of troubled youths. He came out on top of every challenge and obstacle that was thrown in his way. During his journey, Tom learned to rock climb and repel down the side of a cliff. After his first successful climb, he had the opportunity to do it again. The second time was different. If he wanted to do it again, the climb would have to be attempted wearing a blindfold. Tom welcomed the challenge and successfully made it all the way to the top of the cliff. He was a natural in the outdoors. It was the only safe place for him. It was the only place in time during which I could relax. I could feel proud again. I could be happy. It had been five long years.

I could see the envy on the other parent's faces. I could feel their eyes switch back and forth from me to Tom, as I sat there, proud as could be, with a loving grin displayed on my face. I knew what the other parents were thinking. They were thinking that if they had to have a troubled child, why couldn't that child be a little more like Tom? He was going to make it. He came through the program shining. He came through a leader, a friend, a comedian, a big brother. He could make all the parents laugh even when it was a tense moment. Tom was on top of his game, again.

Tom had a knack for making life's minor stressors and uncomfortable situations feel lighter, even humorous. For instance, while out in the middle of the desert, there are no bathrooms. There are no walls to provide any privacy or security for our natural bodily functions. You might be lucky enough to come across a cactus, but even that won't do you any good if you don't feel any movement at that precise moment. Timing was everything.

There is no toilet paper in the desert. There isn't any kind of paper. The only minor comfort to be found at a moment like that, is when your pleading eyes come to rest on the flattest, softest, least threatening stone in your vicinity.

Tom decided to do a reenactment of this situation for the parents. Every child in the group had found themselves in this difficult position while in the desert. It was especially difficult for the girls. He wanted to show us their plight. Tom had the parents, the staff, and his peers roaring with laughter while in his best squatting position and a flat rock in his hand. He had the kids rolling on the floor. Tom could make anyone see the humor in any stressful situation.

There was a quiet girl named Jen sitting on the floor a few spots over from where Tom was sitting. As they were performing one of their skits, Jen unexpectedly released gas because of all the protein they had eaten while in the desert. They had lived on peanut butter, nuts, grains and cheese for the most part. You could see the instant embarrassment begin to flood Jen's face. Tom pounced over next to her and let one rip as he playfully put her in a big-brother head lock. Of course he lifted his behind off the floor to make it as obvious as he could. Everyone laughed and Jen's face reverted back to its normal shade.

Tom had the enthusiasm to lighten life's uncomfortable situations. Who wouldn't be magnetized by that? He had this lovable, little-boy charm that I couldn't help but adore. I couldn't help but to want to help him. I could see where the trouble was going to lead him, when he couldn't. I had a need to put a stop to what he was doing to his life. I couldn't give up. He was my son.

Dave and I heard all about the twenty-eight days that Tom spent in the desert. We saw pictures and met the people that Tom had gone on his journey with. It was quite the adventure. We heard and saw how the kids set up their tents, which consisted only of a small tarp and a rope.

We saw the sixty-pound backpacks that the kids had to carry, sometimes for twelve or more miles in a day. Tom and one other boy had the heaviest packs. They were bigger than the rest of the kids. Some of the girls had a hard time walking and needed to lighten their load, so the two boys picked up their slack.

We heard how the kids learned to read a topographical map. They had a chance to try to follow it and lead the group through part of their hike. Of course, Tom excelled at that. He was presented with a special leadership pin for having led the group through the desert with his topographical map. He stood out, as always. Tom excelled at everything he did, except for life in general. I couldn't understand why he was so capable of most things, but incapable of staying out of trouble.

We heard how the kids had to find water. They put iodine in it so that they could drink without getting sick. The water was brown and had particles of dirt floating around in it. It looked disgusting, but it was all they had. If they wanted to live, they had to drink it. They did drink it. They complained, but they drank.

We listened to the stories about the rock climbing and repelling that the kids learned to do. Tom loved this so much that he wanted to take it up as a hobby as soon as he got home. The program wasn't sounding too much like a punishment to me at that point. Other than the physical challenge of the climb, there was a lesson learned about trust. Whoever chose to do the blindfolded climb would have to trust their belayer for their hand and foot holdings. Tom had no problem trusting his guide. It all came easy to him, which was no surprise. He was very athletic and was sometimes too trusting.

The parents heard all about the coping skills and conflict resolution that the kids had learned to use with each other while out in the desert. They were taught how to use these skills in the real world, if they chose to do so. The kids met with their counselors periodically to talk about their issues.

The parents heard about their children's experience at the homeless shelter. They had spent the last couple of days serving food to the homeless and helping in any way that was needed. At night, they had slept in an old grain silo. The kids loved it because they could take a shower; pretty much the only shower they had had in twenty-eight days. In the middle of their trek through the desert, they had been allowed to take one brief shower. The staff set up a makeshift shower stall with a very limited amount of water. It was more like a quick rinse, so you can imagine how happy a real shower would make anyone after twenty-eight days. Tom's little idiosyncrasies about clean showers seemed to disappear after that trip.

Some of the kids actually liked helping the homeless,

and they talked about where they could volunteer when they went home. It sounded nice. I hoped some of them would actually follow through on what they were talking about.

Tom's vacation was over. It was back to school as soon as he returned home. We met with the principal and the guidance counselor the next day. They decided to let him back into school, even though he had been expelled for possession of pot on school grounds. He would have to repeat the eleventh grade, but he was lucky that they were giving him another chance. They didn't have to. I had helped to sway their decision. I wanted to believe in my child, so I had fought for him again.

The principal gave Tom credit for a lot of the classes he had never finished. They asked him to write a report about his experience in Outward Bound. They would give him credit for a complete course when he finished it. It was a big report. It was another chance they didn't have to give him. Tom was lucky. He would end up only having to repeat half of eleventh grade. And if he took two classes during the summer and an extra class his senior year, he would be able to graduate with all his friends. It seemed too good to be true. It was quite an opportunity, especially after all he had done wrong.

I felt that things were going well. Tom was going to school every day. I didn't get any calls from the school telling me that Tom wasn't there. His second term report card was fantastic. He had A's, B's, and only one C. Tom was capable of getting straight A's, but after everything that had happened, I would have been happy with straight C's. I found my expectations had dropped with every one of my emotional rebounds.

Tom seemed to be staying clean. There were no signs that he was under the influence of any drugs. I could usually tell with him, so I felt pretty confident about his commitment. Tom appeared to be staying away from the friends that used drugs. They weren't calling or coming to the house anymore. He was taking care of himself. He was shaving, keeping his hair cut short, and he was dressing nicely. There was none of the apathy that had been classic with Tom when he was smoking pot. The signs were all good.

Then, out of the blue, the call came. I was at work again. The calls always came while I was at work. I hated that. It was so difficult trying to keep my composure after getting the bad news. It was probably a good thing that I was at work, though. It gave me time to let the information settle before I could react when I got home. It just didn't feel so good at the time. It was embarrassing. I felt trapped between two important obligations; my child and my work. My heart was with my child.

The call came in on my cell phone. I took the call outside, where I could have some privacy, just in case I needed it. It was Tom's guidance counselor. I couldn't imagine why she was calling me because everything seemed to be going so well. I thought, maybe she was just following up on how things were going at home. I stood, with my entire body tensed, waiting for the blow. A pinching pain instantly invaded my neck and began to travel across my left shoulder. It was a familiar pain. It was a pain created by stress.

I was standing behind the hospital, in my usual spot by

the stockade fence. I could feel the sharp pain beginning its descent into the middle of my back. I knew there was a possibility that it could travel further into my left arm. I tried to relax by consciously releasing my muscles from their own grip. Things were good. There was no reason to be tense. It had just become a habit. A habit I would need to break.

"You probably know why I'm calling."

"No, actually, I don't."

"Tom has missed twenty-five days of school and he is flunking every subject." I was baffled. I was speechless. *The report card*, I thought. She was mistaken.

"I saw his report card last week. His grades were good then. I haven't received any calls from you guys saying he was absent."

"You saw his report card?"

"Yeah. He had A's and B's, and one C."

"I have his report card right in front of me, Susan. I'm sorry."

"He must have made it on the computer. We took him out to dinner. We were going to buy him new sneakers. I can't believe this. I'm sorry."

"Why are you sorry? I'm sorry that I have to tell you this. I know how hard you try with him. I know you have done everything you can. You are a good mother. I hate it when this happens with kids from good families." I was crying again. Sobbing, actually. I couldn't control myself. I could barely get any words out of my mouth. I was embarrassed. I felt like such a fool.

"I'm sorry that I talked you and Mr. Knight into giving him another chance. You both went out of your way to help him because I asked you to. I insisted. I believed in him this time, at least more than any other time. I feel stupid."

"Susan, please don't. I wanted to help him. I wanted to give him another chance. I really like Tom. It was for him, too. Not just you. Sometimes school just isn't the right path. He's young. He could still turn out okay. He can get his G.E.D. and take some classes at Cape Cod Community College when he's ready. He's a smart kid. Don't give up yet."

I knew she was just trying to make me feel better. She was trying to ease my embarrassment. It was nice of her, but it didn't change how I was feeling. "Well, I guess I can say thank you for all your help. This is the end of the road. I don't know what else to say. I really do appreciate everything you have done for us."

"It was my pleasure. If there is anything I can do, please call me. Let me know how things are."

"Thank you, again."

I stood for a long time. I stood in the corner of the stockade fence, thinking, waiting for the information to completely sink in, trying to let it settle enough to finish my shift. I was blown away. How had I been so blindsided again? How did he keep doing that to me? How could I be so foolish? I had to pull it together. I had to get control of my tears, but I couldn't. They just kept coming.

It felt so final. It was over. The opportunity for a full scholarship to a state school for scoring so high on his MCAS meant nothing. Scoring 1200 on his SAT's in tenth grade meant nothing. Later, Tom told me that he was up partying all night the night before he sat for his SAT's. He was hung over. It was the beginning of his sophomore year in high school. He scored a 1200 without preparing or even trying. It was all for nothing. It was over. The letter I had received from Brown University regarding a pre-admission program for Tom, all of a sudden, meant nothing. I had to let go of my hopes, my dreams, my expectations. It all had to stop. It was over.

I walked across the street. I needed to look at something pleasant, so I sat on the grass next to the dock leading to the public boat ramp. I looked at the boats for a while, but I didn't really see them. I looked at the ocean, but I didn't really see it. I looked at all the usually comforting sights, but I could only think of Tom. I could only think of giving up, letting go. Not because I wanted to, but because I was out of options.

My mind drifted back to a better time, a time when Tom had only brought me joy. I had twelve great years with him. All twelve were wonderful. All twelve were easy. He was such a good boy. He was loving. I could take him anywhere and he would behave. He was perfect. He always slept well. He wasn't picky. He was a happy child. I could picture his adorable little face. I often watched him play in his own world. He could easily entertain himself when I had things to do. I could watch his smile forever. He was so innocent then. Life had nothing bad to offer. I could sense his joy with the world. His complete lack of knowledge that there was anything bad in the world was beautiful, and I was envious. I needed to spend time with that

Tom, in my head, at that moment. It was the only happy place my mind would allow me to go.

Tom's hugs were not just any hugs. He was so affectionate. He would put his face right up to mine, nose to nose. He would wind his tiny fingers through my long hair and wrap his arms around my neck, squeezing me hard. He would look into my eyes and hold my gaze for long moments.

Tom had never lost his affection for the people he loved. I think that is one reason why it was so hard to accept the way life had turned out. He had never had that awkward stage when he would be embarrassed to hug his mother in front of his friends. Not when he was ten. Not when he was sixteen. Not ever. Some people said it was part of his manipulation. I think he used it, but it was always in his nature.

That part of my life was over. It was time to move on. Tom was not four years old anymore. He was seventeen, and I had to let go. I had to let go of who I thought he was. I had to let go of who I wanted him to be. I had to go back to work, so I wiped the makeup from under my eyes and I brushed my hair back into place. My tears were dried. I had a job to do. I had to go back.

I couldn't wait for the workday to end. I didn't want to go home. The only place I wanted to be was in Dave's arms. I did not want to see Tom. I felt so hurt and angry. I felt so foolish and hopeless. I had fought the best I could. I was stubborn. I loved deeply. I had lost my son to drugs. I had lost the child he was. I knew it, and there was nothing that I could do anymore to stop it. It was a sinking feeling. It had changed me forever. I had become a different person, a person full of anxiety. I was no longer the carefree, adventurous person I once had been.

Tom was not going to sit around the house partying. He was going to get a full-time job, or he could get out. I told him I wouldn't throw him out on the street unless I found drugs, but he was going to have to come up with a plan toward finding his own place.

I called Phil to tell him about the latest disappointment. He was just as surprised as I was. He thought Outward Bound had woken Tom up. He thought Tom had changed. Tom really played a good game. He played both of us. We had fallen for it again. Dave had always been more skeptical, but he would never have hurt me by saying the words. He just stood by and supported me whenever I needed him.

I found out during my conversation with Phil that day that Tom hadn't actually wanted to come home before he went to Outward Bound. He hadn't wanted my help in straightening out his life. Phil had actually kicked him out of his house for sitting around with his friends all day, every day, smoking pot. Tom had completely disregarded Phil's requests that he stop doing drugs in his house. Phil had gotten fed up with the disgusting mess that Tom was leaving his house in, so he threw him out. Tom had nowhere else to go. That's the only reason he had come back to me.

Tom had neglected to tell me that piece of the story the day we had sat in the parking lot of Ocean State Job Lot; the day my hope had come back, the day I had let my guard down again. Phil said he had told Tom to tell me. He thought he had. Tom's whole life was a game and his family members were the pawns. I couldn't believe I was so taken in by him. There was nobody else on the face of this earth that could ever do a fraction of what Tom did to me and get away with it. There was nobody else on the face of this earth who could treat me the way that Tom did and have me come back for more. I never would have associated with them again. There was nobody who would ever be able to manipulate me like he could. There was nobody that I could ever continue loving after the things that he did, except him.

Tom agreed to get a full time job and get his G.E.D. It's not like he had a choice. He had no place else to go. He agreed, but didn't follow through again. Within months of Tom's return from Outward Bound, I found pot and cocaine paraphernalia. He was choosing to be a loser and I was not going to have it in my house, so I threw him out. I was hoping Phil wouldn't take him back in.

For some reason, Phil wanted to give him another chance. He wanted one last chance at turning Tom around. No matter how much Dave and I tried to talk him out of it, he wouldn't budge. Phil admitted that he had been relieved when I took him back in the last time. He couldn't stand to think of Tom living on the streets. I knew that was the real reason Phil didn't tell me he had thrown Tom out.

Not surprisingly, Tom decided to live with his friends instead of his father. He wanted to spend his life hanging out with his friends and being closer to his girlfriend. He spent the remainder of the school year skipping from house to house, spending many nights in his car. I was a wreck, but it was the life he chose. Tom lasted halfway through the summer before he caved and went back to his father's house. He preferred his father's house to mine because he had a lot more freedom. His girlfriend could sleep over. His friends could hang out and smoke pot. It was easier to hide it from Phil and the consequences were insignificant when he did get caught. He liked the lack of structure and rules. He liked not having any responsibility.

Things seemed to be going pretty well, for a while, at his father's house. Tom was working full-time again. He said he was trying to put his life back on track. He said he was staying clean. I didn't believe him, but I was at the point of not wanting to know. I wanted to pretend that everything was okay as long as I didn't know any different. It was a nice break. It was good to pretend that I had a halfway decent son. It was nice not to have to battle for a while. I wanted to be the part-time, oblivious parent. I still loved him dearly. I still had hope. I could always find a reason to hang on. I was about to find out what that reason was.

16

Rebirth

December 17, 2004 was the day my precious little granddaughter was born. It was the same day that my son was reborn, I thought. It actually had started nine months earlier, but the pay-off seemed to come that day.

My son was finally turning into a man. He loved his baby girl long before he ever set eyes on her. He talked to her. He sang to her. He played music for her. He was giddy with the thought of soon becoming a father.

Of course, I didn't find out about the pregnancy from him. I seldom found out anything directly from Tom. We had a close relationship in many ways, but not close enough for Tom to confide in me when he thought I would feel disappointed in him. I overreacted to some things. Tom felt that any negative reaction of mine was an extreme reaction, leading him to feel uncomfortable with confiding in me. The pregnancy wasn't an issue that I overreacted to. I just couldn't think of a baby as a bad thing. Bad timing maybe, bad circumstances maybe, but not something to be disappointed about. There was no way for Tom to know that ahead of time. It was partly my fault.

Bringing a baby into the world wasn't something that Tom could change. We would make the best of it. Tom didn't know I felt that way because he never gave me the opportunity to show him. He had a knack for making things worse by avoiding any perceived unpleasantness at all costs. My worry, my intensity, my occasional desperate yelling: they all fed Tom's tendency to withdraw his emotions, honesty, and trust in other people, especially me. He showed little emotion. I was emotionally out of control at times. While Tom worked on burying who he was, I spent his adolescence in a state of panic.

I didn't panic over Lily May. I embraced the thought of having a granddaughter. I embraced the thought of Tom growing up and settling down. The baby would have to change him for the better. I thought that if it didn't, nothing would, but I was pretty confident in the transformation. He was a caring person. He would have a strong parental instinct. I knew how that felt, and I knew he would feel the same way.

The moment Tom stepped through the door of the labor and delivery room, with the digital camera in his hands, I could only see a man standing before me, a proud man, a happy man. So happy that tears were streaming down his cheeks. He looked like he was about to burst with pride. He looked like he was having the best day of his life.

Tom couldn't wait to show his family and friends the pictures of his brand-new baby girl. The waiting room was full of people trying to get a good look. Dave and I were there. My mother was there. Phil was there. And a couple of Tom's friends were there. We all wanted to share in Tom's celebration.

I will never forget the look on Tom's face. It was the most emotional I had ever seen him. He could barely contain himself as he spoke the words that so many parents had spoken before him. "I know she's my daughter, but she is the most beautiful baby in the world." There were never any words that Tom spoke that were more honest and heartfelt. I knew I was the grandmother, but I had to agree. Except there were two "most beautiful babies"; Tom and Lily. They were identical. Lily May was the carbon copy of her daddy when he was a baby.

I was filled with the joy of becoming a grandmother. I was filled with pride as I watched my son adore his daughter. It was a feeling I hadn't felt in a very long time. I was full of hope that Tom was finally going to grow up. It was more hope than I had had in many years. It was finally over. The bad times were gone. There wasn't a person in that waiting room who didn't agree. Tom always had the charming ability to make people feel that way.

Lily May was even more beautiful in person. I instantly fell in love with the most precious little human being on earth. I held her in my arms. I kissed her tiny, pink, wrinkly forehead. Then I passed her to the next adoring fan. We couldn't stay too long. Angie needed to rest. Lily May needed to rest. Tom needed time alone with his new family.

Little Lily May would have something to do with Tom growing up. I was filled with hope again.

17

Conflict

Tom was in love with his little girl. He didn't want to leave Lily's side. He gave fatherhood his best shot. He was a great father. He changed diapers. He got up at night and rocked his baby back to sleep. He kissed her and held her securely in his arms. It was beautiful to watch how gentle and loving he was.

The stress of living with Angie's parents was getting to him, though. After four months, he couldn't do it any longer. Tom, Angie, and Lily moved into our home. We laid down some ground rules. The only thing we asked was that they pick up after themselves and clean one room a week. They struggled. Everyday life was interfering with just appreciating the baby. The stress of living with me and Dave was getting to Angie. She had never lived away from home before and her parents had always taken care of her. We had nobody to take care of but ourselves, and we liked it that way. It was going to stay that way. We didn't need three children to take of, and they didn't need us to take care of them. They needed to grow up.

While in the Florida Keys, celebrating our fifth anniversary, we got the first call from Angie. She and Tom were breaking up. She had only lasted a little over two months in our home. Her call ended any thoughts of me and Dave recreating the best two weeks of our lives. Our excitement about getting away to one of our favorite places was fading. We tried to put the situation at home on the back burner. We figured it would be there when we got home. It was day one of our vacation and we were determined not to let the kids ruin the entire week.

Angie was going back to her mother's house. She accused Tom of doing drugs again. She heard him talking to one of his old cocaine buddies and she didn't want to go through that again. I couldn't blame her, but I wasn't so sure she was right. I thought that maybe she had old fears that she couldn't let go of. Tom seemed to be doing really well. He was working and helping to take care of Lily. I didn't see any signs of his old ways coming back, but I could have been wrong. It wouldn't have been the first time.

Tom denied all of Angie's accusations. He blamed her. She wasn't doing anything. She wasn't helping him take care of the house while we were away. She wasn't picking up after herself. She was jealous of everyone he talked to. She was constantly bitching at him. He couldn't take it anymore. Both of their stories were believable, but Dave and I didn't want to get involved. We just wanted to enjoy our vacation.

I could tell by Angie's state of mind that the break-up was

not going to end well. She was crying uncontrollably when I spoke to her on the phone. There was no reasoning with her at the time, and we couldn't do anything about it from where we were. We figured it would blow over, or at least settle a little by the time we returned home.

Our minds wouldn't allow us to put the situation aside. We were too worried about our home. We didn't know what was going on. We knew the police had been to the house because Dave had received a message from the Plymouth Chief of Police. They had been called there by Angie because Tom wouldn't allow her to take all of Lily's belongings. It sounded like it was a bad scene. I felt embarrassed, even being two thousand miles away. I could only imagine what the neighbors had witnessed. I could only imagine what my house looked like. I hated not having any control over my own home.

Dave returned the chief's call. He told us that Angie had been running out of our house with armloads of stuff and throwing it in her car. There had been stuff all over the hood when they had arrived. Tom had tried to stop her, so she had called the police. The chief asked us who was allowed in our home while we were away, in case he received another call. We told him that nobody but Tom was allowed in our home until we returned. It was the only control we had from where we were. It was the only way of trying to diffuse the situation. We didn't want a free-for-all going on in our house. Any more exchanges of possessions would have to wait until we returned home. We told the chief that Tom was responsible for the house while we were away. He would have to make all other decisions for the time being. It wasn't a comforting thought.

Tom called us to apologize for what was going on. He said he would handle the situation. He just didn't know what to do about dividing up the rest of the baby's belongings. Angie had already taken everything but the crib, the toy box with a few toys in it, and some clothes. Tom planned to have Lily as often as he could, so he would need some of her things. He would need all that he had left. I could hear the stress in his voice. It was a big issue with Angie. She wanted everything, and he didn't want to make matters worse. I told him not to do anything until we returned home. I told him that we didn't want anyone in the house, and we didn't want anything else to leave the house. She already had what she needed for the week. We didn't want any more disturbances while we were away. Everything could be sorted out in a few days. He agreed.

Tom told us that he couldn't stand living with Angie any longer. He was trying to take care of the house alone. He was doing all the cleaning, tending to the lawn, and taking care of our dog while working and helping to take care of Lily. He couldn't stand watching her sit on the couch anymore. He was sorry that it had blown up while we were on vacation.

We heard a different story from each of them. We didn't want to hear either one. We didn't know what was true and what was not. We figured there was some truth to both sides. Dave and I didn't want it to be our problem. We just wanted to relax. We needed to get away from all the trouble at home. We just wanted to be able to enjoy each other, stress-free, for the first time in five years. That was taken away from us on the first day of our vacation.

Dave and I shut off our phones. We had six days left to be away from all the stress. We were determined to have a good time, but our minds wouldn't allow it. I kept thinking about Angie's words. Even though they were mostly irrational, I knew there might be some truth to them. I didn't want to go back there. I couldn't go back there. My mind was tortured by her words.

Dave couldn't stop thinking about the safety of his home and the condition of his wife's mind. He didn't want to see me go through turmoil again. He hated what Tom did to me, and that there was nothing he could do to stop it. We hated that there was now an innocent baby girl involved in the whole mess.

We kept trying to forget. We sipped margaritas by the ocean, but the alcohol intensified our fears. We took walks on the beach, but our conversations were about the troubles at home. We awoke in the mornings in hopes of reliving the adventures of five years earlier, but we had a hard time getting going. We finally gave up a day early. We ended our vacation and headed home. We couldn't trust that our home was safe. My fear that Tom hadn't changed a bit was heightening every day.

The situation didn't get any better when Dave and I returned from the Keys. Things were about to get worse; worse for Tom, worse for me and Dave, and worse for Lily.

Angie wouldn't allow Tom to see his daughter. He went to the police, before we got home, to see if they could help. They told him that he would have to file some paperwork with the sheriff's office and take her to court. There was nothing that he could do to see his daughter immediately. He had no paternal rights until the court decided if he was to have any. It wasn't fair to Tom. It wasn't fair that Angie had all the rights, and all the power, just because she was the mother. It wasn't fair to Lily. She didn't deserve to have her daddy taken away from her. She didn't deserve the damage that it was doing to her. It was killing Tom, but he had no choice. He would have to wait for court. He filed the paperwork immediately, but it would take time to get a court date.

In the meantime, Tom pleaded with Angie to let him see his daughter. She refused. He got angry and yelled at her. She had no empathy for him whatsoever. She didn't budge. He cried and begged her. She still did not budge. It seemed that the harder he tried, the firmer she held her ground. She was angry and she was determined to make him pay for it. She was doing a good job. I couldn't think of anything more painful than losing your child. I couldn't think of anything more evil than taking someone's child from them. I wanted her to suffer for what she was doing to my son, for what she was doing to my granddaughter. I didn't know how Tom was capable of dealing with that. I knew that I would not have been able to. I could never allow anyone to keep my child from me, but the situation was hopeless. It was destroying him, but he knew his only chance was with the judge. He was getting nowhere with Angie. The only thing he could do was to wait for his court date and hope the judge would give him some rights.

Dave and I figured we would take Lily for visits. She

could spend time with her daddy then. We couldn't wait to see her. We called Angie as soon as we returned from our trip to set up a time.

Angie didn't have good news when she returned our call. She went back on her word. We weren't going to be able to see our granddaughter after all. Angie said she didn't trust us. She said, "I don't know what you will do to her because you wouldn't even let her have her bed." I tried to explain that we just didn't want a free-for-all in our home while we were away. Lily wasn't sleeping in her own bed yet anyway. It would only have been a few days until we were to return and things could have been sorted out then, but Angie didn't want to hear it. She was being completely unfeeling and full of control. It made me angry, so angry that I couldn't control my thoughts. I was unable think about the most logical way to deal with this person in order to get what we needed. In order to get what Lily needed, our love. I was blinded with rage.

I was insulted and hurt by Angie's words. I was angry that she was using Lily to get back at Tom. I was angry that she would hurt her own child to get even. I was angry that she was depriving her daughter of our love, and her father's love. I didn't handle the situation very well. My anger clouded my judgment. I was ready to fight. I would fight to the death for our rights as grandparents. I would fight for my son's rights. I would fight for Lily. I couldn't see any other way. Angie was irrational. Her thought process was impenetrable. The fight was on.

It broke my heart to see the pain that Tom was in. He begged Angie every day to let him see his daughter. Several times a day, in fact. He cried. He got angry. Nothing worked. She had all the power, and there was nothing he could do about it. The wait for his court date was tearing him apart. I watched the deterioration and there was nothing I could do to stop it. I hated Angie for what she was doing to our family. I hated her even more for what she was doing to Lily. There was no getting through to her. She was determined to be as nasty as she could possibly be.

I asked around work for the name of a good custody attorney. The same name kept coming up. Stacy Freedman was the best around. She was a "pit bull." She was cut-throat. There was nobody that she couldn't beat. Stacy was the lawyer for us. We needed someone like her with what we were facing. The situation was grim and we needed all the ammunition we could find. After discussing it with Dave and Tom, I made an appointment for the three of us to meet with her.

Our initial meeting was empowering. Stacy told Tom that he should go for full custody because of the things he told her, even though he had no evidence to back up his words. Angie's state of mind was unstable. The court would have to see that. He would shoot for the stars. If he ended up with fifty-fifty, that would be okay with him. He had nothing at all to start with.

Stacy also told us that Tom had no rights to his daughter until paternity was established. He would have to be DNA-tested if Angie denied he was the father. Tom knew she wouldn't do that, so it was not something he worried about. It didn't sit right with me, though. It was wrong. How could he not be considered Lily's father? It wasn't fair. It was unjust. Keeping her away from Tom was child abuse and our justice system was the cause of it. How could that be, in a civilized country? Why was nobody doing anything about it? It would never be that way for mothers, but we couldn't change the system. We just had to fight to get what we could at the time.

Father's Day was coming up. Tom begged Angie for a little time with his daughter on Father's Day. He tried rationalizing with her. He tried charming her. He got angry at her. He yelled. He cried. He begged again. Finally, she agreed to a couple of hours, but that would be the only time Tom would get through to her. The next time, he begged again. He yelled and cried again, but she just yelled back with words that were only meant to maim the heart. She yelled, "You're never gonna see her!" Then she hung up the phone. Angie literally brought him to his knees, leaving him on the kitchen floor, holding his head, sobbing for the loss of his daughter. She crushed his heart and took away all the power and dignity he had left.

I didn't know what to do. I couldn't talk to her. I was too angry to pretend I had nothing but pure hatred for her. I tried to put it aside. I didn't want to hate Lily's mother. I knew Angie couldn't separate Tom's feelings for her, from the ones he had for Lily. To her, they were a package deal. If he didn't want one, he couldn't have the other. I knew she was just immature and histrionic, but I couldn't do it. I couldn't maintain control of my emotions. I wanted to cause physical harm to her. I wanted to hire a private investigator and have her followed, hoping to catch her doing something illegal that would send her to jail. I wanted to install surveillance equipment to catch her in her lies when she accused us of something completely fabricated in her mind. I wanted to have one of Angie's psychotic episodes caught on tape. I couldn't talk nicely to her no matter how much I wanted to, no matter how much I knew I should. I just wasn't capable at the time. Dave decided to give it a try. He dialed Angie's number. She picked up on the third ring. "What!"

"Angie, it's Dave."

"Whaaat! Whaaat?" Her words were cold and whiny. We were just bothering her. She had no desire to meet any of our needs whatsoever. She loved the power she had over us and she was going to take it as far as she could.

"Can I talk to you for a minute?"

"What? What do you waaant?"

"I want to see Lily, like everyone else wants to see Lily."

"Yeah, I know, so come to my hoouuse!"

"We were told not to do that because of everything that has happened."

"Well, what's your lawyer's name?"

"Stacy Freedman."

"Ok, this is sooo ridiculoouus. I'm done with everythinngg." Dave's voice tried to break through her whining, but Angie kept going. "I just don't want to bring her oouut. Everyone is just being ridiculoouus. I'm not dealing with it at all. My lawyer told me that I can meeeet with you guys on myyy terms, and I don't have to let you guys see the baby, so you guys can either meet with us on myyy terms, or you can't see her! Soorrry!"

"Yeah, I'm sorry too. This is just not in the...." Dave stopped mid sentence. He was trying to choose his words very carefully. He was walking a tightrope. One slip and it would be all over. "There's nothing that we want to do for that baby except love her and be with her, and this is just...." He stopped again to find better words to use with Angie. I didn't know how he was doing it. I would have lost my composure, but Dave was remaining calm. "There's no reason for this."

"Well, every time I call there, I get attituuude!" Angie's whine was drawing out further and further. Her pitch was getting higher. I didn't know how Dave could bear to listen to it. "I'm sick of everythinngg!"

"So are we." Then, Dave quickly said, "We just want to see the baby." He knew he may have chosen the wrong words. Words that may cause Angie to hang up, blowing any remote chance we may have to see Lily. "We won't give you any attitude. Nobody here wants to give you an attitude. We just want to...." Dave's words were cut off.

"Every time I call there, Susan's giving me attituuude! I'm sick of it."

"I was there every time she talked to you. She's never raised her voice. She was up...." His words were cut off again.

"I didn't say she raised her voice. She gave me attituuude!"

"She was upset because she couldn't see her granddaughter. Can you blame her?"

"So! People called DSS on me and my mother!"

"Angie. I don't know what went down here while we

were gone." She cut him off again.

"No, you guys don't know what went down there, and that's the thinngg! You believe everythinngg that Tom says! And that's not what really haappened!"

"I'm not saying that I believe everything that Tom says. I'm telling you that what it comes down to is, all we want to do is see the baby."

"I want you guys to see the baby." Dave had said the right words. He had said we didn't believe Tom. Those few words seemed to be turning Angie around a little. Her whining diminished.

"Can we please meet someplace neutral so we can just see the baby for a little while? Nobody's gonna give you an attitude. Nobody's gonna give you a hard time. All we wanna do is just be someplace neutral so that nobody has any problem and nobody gets in any trouble. Nothing gets, you know, out of hand or anything like that."

"The baby's been out all dayyy! She's tired. She wants to be hooome." I was afraid he had blown it. Angie's voice got louder and her whining picked up again.

"Angie, do you really think another hour is gonna make a difference if we bring her someplace with AC?"

"My house has air conditioning!"

"I understand that, but we can't go to your house. We've been told not to. It's not a possibility."

"I'm sorry."

"I'm sorry too. Can you do something for us? Please?" There was a hesitation.

"Fine, then we'll meet at Independence Mall."

"I appreciate that very much."

"I'll meet you there at, like, four-thirty."

"Whereabouts?"

"The food court."

"Ok, thank you."

"Yup."

"Thank you."

"Bye." Angie hung up the phone.

She finally had granted us a short visit, supervised by her and her mother. Tom was glad that Dave and I were going with him. He wanted us to be there as witnesses. He wanted us to be able to see our granddaughter. He knew it may be a long time before he was given another chance. He was grateful to Dave for getting him what he so desperately needed. I was grateful also. I couldn't have done what Dave did. He was there for us again.

The visit was humiliating. It was wonderful to hold Lily in our arms. To tell her how much we loved her. To kiss her, hold her, savor every second we had with her because we didn't know when, or if, there would be another.

It was difficult not to let our negative feelings affect Lily. I struggled to ignore my anger when Angie's mother kept talking to Lily during our time with her. She kept saying things like, "It's okay. I'm right here." Lily wasn't crying. She was smiling. She was happy to see us. She felt loved because she was loved, deeply. Their words were meant to hurt us, to keep control, to humiliate us. I knew that, and I was not about to let them win.

We would not let them win. We blocked them out of our minds, as much as we could, while they sat next to us, watching every move, listening to every word, monitoring every action. It was worth it just to see Lily. That was the last visit Tom was allowed for a while. It was the only time he was given to see his daughter that month. The next time would have to be decided by the court. We had hope because we had the best lawyer around.

Stacy Freedman didn't show up at our first court appearance. She sent one of her partners. Our hopes began to fade quickly when our case was called. The partner submitted the paperwork to the judge in the wrong order. He angered the judge right off the bat. The judge rejected our motion for emergency temporary custody.

Stacy had said our chances would be better if Dave and I requested co-guardianship. I had questioned how that would make Tom look, but she had the reputation. She had the track record of a winner, so we followed her advice. We looked like idiots to the judge. He wouldn't even consider it. I could tell he was disgusted. Tom would have to wait until the next court date just to find out if he could have visitation with his own daughter. Our first day in court was very disappointing. It diminished our hopes of getting what was right.

The next time we went to court, Tom was finally granted temporary visitation. He was allowed every Tuesday and Thursday evening for three hours, and every other Saturday for eight hours. Angie was to bring Lily to our house for her visits with her father. Tom was to do all the drop-offs at Angie's mother's house. Tom was only allowed fourteen hours a week with his daughter, but I was relieved that he had gotten something, even though the day in court had been very frustrating.

The judge wouldn't listen to a word Tom had to say, even when he had evidence or documentation. He refused to look at anything Tom had. He wasn't interested. Angie didn't need any evidence. The judge believed everything she said, no matter how ridiculous her statements were. She had no proof of anything she was accusing Tom of, but it didn't matter. The case was completely one-sided. Angie was going to get whatever she wanted. The judge was going to keep Lily away from her daddy as much as possible.

Angie never let up. She kept running to the courthouse to file gross complaints against Tom. She even filed one against Dave, and the judge believed everything she said, even though we had evidence to the contrary.

Angie was observed by one of our neighbors walking around our house while we were away. She tested every door to see if she could get into the house. Then she walked into the backyard. It wasn't known if she actually broke into the house, but we couldn't take any chances, so we obtained a no-trespass order against Angie, with the exception of dropping off the baby. Dave had to hand her the order the next time she came to the house. He just handed her the paper and took Lily into his arms. He walked away without any unpleasant exchange of words.

Angie went into court and said that Dave had threatened her and she was afraid for her safety. She said that he was yelling at her, and his size and tone of voice scared her. The judge ordered that Tom would have to do all the drop-offs and pick-ups from then on. The judge just believed her, no questions asked. The turmoil never ended. Angie was relentless in making our lives a living hell.

I was getting very worried that Tom was sliding further and further into a desperate, hopeless abyss. I thought that he might be abusing drugs again. I knew it was the wrong thing to do, but I understood. I don't know what I would have done if I were in his shoes. What do you do? You can't just check out of life. There is always some hope of getting your child back as long as you're alive. But how do you numb the torturous mental anguish of having your child taken away from you? I knew, from where I was standing, that the only option was to remain as level-headed and as clear-headed as possible. To keep fighting as long as it took to get what was right, but that was easy for me to say. I didn't lose my child. I can't say that I wouldn't have needed to kill the pain once in a while. Given the circumstances, it could have been very possible for me to use the same coping mechanism. I couldn't say that to Tom, though. I couldn't say that I understood. I was afraid that if I did, he might feel like I was giving him permission to fall even deeper. I had to keep telling him to stay in the fight, to keep a clear head. But my words were insignificant in the whole scheme of what he was dealing with.

Tom had lost his daughter. He couldn't take that. He couldn't take the pain. It was worse than anything he had ever been through. Losing his child was worse than being raped. It was worse than losing basketball. It was too much for his heart to bear. I was relieved when he gained a little ground. What little time the judge granted him was a saving grace, I thought.

Our lawyer suggested that we have Angie drug-tested. Tom knew she was smoking pot and it was the only leverage we could get because she was the mother. Tom rejected the lawyer's suggestion. He told us that he would test positive also. He said that he had gone to a party and smoked pot because he had needed to escape his problems for a night. He couldn't get tested.

The law partner pressed the issue. He said that Tom could strip and bleach his hair to mask the test. They would have Angie tested right there in the courtroom. It was the only way. We needed something, so after several phone calls, Tom finally agreed against his better judgment.

The brilliant tactic was disastrous. The court ordered that both Angie and Tom be hair-follicle tested, as expected. It was not going to happen in the courtroom that day, though. It was to happen the following day, at the lab. We knew that wasn't good. Angie would have the chance to find out how to beat the test, but Tom had no choice but to follow orders at that point.

He had his hair stripped and bleached. He did everything he could do to come out on top for once, but the lawyer neglected to tell him one important detail. Tom's hair was too short to test. They had to take a leg hair. He knew he was in trouble. He knew he had made the wrong decision to agree with the lawyer, and the consequence would be devastating. He had made the wrong decision to use drugs to cope. He had made the wrong decision trust the lawyer, but there was no turning back. Tom tested positive for cocaine. Angie was told about a hair rinse that she used to ensure a negative test result. She beat the test, and Tom's visitation was cut to six hours a week. He was only allowed to see his daughter for six hours every Saturday. He would be subject to future drug tests and he was ordered to go to parenting classes, even though he was a great father. The judge didn't believe that. He treated Tom like he was a low-life. He couldn't see Tom's strong paternal instinct or how much he loved his daughter. He couldn't see that Angie was being vindictive and he was granting her the permission to destroy someone's life and hurt their daughter in the process.

I was angry at Tom for not being completely honest with us about his drug use. He was hurting himself and his daughter by giving Angie and the judge ammunition. I was even more angry at the lawyers. They were making a horrible situation worse, so I fired them.

Tom was on his own. I worried about what was going to happen. I worried that the situation was hopeless and that he no longer had any help, but I couldn't do it anymore. We had put out ten thousand dollars and he had lied to us. We couldn't take any more chances. We didn't have any money left. He would have to fend for himself. I didn't have faith that he could hold it together because he was already feeling hopeless, but there was nothing left for me to do.

I was worried about how he would cope in the long run. I had a bad feeling that he wouldn't be able to keep it together long enough to get what he needed. He had never been able to work hard for anything he wanted. Tom always needed instant gratification and this was going to be far from instant. Everyone knew that the case was going to be a long, hard, fight. Tom had a long road ahead of him. He had started with nothing, gained a little, then lost most of what he gained. He would have to start over and it was just the beginning. I hoped that the love for his daughter would be enough for him to hold it together.

To add to Tom's stress, I received a letter from the parole board. It seemed so soon, only seven years. I thought we had two more years to be free from it. Eugene's sentence was nine to thirteen years. I didn't understand the justice system. I figured he must have been awarded the opportunity for early release because of good behavior. We had all pushed that part of our life aside. It was our past. Our past was coming back to haunt us. It was the worst possible time for Tom.

The parole board wanted to know if Tom and I wanted to be present at the hearing. I didn't want to tell him. It was bad timing. I was afraid it might be enough to push Tom over the edge, but I didn't have the right to keep it from him. I just needed to be as supportive as I could. It was Tom's decision. I would be there for him.

Tom seemed to take the news in stride. He always did, on the surface. I was just afraid of what he would do when nobody was around. When his family wasn't around. Especially when his little girl wasn't around. I was afraid of what Tom would do to escape his troubles. I was afraid he would return to drugs. He had already slipped a couple of times, but I had no control over Tom's actions. I could only hope that he would be okay. That he would make the right choices.

Tom wasn't okay. I started to find things again. Things that told me he was falling back into his old ways. I was so hurt, not just for myself or my husband anymore. We would survive. I was hurt for Lily. She needed her Daddy to stay strong. She needed to know that he could overcome anything for her. He didn't feel he had her, though. Any little time he did have, Angie would turn into a drama scene. She would call the police on him when he dropped off the baby. She would yell and scream at him in front of the baby. It was bad for Lily. It was hopeless. In his mind, he had lost her. He was giving up.

As sad as I felt for Tom, I had to show no tolerance. Using drugs as a coping mechanism was not okay. I felt bad for him. He didn't deserve what life was handing him. I understood how awful his life was at the time, but I knew that drugs would only make it worse. I knew that the hard times would pass, or at least ease up. They always did. I told him that, but I don't think he was capable of seeing through the mess. He was trapped in a solitary painful existence.

I couldn't watch Tom destroy himself. It was too painful for me. Watching his decline was too disappointing. I had to ask him to go back to his father. Not because I was angry, but because I just couldn't watch him unravel. Dave and I were doing everything we could to help him. We gave him our love and our encouragement. We had helped him by paying for the custody attorney, but we could do no more. We had to watch from a distance. We didn't withdraw our help, our love, or our hope. Just our money and daily involvement.

I functioned better with Tom living apart from me. It was easier not seeing the mistakes, the escapes, the lack of insight. We got along better. I could close my eyes. He didn't have to feel judged. We could still have a good relationship.

Tom couldn't go to the parole hearing. His custody hearing was the same day. He had to fight for his daughter. He needed her in his life. Six hours a week was not enough. Lily was his priority.

Dave and I went to the parole hearing for Tom. Dave couldn't attend the proceedings. Only victims and their parents were allowed in, but Dave didn't mind waiting outside. He just wanted to be there for me. We both knew it would be a difficult day.

I wished Tom had the opportunity to face his demon, but I agreed that he had more important things to do that day. Tom wasn't allowed to change the hearing date. It would be held, whether or not we could attend. I wasn't sure if he was ready to face it anyway. I would do it for him. It was my demon also.

18

NOTES

I couldn't wait to talk to Tom so I could tell him the good news, but he wasn't answering the phone. I thought he must still be in court and that he had his phone turned off. I had this nagging feeling in the pit of my stomach that something wasn't right, though. I hoped his court hearing was going well. I hoped my news would soften the blow if it wasn't.

I paced around the house. I needed to busy myself, so I did a little yard work, trying to ease the pangs of anxiety jumping in my stomach. I dialed his number a few more times throughout the afternoon, only to get his voicemail every time. I would just have to wait to hear from him.

It was an exhausting morning, facing the man who had assaulted my son. It was emotionally draining, but satisfying when the parole board turned down his release. I don't know how much my statement helped, because he lost his case all on his own. Eugene wasn't exactly a model prisoner. Whether or not I had anything to do with his continued incarceration, I would be there every year. I hoped Tom would be able to come with me the next time. I hoped his custody situation would be resolved by then. This time, his daughter was more important than the lowlife he had the chance to face, regardless of how it turned out.

The phone, almost expectedly, began to assault my ears late that afternoon. I couldn't wait to answer it in hopes that it was Tom, but I had come to dread answering it after years of bad news coming from the other end. I picked up the receiver, as I always did, regardless of my fears.

"Sue... I... d-d-don't... know... what t-t-to d-do." I knew it was Phil on the other end of the line. He could barely get the words out, but I knew his voice. He was struggling with every syllable. There was a long pause between every word.

I knew he had had a stutter as a child, but he hadn't had it for many years. It had been gone before I met him twenty-three years earlier. Sometimes he would stare at the ceiling while he spoke. I assumed that made it easier for him to talk. I knew he was taught to do that if he was having a hard time with a conversation. Phil would stare at the ceiling when he was excited about something that he wanted to tell you, and he would stare at the ceiling when he was angry or upset. But he never had the stutter, at least not in the many years that I knew him. Something was very wrong.

"What's wrong, Phil?"

"T-T-Tom. H-he t-t-took s-s-something." Then there was nothing until I heard men and scuffling in the background.

"Phil! Phil! What is going on?" There was a brief hesitation before he came back. It felt like an eternity. It was driving me mad. I needed to know more. I needed to know immediately. I wished I could have gotten through that phone.

"I-I-I g-gotta go."

"NO! Tell me what's going on! Phil, just calm down for a minute. Please tell me what's going on. Did you say Tom took something? Please, Phil. Just calm down and tell me." I dropped my voice, almost to a whisper, hoping that Phil would follow my rhythm and tone. He did, a little.

"I-I c-c-came home f-r-rom w-w-work and f-f-found T-Tom unconscious on th-the b-b-bathroom f-f-floor. There are p-p-pills all over the f-f-fucking p-p-place. I-I-I t-t-tried t-to p-p-pick him up t-t-to w-w-walk him, but he w-w-wouldn't w-w-wake up." Phil hesitated so that he could give his tongue a brief rest. "I-I-I w-w-was just d-d-dragging h-him, b-but he w-w-wouldn't w-w-wake up. I-I-I c-c-called 911. T-they are here n-n-now. I-I have t-t-to g-go."

"Wait! Where are they taking him? Does he have a pulse?" I was so frustrated with him. I knew he couldn't help it, but goddamn it, he was my son too. I had to know. That fucking stutter was getting in my way. It was getting in his way. I felt bad for him.

"Y-Y-Yes. B-B-Brockton Hospital." He answered in the order that I needed.

"I'm on my way."

When I hung up the phone, I didn't know how long I could keep my legs under me. I just knew that, somehow, I had to. My legs were burning and weak. They weren't meant to hold my weight at that moment. I had to get to the car. I had to get to the hospital. If I had to, I would crawl. They were just so weak and tremulous. Pure adrenaline got me to the passenger's side of the car. Thank God Dave was there, as always. I don't think I could have driven. I could barely walk.

My cell phone rang as we drove the painful, eternal route to Brockton Hospital.

Is it good? Or is it bad?

Is it good? Or is it bad?

Those seven words must have repeated themselves twenty times in my head in the few seconds it took me to answer the phone.

"Hi." It was Phil. He sounded much calmer.

"Is he going to be okay?" My voice was pleading. I just wanted to hear there was some sign of consciousness.

"I think so." He got out an entire statement without a stutter. A short one, but a complete one. Tom must be a little better, I thought. "He moaned a little and t-t-tried to open his eyes before th-they put him in th-the a-a-ambulance." The stutter was almost gone. I imagined he was staring at the roof of his car. I imagined Tom was better. It's amazing how many thoughts you can have in your head at the same time while in a crisis like that.

"Sue. Th-that was terrible. When the police got there, I couldn't speak. I was crying. My tongue was stuck on the r-r-roof of my mouth. I mean stuck! My eyes were stuck up at the s-s-sky. My God, I couldn't say a word. My s-s-stutter. It came back. I was trying to t-t-tell them where he was. T-to help him. Sue, I couldn't get it out. I haven't had that in years."

As Phil was speaking, tears were steadily flowing down my cheeks, onto my shirt, creating a big wet area across my chest. I was crying for Phil. I could picture the condition he had been in while trying to help his son. I could picture him dragging Tom's lifeless body around his apartment. I could picture his stuck words, his desperation, his frustration. It was awful. I was crying for Tom. I could imagine the pain he had to be in. It was too much for him to bear. The situation with his daughter felt hopeless. Eugene's potential release from jail was too much to take. I knew he couldn't take much more without breaking. I was also crying for me. My child would rather take his own life than live on this earth.

"The cop yelled at me to calm down. Two of them had to physically walk me into the house and sit me down on the chair. They kept saying, 'It's okay, sir. Calm down.' They had to go find him on their own. That r-r-really sucked."

People lose their quota of body fluid each day through sweat and urine. Some moisture escapes through the mouth in tiny droplets riding on words and breath. I felt I had lost most of my body fluid for the last five years through tears. It's amazing how much water the body can produce to carry out the functions it demands. I didn't think I had any more tears in me, but they kept on coming.

I couldn't imagine living in a world without Tom. It's funny how that happens. You get through life just fine before a special person enters your life. Then, once they are there, it doesn't seem possible to live without them. Life would never be the same without him. I kept envisioning him lying lifeless, lying expressionless, lying forever in a coffin. I wouldn't be able to take that.

I wouldn't be able to make all the arrangements that I would be expected to make. I wouldn't be able to make phone calls to the funeral home, or order the flowers. I wouldn't be able to meet with the priest. I couldn't be the one to make all the arrangements. I don't think I would even be able to get out of bed. I couldn't tell people that he was dead. I couldn't say the words. It was unbearable to just think them. How does a parent bury their child and keep functioning, even in the most basic ways? How do they talk? How does their body not refuse to work? How does your heart keep beating? How do you find any desire to live?

I couldn't bear the thought of living the rest of my life not seeing that beautiful face. I couldn't bear the thought of never again witnessing him standing in the middle of the back yard, in only his boxer shorts, in a muscle-man pose, saying, "Mom, look how big I am." That funny look on his face. Cocky eyes and lower jaw jutting forward saying, "yup, I'm huge." So full of life. I couldn't bear the thought of never again watching a Jim Carrey or John Edward impression. I could not bear the thought of never feeling Tom's arms wrap around me from behind. Of feeling his kiss on my cheek. Of hearing the words, "I love you, mom." I couldn't bear the thoughts.

I was pleading with God. I promised everything. I promised to go back to church. I promised to never ask for anything again unless it was for someone else. I promised anything, if God would just let me keep my son.

It was a long ride to Brockton Hospital. As we passed all the familiar landmarks, I guessed how much longer it would be. I wanted to see him. I needed to touch him. I had to kiss him and tell him that he would get through this. I had to tell him that I loved him, just in case. I wanted to tell him that this would pass, whatever he was going through. It would pass. It always did. I could promise him that. I wanted to hold him.

The large, automatic doors parted, inviting Dave and me into the waiting area of the emergency room. I approached the first employee I saw sitting behind the desk. He was wearing a security uniform. I didn't notice the name on his badge, if there was a name at all. I didn't notice what he looked like. I didn't care. I was there for one reason. To see my son.

"Hi. I need to see my son. He just came in by ambulance."

"Only one person can go back. Did anyone come with him?" This was no time for rules. Couldn't they see how desperate I was? Couldn't they see my blood-shot eyes and swollen face? I could feel it. I was becoming accustomed to my sandpaper eyes.

"Yeah, his father. Can you just tell him that I'm here, please?" I was impatient. I was disinterested in their rules, but I was still logical. It wouldn't get me anywhere to make enemies. I could hear my mother's voice, "You get more with sugar than you do with vinegar." She was right. The security guard picked up the receiver. I didn't need to listen. I knew what his words would be.

The waiting room, across from the security desk, was full of people. Sick people. Loved ones of sick people. People in wheelchairs. I briefly wondered what they were there for. Was anyone feeling what I was feeling? Did they have a broken bone or a sprained ankle? If so, then I'm next, I thought. My situation was more urgent. At least it could be and I needed to find out.

I kept my eyes focused on the emergency room doors. It felt like a lifetime had passed before Phil finally walked through them. He looked rough. His eyes looked like mine felt. I couldn't read his face. There was not enough information there. At least not the information that I wanted.

"How is he?"

As Phil spoke, he reached for his cigarettes which were safely locked in his front shirt pocket, too safe for trembling hands. "He's in and out of consciousness. I think he's gonna be okay."

"What did he take?" I quickly asked before entering the doors that would lead me to my son. I didn't want to wait for answers from the busy staff behind those doors.

"A bunch of my sleeping pills. A bottle of Advil, I think. I don't know how many."

"Did he drink any alcohol?"

"I don't know. There was a bottle of Captain." I rushed by Phil and left Dave to get more information from him in my absence.

It sounded better. In and out of consciousness.

In and out.

In and out.

In and out.

In.

That was good. In was good. He was coming through it. Tom would be okay. *How is his liver?* I thought. *Did they run any tests?* I had so many questions. But first, I had to see him. To touch him. To tell him, "I love you."

I followed the nurse around the corner, trusting that she would get me to where I needed to be. She did. There he was. Tom was lying in a stretcher alongside the hallway. It was just like them to treat a psych patient that way, I thought. It wasn't important. I could go to him. That's all that mattered. His eyes were closed. There were no tubes. There was no oxygen. All good signs. His sleeping expression was strange to me. I had seen that look one time before. It was desperate. It was sad. It was lost. My tears began to flow again. My child was in pain.

I gently sat on the edge of his stretcher as I took his hand in mine. Tom's eyes opened slightly as I softly pressed my lips against his clammy forehead. I wanted to take his pain away. I wanted to fix this. I felt hopeless. Tom's eyes struggled to hold a sliver of light. His lips pouted against the better judgment of his orbicularis oris muscles, as he tried to speak. He looked like an injured little boy. I leaned forward and whispered in his ear, "I love you."

Tom's blotchy, clammy face was now streaked with tears. "I'm sorry, mom. Did he get out?" Tom's voice was strained as he forced the words out. He was heavily sedated. He was distraught, but he was speaking. It was a low whisper, and he had difficulty completing a sentence, but he was speaking.

"No, honey, he didn't. And if you ever do this again, I will kill you. Do you hear me? You have two choices, Tom. You can kill yourself and leave Lily screwed up and fatherless for the rest of her life because you didn't love her enough to stay alive, or you can get through this another way and make her proud of her daddy."

At that moment, I was relieved. I was angry. I was sad. Mostly, I was relieved. There was time to deal with the other stuff. I just sat and held Tom's hand as he drifted back to sleep. He looked so small. He looked a little more at peace. He looked okay to leave for a moment. I wanted to talk to the doctor. I had questions.

If I couldn't keep my son from wanting to die, I could get him the best help there was. I was a psych nurse, and at one time, I had worked for one of the top psychiatric hospitals in the world. I was going to use my connections if I had to. First, I had to make sure Tom's physical health was stable.

I walked up to the nurses' station and asked to talk to Tom's doctor and case manager. His case manager was sitting behind the desk. She was on the phone, already trying to obtain insurance approval for an in-patient admission. I introduced myself as Tom's mother.

"Did he leave a suicide note?"

"Yes."

"Can I see it?"

"We need a release from Tom. He's an adult." Tom

didn't seem like an adult to me. He was still a little boy in so many ways. He was living in an adult world because technically, he was an adult. He was eighteen years old. He was playing adult games. He was a father. He had a full time job and a car payment, all adult things. Apparently, he couldn't handle the adult world. He couldn't take the pressure. He wanted to; he just couldn't.

"I only want him going to McLean Hospital. I worked there as a nurse. It's a good place."

"I'll see if they have any beds."

"We'll wait if they don't." I wouldn't allow Tom to be admitted to any other hospital. I had worked in a few of them. I had worked in the best, I had worked in the average, and I had worked in the worst. I knew if Tom was going to get any help at all, it would be at McLean Hospital. I knew the doctors. I knew the medical director. I knew the program director, the case managers, the nurses, the mental health workers, and the group therapist. They would take good care of my son. I would make a call if there were no beds.

I went back to sit with Tom while I waited for word on the bed. He was still sleeping, until the commotion started in the stretcher down the hall from us. A female patient wanted to leave. She was another psych patient left out in the hall. Her husband was with her. Her voice began to rise because she wasn't getting what she was asking for. She was getting more and more demanding. The woman's nurse tried to explain to her that she couldn't leave. That she needed help. She said her voices were making her hurt herself. The woman's husband jumped to her defense. He was also getting loud and demanding. He promised to take care of her if they would let her go. It was obvious to everyone that he wasn't able to do that, from the blood-soaked bandages on his wife's wrists.

The atmosphere was tense. It was a familiar feeling to me. I knew where this was likely to lead. I was worried about Tom. Situations like that can be scary to someone who doesn't understand or have experience with them. The yelling was bringing Tom to consciousness.

The security officers arrived. All involved staff stood by with latex-gloved hands. The psychiatrist and nurse pleaded with the husband to walk with them to discuss the situation. They were trying to separate the husband and wife. It would be easier to get one person under control without the other jumping in. I knew the drill.

All hell broke loose. Tom's eyes opened wide, under the resistance of the sleeping pills, when the scuffle began. There was yelling. Beds were crashing into the wall. Once the husband's route was blocked, the psychiatrist rushed back to the scene to help get the situation under control. The husband was yelling for his wife. He was trying to push his way through the human blockade formed by more staff. His fight was to no avail. It wasn't happening for him, and his anger was rising fast. The staff managed to get the woman through the entrance of the "quiet room." That term always made me laugh. The only time the "quiet room" was ever quiet was when nobody was in it.

Even though I couldn't see it, I knew what the inside of

the quiet room looked like. It was empty, except for a single, heavy, wood-framed bed that was bolted to the floor. No sheets. No blankets. No pretty pictures on the walls. The walls were painted a drab color, as if that was necessary for safety. There was nothing that could hurt the patient, nothing that could hurt the staff. No blankets or sheets for choking or hanging. No loose objects to throw at people. No sharp edges or objects for cutting. The restraints were safely stored outside the quiet room, close by. It was a safe room, rather than a quiet room. Not exactly the same thing, but it sounded better than the "restraint room".

Tom's eyes were open, but he lay still. I could tell the sedation was wearing off. His eyes were a little less heavy. He was awake for longer periods of time, and he was putting full sentences together.

"Are you okay? You're not used to this kind of thing." Tom nodded his head. A slight grin appeared on his face to let me know he really was okay with what was happening around us.

The psychiatrist and nurse exited the quiet room and approached Tom and me. The psychiatrist had taken a blow to the side of her head. She was softly rubbing the area as she stood, speaking to us. They were disheveled. The perspiration had become apparent under their arms and down the centers of their backs. It was showing through their familiar green scrubs. The nurse left us to get the doctor an ice pack for her head. All in a day's work.

"Are you guys okay?"

"Yeah, I'm a psych nurse." Tom nodded his head again.

"I don't know how you do it on a regular basis. It takes a certain kind of person."

"Never a dull moment." *Let's get on to the business of my son,* I thought.

"I'll be back to talk to you." The psychiatrist walked away. No doubt to attend to her injury and collect her thoughts. There would be a debriefing immediately following the restraint, a chance for the staff to vent, to check on each other. To discuss what went right, what went wrong, what could be done better. The debriefing was a good idea.

I asked one of nurses if it would be okay if Phil could come back. I felt that he should be there when we talked to the doctor. Tom would want him there, and Phil would want to be there. I was starting to feel guilty about hogging all the time with Tom. It was a stupid rule not to let both parents be with their child.

When Phil and I returned to Tom's area of hallway, the doctor was already there. Tom was signing a release so that the doctor could talk to us. Phil and I followed the doctor down to the other end of the hall where it was less chaotic. We headed for the couch next to the elevators. The doctor was holding Tom's chart as we walked. Phil and I were holding Tom. He was weak. He was slow, but he was walking. It was a much different picture than I had expected when driving to the hospital. It was better.

"I have to admit him. I think he knows that he needs to be in the hospital. He signed a voluntary."

"I agree. I know he needs to be in the hospital. We can't trust what he will do at this point. Do you know if there's a bed available at McLean?"

"There is." That was a relief. I wouldn't have to ask for any special favors.

"You asked to see the suicide note? You can read it. Tom gave permission, but it has to stay in his chart."

"I understand. I just want to try to understand this a little better. I know he's going through a lot right now. I don't know how I would handle all of this myself. I just want to try to help him."

There were two notes. One to me and Phil, and one to the parole board. The note addressed to the parole board begged them not to let his perpetrator out of jail. It stated that he had taken his own life so that they would see how important it was to Tom that this so-called "man" would not be given the chance to hurt any more young children. My tears began to break through again. There was no resistance. There was no more lump in my throat. It had decided to give up the battle, just lay flat, and let it happen.

The note to Phil and me explained how sorry he was for being such a disappointment to us and everyone else, for being a loser. He had lost his daughter, for the most part. He just couldn't live without her. The note stated that maybe it was best for Lily that way. It was so hard to read Tom's words, but I kept reading through my sobs, because I needed to know what was going on in his head. I wanted to help him. I could not lose him. His words were so painful to read.

Phil recounted the events of the day. We both gave some background information to the doctor. The doctor asked a lot of questions. Most of the time, I knew the questions behind her questions. She was checking for chronic mental illness.

I didn't go to McLean Hospital that night with Tom. I wanted to, but I knew the drill. I knew how the staff would want it. No family. No friends. They would want to talk to Tom alone. They would want to get the admission done, then they would tell him to go to bed. His doctor and case manager would be assigned the next day. They would get all the family history then. I planned on being there as early as I could, either for a meeting or for visiting hours. I hoped for both.

I arrived at McLean Hospital at noon on Friday. I pulled into the long, winding driveway and followed the signs that led to McLean South East. The red, brick buildings were old and a little creepy. They were all similar in appearance. The building I was looking for sat at the back of the property. It was as far away from civilization as possible. It wasn't very far, considering it was situated in a small city.

I couldn't wait to see Tom. I was a little hesitant to walk through the large locked doors that lead to the inpatient unit. I knew there would be someone there who I had worked with in the past. I was easily able to bury any embarrassment that I had. I knew it was a good place, filled with good people. I looked through the long, rectangular window in the door, watching for someone to answer our call.

As I had presumed, there were several people who I knew working that day. Everyone assured me that they would take good care of Tom. I was desperate for help and would take it from anyone who was offering. It was strange viewing and feeling the process from the other side. We were lucky enough to get a family meeting on such short notice. I was sure they had made special arrangements. Dave, Phil, and I had taken the day off, just in case.

One of my favorite case managers, Jack, was assigned to Tom. He set up his after-care to include a therapist who was an expert in trauma, especially with male patients. I already had a psychiatry appointment made for him. The only thing left to do was work out the family issues, to figure out how best to help Tom. I felt good about things after the meeting.

Tom, Phil, Dave and I followed Jack out of the unit to his office. The black motorcycle helmet, sitting on the slightly cluttered desk, helped to make Tom feel more comfortable with the process. The modest, plain surroundings also set an unpretentious mood.

Tom said all the right things, as far as his safety was concerned. I really felt that he meant what he said. He regretted his suicide attempt. He realized that there were better ways to deal with things. He told us about all his debt. He was three months behind in his car payments, two weeks behind in his child support, a month behind on his cell phone, and a couple of weeks late on his car insurance bill. Every bill he had was late. He had blown all his money on drugs. He had nothing. We agreed to help him as much as we could until he got back on his feet.

Dave and I made two car payments and one child support payment. That killed me. I hated making any child support payments. That was Tom's responsibility, but I was afraid of him getting overwhelmed. He needed time. He needed a fresh start. He needed another chance, or so we thought. I thought. Dave would have done things differently if he felt he could, if he had come into Tom's life earlier.

The court case for his daughter was another story. Between the expensive, terrible lawyer we had gotten him, and Tom's own stupidity, he was buried. Tom would have to work hard to pull himself out of that situation. He would have to do it quickly if he wanted to see his daughter for more than six hours a week. The custody was the most hopeless issue, and it was the most important one to him. That worried me, but it was his battle. There was nothing more I could do for him as far as the custody case, except to be supportive.

Tom was coming home Monday morning. He would have a fresh start again. He was lucky he had such a supportive family. I don't think he realized the importance of that. How could he? Tom had never gone without. I was hopeful that he would be okay. He seemed happier. I had always hated to see him unhappy. I was just relieved to have my son back. He was alive, and that's all that mattered to me. My tears, that morning, were of gratitude.

19

LETTERS

I came through the back door as usual. I placed my bag down on the edge of the counter next to the door. I hung my keys on the hook above my bag. Dave was not home yet. I had time to start dinner.

I took the marinated chicken out of the fridge and placed it on the counter while I got the frying pan heated with olive oil. Just as the chicken started to sizzle and spit its angry, hot pellets, the back door opened. It was Dave. He had his old, dark grey, Ralph Cramden lunch box in one hand. The day's mail was in his other hand. He wore his battered, navy blue-lined work jacket. I could feel the cool November breeze slip in behind him as he shut the door. Things were as usual. I always looked forward to that time of day. I couldn't wait to see my husband. I couldn't wait to get my kiss and to talk about our day.

My life was good. I had a good marriage. I had a man

who kept me on a pedestal. I don't know who adored whom the most. We had a beautiful home that was a short walk from our private beach. Dave and I took advantage of it as often as we could. We had a small, two-bedroom second home in Florida. It was just across the street from the Intercoastal Waterway. We had good friends and good jobs. I felt lucky. I was blessed with so many wonderful things.

There was just one thing that kept nagging at my brain all the time, night and day. It refused to loosen its hold. Other than my husband and our friends, nothing else but this mattered to me. My heart was heavy. As hard as I tried, I couldn't really enjoy anything. My worry consumed my heart and mind, immersing itself deep in my soul. I tried to occupy my mind with work, but the question was always there: will he be okay?

Dave gave me the kiss that I anticipated every morning before he left for work and every night as he came through the door. Just as I set the plates down on the snack bar, a place where Dave and I liked to eat our meals when it was just the two of us, the phone rang.

"Hello?"

"Hi Sue. Have you heard from Tom?" It was Phil.

"No, why?"

"He left his friend here at my house while he went down to the court house to file some papers for a hearing. He was supposed to be back at two o'clock. It's almost five and we haven't heard from him yet." I could hear the anxiety in Phil's voice starting to climb the longer he spoke.

"He's probably just talking to a lawyer or something. You

know how he is."

"Yeah, you're probably right. Call me if you hear from him."

"You do the same." I hung up the phone. I could feel my own anxiety creeping into my stomach. I was trying to blow it off. With Tom's history, I just never knew.

Dave and I finished dinner. I was placing our dinner plates into the sink when that hated noise began to assault my ears again. "Hi. It's me again. I just called the court house. They're closed. Nobody is there. It's almost five-thirty. I'm getting worried, Susan. What should I do?"

"Why don't you take a ride down to the court house? Just follow the route that Tom would take. Maybe his car broke down on the way home."

"He would have called."

"Maybe his phone is dead. You know how he is. It's dead more often than not."

"Yeah. Y-y-you're right. I'll call as s-s-soon as I f-find him." His stutter started to unveil itself again. It had begun to have a mind of its own when Phil was extremely stressed. No matter how much training he had had, he suddenly couldn't control his stutter at certain times.

My own anxiety began to turn into panic. I was struggling to remain calm. I was focused on keeping my breath steady. Every time I looked at Dave, I could see the concern on his face. I tried not to look at him. I had tried to busy myself with the dishes. I didn't notice that I had stopped in the middle of what I was doing and had begun to pace the kitchen. Dave picked up where I left off with the dishes. We both knew what the other was thinking, but we didn't need to ask. We were silent. We were waiting for that hopefully wonderful, dreadfully terrifying, sound to come again. When it did, my heart stopped for just a fraction in time.

"Hello?"

"S-S-Sue. Th-this i-i-isn't good." There was pure panic in Phil's struggling words.

"WHAT?"

"I f-f-found his car, but he's not here! His c-c-car is parked r-r-right across from the courthouse. It's unlocked. His k-k-keys and w-w-wallet are s-s-sitting on the front seat. There's nobody around. W-what should I d-d-do?"

"We're on our way. You go to the police station. See if they know anything. File a missing persons report. Call my cell as soon as you find anything." I thought my heart couldn't possibly take anymore.

My first letter to Tom:

Dear Tom,

I miss you, but even more, I miss the son I had a long time ago. I wish I could bail you out, bring you home and everything would be okay. But that wouldn't happen.

I felt that giving you six months was pretty extreme,

but maybe this is what you need. Maybe this is what you deserve. Maybe that judge is doing something for you that I never could. Maybe this will force you to grow up.

You can sit there and blame Angie. You can blame me for not getting you out of another major jam. You can sit there and wallow in self pity. Or, you can use this time to do some serious soul searching. You can grow up, take responsibility for your own actions, and maybe decide to join the world as a decent, honest, responsible man. It is all up to you now. Nobody owes you anything. You owe everyone who loves you, especially Lily. You need to stop hurting everyone around you.

You need to stop believing that everyone has to serve your immediate needs. You need to stop thinking that what Tom wants, Tom should get. You need to stop being so selfish. The world doesn't work the way you think it does. You don't always get what you want. You don't always get what you need. You only get what you work hard for, and even then, there is no guarantee. But if you're a good person, a responsible person, life seems to go so much easier. Better things seem to come your way. And it feels good, just to be a decent person.

Why should you feel that you don't have to pay any bills? Why should you feel that you don't have to work for anything and that I will always take care of things? And if I don't, somebody will. Why should you feel that you can hurt anyone you want and you will be forgiven if you just charm them a little? Do you really feel that you are that superior in this world? Nobody else gets to do that. I guess you're not because now you are sitting in a jail cell.

I know that what I have to say to you now won't make any difference. But it just might make me feel better. Wednesday night, when you didn't show up at your father's house, it was the absolute worst night of my life. Even though I thought you had already given me the worst night of my life, you topped it again. Let me tell you what happened the night you went to jail.

Your father called me just before five o'clock in the evening to say you left your friend at his house and that you were just running down to the courthouse to file a paper. You were supposed to be back around two o'clock. A few hours later, you still hadn't shown up or called. Being the fool that I have always been for you, I said, "He's probably just talking to a lawyer and lost track of time." At five-thirty that night, your father called me again in a panic. He had called the court, but it was closed and he still hadn't heard from you. Now I really started to worry, something I will never get used to. Your father decided to go look for you. I got the third call from your father shortly after. More bad news. He found your car across the street from the courthouse. It was unlocked with your wallet and keys on the front seat. It appeared that something very wrong had happened to you. Your father headed for the police station to file a missing persons report and ask for help in looking for you.

Dave and I were on our way to your car to wait for you, to look for you. We really didn't know what to do. We just knew your car was the only connection we had to you. As we were driving, we both realized that our entire bodies were seized up with fear. I had the chills. Not because I was cold. I think I was in shock. I knew something had happened to you.

I called Nana to have her say some prayers because I knew they usually work. Through her tears, she called her priest who agreed to pray and say a mass for you in the morning.

Dave and I got to your car. There was still no sign of you, just your car and your distraught father. My shakes got worse. Dave immediately took off into the parking garage to search every level, every stairway, every inch. With your picture clutched in our hands, your father and I took off in different directions in the pouring, cold winter rain. We stopped every crack-head and store clerk to ask them if they had seen you. Our eyes were begging as we held out your picture.

While on the hunt, I was calling everyone I knew. Everyone you knew. I asked them to come and help with the search. Pedro was on his way with a carload of friends. Uncle Connor and Aunty Bea were on their way. Rob was printing pictures of you so that everyone in the search party would have one. Aunt Shannon and Kelsey were on their way, calling periodically for updates. I even called one of the doctors that I work with to ask her what the chances were of the medication you started causing memory problems. Maybe you were walking around lost, scared, and cold. Your father had a call into Fox 25 news. He was convinced you had wandered off and just jumped into a river or something. He thought you were dead. I could see it in his eyes. He really believed that. It was something that none of us but him were willing to admit. My chills didn't go away for days.

I had to hear from Angie eight hours into our search that you were in jail. That you lied about court, that you lied about paying child support, that you lied about so many things, again. The only thing I was grateful for was that you were alive. I know nothing I have ever said to you has made a difference. I just wanted to let you know what you did to us. Why don't you try to imagine that you are walking Lily in the mall? You stop and turn to chat with a friend. You turn back and Lily is gone. No sign except the stroller she was in just a moment before. Can you imagine what that would feel like? Maybe you can, but to find out that she purposely put you through that? You cannot imagine that.

Now, you can become an angry person and go on blaming everyone else. You can do the ultimate selfish, cruel, cowardly act of killing yourself and leave everyone around you in complete despair, some of us for the rest of our lives. Or, you can grow up, take responsibility, and make up for all the pain you have caused. I don't know what your problem is because you refuse to be honest. You can't blame it on ADD because, even if it's as bad as you think it is, there are millions of people out there that don't lie, and they are not in jail. You can blame it on all the bad things that have ever happened to you, but there are millions of people out there who have risen above some pretty horrible, traumatic things. You can blame yourself because of the choices YOU decided to make. You can decide to stop making these bad, immature, selfish choices. Only you can change your life.

All I can do now is pray. All I can do now is hope. That is all I have left. I can hope that some day, I can be proud. I can hope that some day, Lily will have a father that she can look up to. That she can respect. That she can feel safe with. For once in your life, make the right choice, even if it is hard.

With Unconditional Love,
Mom

The night I spent in Brockton was the worst night of my life. It changed me forever. I couldn't take anymore. They say God won't give you any more than you can handle. I was thinking that someone made up the saying to get through a difficult time in their life.

I didn't know if my preppy-looking son was sitting in some crack-house with a bunch of lowlife drug addicts. I asked people on the street where I could find these places. They were reluctant to tell me. I could see the warning in their widened eyes. I think they knew that I wouldn't take no for an answer because they eventually told me. I didn't care. I was not afraid. I had no room in my heart for fear of scary places. I was filled up to the brim with the fear of where my child was.

Dave joined my route after he searched the parking garage. We decided to drive up and down the streets to cover more ground. We stopped every pedestrian to show our pictures of Tom. We went into every store along our route as we headed toward the drug-infested area of the neighborhood.

Our search ended seconds before we entered a sleazy bar on the corner. It was a place several people told us to check. They said, if my son was looking for drugs, that would be a place to look. It didn't matter that Tom was only nineteen years old. He could get in, they said. I didn't care about walking through the shady, dark doors. I wasn't afraid of the skinny, disheveled, hardened men coming and going. I was not afraid. I would have walked through the gates of hell that night. I would have found my son at any cost. My husband was right by my side. He kept telling me to wait in the car, but I couldn't. I had no control over that. Nothing could stop me from looking for my child. I had to search until there was no place left to search, or until he was found.

As scared and upset as I was for Tom, I refused to think that he was dead. The thought kept trying to creep into my brain, but I would quickly kick it out by replacing the thought with some better, but not so great, alternate scenario. I hoped my other scenarios were true only because it meant he wasn't dead. He was lost. He was sick from the medication he had tried for his ADD. I thought he might be in a crack-house. He had given up on life and decided to waste away time, where time didn't matter. Where there was life, but barely. Not dead.

Not dead.

He can't be dead.

God, please. He can't be dead.

Then we got the call from Angie.

The next morning, I was awake, but I had no desire to open my eyes. I had no desire to get out of bed. I didn't want to face the world. I couldn't take any more. I just wanted to stay where I was. I wanted to keep the blankets pulled up over my head and just sleep the day away. It had been a very long time since I had felt that way. I had no desire to participate in life.

While I was lying there, trying to fight back my intruding thoughts, Mary's voice came to me. Mary was an older Irish lady who I worked with. Her words motivated me to move in the right direction. She spoke to me as I laid there in despair.

She said, "Honey, some days, you just have to get your feet on the floor." She was right. I could do that. I could just sit up and put my feet on the floor. It was a start. So that is where I started. I got my feet on the floor. I had two choices from there. I could go backwards and lay my head back down on my pillow, or I could keep moving forward. It would have been easy to lie back down, but I wouldn't allow myself to go backwards. The next thing I knew, I was dragging myself to the shower. Every step was a chore, but I had to keep going. I did my best, even though I had no desire.

I tried to go to work, but I couldn't last more than a couple of hours. I had hardly slept a wink the night before. My stomach was sour. I wanted to see him. I wanted to confront him. I tried to stop sobbing from behind my locked office door. I was tired. I didn't think I could cry anymore, but it kept coming, and so did my lack of stomach contents every time I heaved over the toilet. I concentrated, intently, on slowing down my breaths. My stomach began to settle enough that it stopped rejecting itself, only after there was nothing left to reject. I patted my face with cold, wet, paper towels. I had to leave them there for a while to bring down the swelling and blotchiness. I needed to go find out what prison my son was in.

I went to the doctor whom I had called the night before. She was amazingly understanding. I knew she could see the pain in my eyes, in my body language, in my presence. She told me to take all the time I needed. I was embarrassed, but grateful that I had so much support. It helped.

On my lonely drive back to Brockton, it hit me like a ton of bricks. I was never going to get my perfect little boy back. He was gone. In a way, he was dead. I was grieving. I also realized that I could not force a good man into him. I had no control. I had to give up my fight. It was over. I had lost. The hardest part was that my love never diminished. I had no control over that either. It would have been easier if I could hate him, but I couldn't. No matter who he was. No matter what he was. No matter where he was. I loved him deeply, but I had to let go.

I called Phil and told him to get Tom's car and leave it at his house. I just wanted to see it. It was something of Tom's. I didn't know if I could see my son, so I would need to see his car. I didn't understand it; I just knew I needed it.

I found out, at the courthouse, that Tom owed sixteen hundred dollars in child support and fines. He had to pay for Angie's lawyer for the court date he had missed because he was lying on his father's bathroom floor, hoping to be dead. Hoping he would be out of the pain of losing his child, who the judge had helped to take away. And just to make sure Tom knew he would never get what he needed through court, the judge had put him in jail. He wanted to finish him off. The judge had sentenced him to six months in jail for sixteen hundred dollars. Eight hundred of that for child support. I couldn't believe it. I could remember hearing about guys that owed several thousands of dollars in child support and they were still free. Why Tom? Why for eight hundred dollars? It seemed harsh.

I wondered what had happened in that courtroom. I knew Tom would never be disrespectful. I couldn't imagine what had happened. I thought, maybe the judge saw something that nobody else did. Maybe he didn't fall for that little-boy charm. Maybe Tom didn't try. Maybe he was angry and he shut down. I had seen that side of him many times before, but could he be that stupid in court? Maybe the judge knew that Tom needed to grow up, fast. I knew there was nothing that I could do to make that happen. And I was not going to do anything to prevent the judge from trying, even if it killed me.

I found out that Tom was in the Plymouth County Correctional Facility. I found out that I couldn't visit him for ten days. I could bail him out because he was there for contempt, but I couldn't see him otherwise. I would not bail him out again. I would just have to deal with not seeing him.

I thanked God that I had the husband I did. If I didn't, I might have ended up in one of two places; the psych hospital or the grave. I couldn't eat. I couldn't sleep. My heartbeat decided to create a new type of rhythm that was unsettling in my chest. I lost ten pounds in two weeks. Dave was there for me every step of the way. I was grateful for having something so positive in my life. I was grateful for his love and support. I needed him more than ever.

The first letter from Tom, written before he received mine:

I love you, Mom. Angie and her attorney are charging $1650 in lawyer fees because I was found in contempt. I need $1650 to get out. If you can come up with the money I will pay you back. Or if not, can you bring me money for canteen? I'm so hungry, I need some food. I love you and I'm sorry you have to hear this.

I love you,
Tom

Boy, I would have loved to be a fly on the wall when he read my letter. I could almost feel the blood rush into his face as it quickened inside his vessels. He probably hadn't given his letter a second thought. I would just do as he asked. He would have to put up with a lecture, but in the end, he would get what he wanted. He never considered the possibility that Mom was going to leave him in that tiny, cold, lonely cell because of a measly sixteen hundred dollars. My letter must have been hard to read, especially being in a place where he wasn't allowed to show the type of emotion the letter may provoke. He wouldn't be able to cry if he wanted his pretty face to remain the same, at best. I wouldn't allow myself to think of the worst case scenarios. I wondered if any of it would make him grow up at all.

I was sure that after Tom read my letter, he would somehow have to force his emotions into a prison he well understood at that moment. Then he would come up with a plan to get what he wanted. After all, he was a master of manipulation. It had always worked in the past. This time it would just take a little more effort to get his way, to make him more comfortable. To let him do what he wanted to be doing: hanging out with his friends, smoking pot, snorting lines. Having no rules, getting his freedom back.

Tom's response to my letter:

Mom,

I never imagined in a million years that I could cause as much pain as I have. I could write an incredibly charming and persuasive apology telling you how sorry I was, but that would probably be a waste of my time to write and your time to read. I will say sorry for everything and at the same time thank you. Thank you for all the help, all the encouragement, and most of all, all the love you have shown me throughout my life. I love you and respect you so much. I don't know what is wrong with me. I mean, I care about the people who love me and the people I love, but I lie constantly to cover up what is going on in my life. I am afraid of disappointing everyone, but I only disappoint so much more by lying. I don't get why I do. I can't blame anyone but myself for the situation I am in. The decisions I have made all my life have been horrible. I honestly feel like an asshole, scumbag, and so many other things I can't explain right now. You have raised me to be respectful, honest, hardworking, and charming. I have the respectful and charming thing down pretty good. I work hard once in a while. But I don't get how I can be so deceitful, so dishonest, coming from such a good, hardworking, honest family. I love you, Mom, so much, I really do, straight from the heart. You deserve a son that you can be proud of. A son that has accomplished something other than getting his G.E.D. and receiving a 6 month sentence to the house of corrections. You have worked so hard in your life to get to where you are now. You deserve the best. You are an amazing woman, I'm so sorry I couldn't be the son you hoped for. I will try to do something with my life when I get out but I don't know what. School is all messed up, I'm so far in debt and everything just looks horrible. Don't worry I wouldn't further the pain of everyone I love by killing myself. I learned my lesson the last time.

It will be a hard 6 months, I mean real hard, missing all of the important times coming up. Thanksgiving, Lily's Birthday, and Christmas. I will miss you constantly, and think of you just as much. You have showed me unconditional love only a mother could show through all the shit I've put you through. Thank you. Someday I hope to make Lily as proud of me as I am of you. It kills me to know she has to go 6 months without seeing her daddy, and hurts so bad to know I won't see her. Please send me pictures when you write next, hopefully soon. I really miss her like crazy and it's only been a week.

It took me about 2 hours to read your letter. I had to keep stopping to hide the pain and tears about to burst out of me. It's not accepted around here. After I finished reading, I felt a guilt I've never felt before. I felt ashamed, embarrassed and horrible. I can't believe I put so many people I love through that, for some reason, again. I tried so hard to get a message to someone about where I was because I feared everyone would be worried. I need to tell you how guilty I feel, how embarrassed and sorry I am for this situation. I was so excited to hear the C.O. say I had mail, then I started to read and my heart shattered. It was so hard to hold my emotions in and not show everyone my weakness. I climbed under my blankets after reading and put my head under my pillow to let some emotion out.

I feel so out of place here. No one is like me. No one seems to relate to me. Everyone is so used to this place and so cold it's scary. I talk to this one old man that gives me a lot of advice, he's all right. Everyone calls me the young kid and doesn't give me too hard of a time. I get picked on once in a while because I'm pretty naive in here. I don't know much, but hopefully that will get better. The food here is horrible and small portions, just enough to keep you up and living, but hungry most of the time.

At first I thought I had 60 days, that wasn't bad, but I've found out that I really have 6 months which wicked sucks. I thought you might bail me out at first, I had a letter all written out ready to send to you. I was just awaiting an envelope and stamp. I promised to pay you back the money and blah blah blah. I hadn't realized the pain I had put you through and everyone else. Now I don't even want to get out, not that I don't want to, but I wouldn't want or expect anyone to pay for my sorry ass to get out of jail. Maybe I'll write to Santa and ask for a get out of jail card for Christmas. LOL. I was just being selfish and ignorant by thinking you would bail me out. I just was so shocked about being in here I thought I needed help.

I am going to get classified and housed in the General Population within the next week. Right now I am in the unit everyone goes into first. Then I can make a new call list. I think I messed up putting our number down because I was so confused, lost, shocked about going into prison. So hopefully I will be able to correct the number and be able to call you. You can also try to call to see if you can set something up so I can call. Tell dad to call that number I gave you too. I have his number on my list.

Right now I can only have non-contact visits. Well, I can't have them until I've been here for 10 days, which is Friday 11/18. The visiting schedule is: Thursday 9-11am and 1-4pm, and Sundays 9-11am, 1-4pm, and 6-10pm. I can only get 1 visit per day, but I think more than one person can go. After I get classified, hopefully I will get contact visits.

Well, so you know, I love you and will be thinking long and hard about everything. I will miss you so much and think about you and everyone else that loves me every day. I do have one favor to ask. Could you drop off some money so I can buy stamps and envelopes and maybe some snacks? I hope to hear from you soon and get some pictures of everyone. I love you.

Love,
Tom

Every minute of every day was a chore to get through. Some days, it was all I could do to just get my feet on the floor. It was difficult to work, but it was something to focus on. The co-workers who knew what I was going through were very supportive. It helped working in child and adolescent psychiatry.

There were moments when I would lock my office door and sit at my desk sobbing. I sobbed for the loss of my son, the son I had once had, the son that I wanted him to be. I sobbed for the troubled son that I had ended up with. I was very sad.

I knew I could not bail Tom out of jail. I knew that would be the absolute worst thing that I could do to him. He needed to fix this one on his own. I was determined to stick to the plan, even though it was torture to my mind. It was the only thing I had left to give him: freedom to grow up, freedom to fight his way through life, freedom from me.

I couldn't picture Tom surviving in jail. He was so naive.

He was clean-cut, when he was living at home and had some control over his drug use. He was just a fair-haired, blue-eyed kid from the sticks. Tom may have thought he was tough when it came to his friends in Plymouth, but prison was a completely different story. I didn't know how he was going to defend himself. I didn't know how he was going to figure out the system. I didn't know how he was going to respond in order to avoid too much trouble. Could he find that line between authority and self-respect? Tom looked like an easy target. I couldn't wait to see him so that I would know he was okay.

The tenth day came. I left work an hour early to get in line at the Plymouth County Jail. I reluctantly walked through the large glass double doors. The lobby was new. It was cold. I could see the security guards through the glass where I was to check in to get my number. It wasn't a place where they knew their residents by name. It was not school or therapy. It was prison. It was a place where nobody cared, a place that housed the boils on the asses of society. The security guards didn't care what the story was. All the prisoners had one, and they had heard them all. They didn't care. I got in line.

There were all different types of people waiting to see their loved ones. Many of them acted like it was just a Sunday afternoon picnic in the park. There were young, overweight ladies dressed in under-sized clothing. There were children running around, excited to play with their daddies, as if it were part of the routine in their young lives. There were people who stood there with flat expressions on their faces. There were concerned-looking grandparents. And there was me. The distraught mother, afraid of what I was about to see. My child, behind a window. My child, dressed in prison garb. My child, in a place that I felt was only a step above death. I didn't know how I was going to get through it, but I went through the degrading body search and all the metal detectors. I went through the embarrassment for my son. I didn't belong there, and my child didn't belong there.

As it turned out, I didn't get through the visit very well. The figure that looked at me through the glass was disturbing. He looked awful, sitting there in his orange jumpsuit. Tom was unshaven and his hair was cow-licked. He looked like he hadn't slept in the ten days he had been there. He had a rash all over his face, neck and chest. He was trembling and looked cold and scared. He looked beaten by life.

I could see flashes of my little boy. He was wounded and needed his mother. I couldn't get to him, though. That fucking piece of Plexiglas was preventing me from reaching out and grabbing my child.

Then I realized that it wasn't really the glass at all. It was that person that had taken over my little boy's body. My little boy's mind. That person was much stronger that the glass. The flashes of my little boy were fading. That man was becoming more and more evident. There were two sides to him: one bad, one good. Who would win? I couldn't take it. I didn't want to leave, but I needed to. I couldn't see him like that any longer. The liquid inside my stomach churned and gurgled, lurching its poison up into my throat, burning the pink, wet flesh, leaving a rancid taste in my mouth.

My heart couldn't take it. I could actually feel it breaking. It was a heavy, aching feeling just inside my chest where my heart sat. It felt deeper than just under my rib cage. My pain went to a place that no human being should ever have to endure. It reached down into my soul and grabbed tight until I felt an awful ache. My hand went to my heart as I sat in the parking lot of the Plymouth County Correctional Facility. I couldn't turn the key. I couldn't step on the clutch because my legs were heavy. I couldn't move, so I sat for a while, holding my chest.

All the visitors were gone. I was the only one left in the parking lot. I sat in my car and I prayed to God. I didn't pray for Tom anymore. I had done enough of that. I had spent years begging, pleading, bargaining with God to help my son. It had never worked, so I prayed for me. I begged to please stop the pain. I asked if that phrase were true. The phrase about how much a human being can take. I had all I could take, and I needed Him to know that. I had all that I could handle. *Please, make it stop!* My heart was battered and I didn't want it to die. I still had Dave.

Eventually, I drove home. I couldn't eat. I spent a little time in the bathroom, visiting the toilet until my stomach stopped heaving. I lay down and tried to sleep, but my mind refused to stop. I had no happy place to go to anymore. My thoughts wouldn't allow me to get there. My pain did not stop that night.

I must have gotten a little sleep because I woke to my alarm clock. The last thing I remembered was seeing the green neon light of the clock on my bedside table show 4:00am. Then nothing until the beeping startled me into reality at six.

I felt different. I had somehow changed during the night. I didn't feel as sad as I did just a couple of hours earlier. My tears had dried into a white, crystallized, powdery substance which left a trail of evidence down my cheeks. No. I wasn't so sad anymore. I was angry.

My second letter to Tom:

Dear Tom,

When you first went to jail, I was relieved that you were alive. I was angry that you had lied again. I was disappointed that you were still so irresponsible. I was hurt. God, I can't begin to describe how hurt I was. I was worried. I was worried about how you were holding up in there. I was worried about so many things.

Today, I am just angry. Maybe because I know you are okay. I don't know, really. I just know I am angry. I am angry for all the pain you have caused me. The deepest pain I have ever felt in my life. I am angry because you have made such a fool out of me over and over again. Every time I stand up for you, you have let me down, hard. You made a fool out of me with the entire family. You have made a fool out of me with the school system. You have made a fool out of me with every situation I have ever helped you with, bailed you out of, stood up for you, and protected you. With everyone. And I just kept coming back for more.

There is nobody on the face of this earth that could have done to me what you did. I guess, sometimes unfortunately, you can't just stop loving your child. I let you do that to me. I would never allow anyone else to treat me the way that you have. I guess I can take some of the blame. It was my stupidity. I don't even remember the last time that things were good with you. I don't remember what it feels like to be at peace. You took that from me.

I am angry that you have caused me to have anxiety problems. I never had any anxiety until six years ago when you started all this. Now, I live with it every day. Now, sometimes, I have panic attacks. I never had that until you went into the hospital.

I'm sure this letter must be aggravating you, maybe upsetting you. I can't be sure. But I don't care. I want you to hear it. I want you to be in a place that you have to listen. You have no choice but to think about it. You can't run to drugs this time. You have to face it, if you have any bit of decency in you.

I want to know why you didn't pay any of your bills. That's right, I know. You paid nothing. You lied to us when you were in the hospital. You took advantage of us. The only bill you paid was your phone bill and that was always by Western Union. I'm sure the only rea-

son you paid that was so you could find drugs and get high with your friends and laugh about how you manipulated your mother big time, again.

I want you to answer my questions. I want to know why you never paid your bills. I want to know what you thought was going to happen. I don't want to hear any bullshit. I don't care how hard it is for you to answer. I want an honest answer to these questions. I would be careful if I were you. You can't bullshit me anymore. I deserve to know since I have been the one to pay, in more ways than one. I have paid dearly for every jam you have gotten yourself into. I would like to know how much jail has really affected you by the way you answer my questions.

Saying sorry isn't nearly enough anymore. So you better think long and hard before you answer my questions. Just don't give yourself enough time to hand me a line of shit. There is nothing you can say to hurt me except for more lies. I already know what you are all about, so there is nothing to hide from. I will be waiting to hear your honest answers. Don't bother sending me a letter if it's not the truth.

And yes, still,
With Unconditional Love,
Mom

I was filled with six years of anger. My questions were just the beginning. I was angry that he had started using drugs to begin with. I was angry that he was so disrespectful that he had completely disregarded any and all rules that I had. Tom had completely disregarded everything I had ever said to him. I was angry because he had either blown off every consequence I had ever set for him, or just accepted it as something he would just quietly deal with until it was over. Then he could go back to what he wanted to do, regardless of who he was hurting, including himself. I was angry that Tom would never tell me what was bothering him. He never gave me the chance to try to help him. He had played head games with me for six years. He acted like the good boy, the remorseful boy, the loving boy, who just kept making these stupid mistakes. Except he wasn't stupid. He was highly intelligent. He didn't have a mental illness that made it impossible to control his impulses. He was just a master manipulator.

I was angry that Tom had swindled me out of thousands of dollars, all the way up to the end. I had fallen for his story over and over again. I guess I was angry at myself too. Get me once, shame on you. Get me twice, shame on me. How about, get me ten times. Get me twenty. What does that make me? Pretty stupid.

The suicide attempt was a good one. How could I not fall for that? Even though I had briefly questioned it later, how could I take the chance? I would probably lose that game again if it was played over. I couldn't play with Tom's life being the consequence, but he should have never played with those stakes. That was cruel. It was all cruel. It had left me feeling that I had to do anything that I thought would prevent him from ever wanting to take his own life again.

I had made two of his car payments, only to find out that he had never made one payment from the day he bought it. Not one. He had just gone out and bought this car and figured he didn't have to pay for it. He must have figured he could get something out of me, but how long did he figure that would last? I didn't get it. What I did get was mental suffering, financial suffering. I threw all that money out the window and in the end, the vehicle was about to be repossessed. Tom had known it. He just let me pay. After all, I didn't want him to try to kill himself again. I knew that he was in a lot of pain then, but I was still angry.

I had been very hesitant to pay any of his child support. That was his responsibility, entirely. It didn't feel right. But I was scared, so I had paid what I thought to be a nominal amount in exchange for his life. Look where that got me. Tom was sitting in jail. He had never paid one week of child support. The only weeks that were paid were the two that I had stupidly dropped in the mail. Wow, what a slap in the face. If he wasn't my son, if I didn't love him, I would have walked away and never turned back. I had been used.

I was so angry, Dave and I brought Tom's car back to where he bought it. We handed them the keys and told them to repossess it. We told them that Tom was in jail and could no longer pay for it. Not that he had ever paid for it. I was so angry, I sold everything Tom had except for his bed and dresser. I sold all his movies. I sold his Play Station and all the games that went with it. I sold some of his sports collectables. Everything went on eBay. I didn't care anymore. He could come home and stare at the walls. Or better, he could get out and get a job. Start living his life. Work towards getting his life back on track. He could use the money to pay his child support while he was looking for a job, but it would be controlled by me. The money would be locked in my safe. I would watch him put the money order in an envelope and mail it. He would not blow it on drugs. Other than that, he was on his own. I was through with him.

I know a couple of car payments and a couple of child support payments didn't sound like much, but there were two major problems that I had with it. One: we had already wasted tens of thousands of dollars on bailing Tom out of one jam after another. Two: none of it meant anything to him. It was all a game. It was all smoke and mirrors, just to make himself look good. Just to hide what he really was. It had cost us, and not just financially.

My husband was a saint. He knew all along, but he also knew that if I didn't try everything I possibly could to help my son, I would have regrets. He also knew that he needed to support my efforts when it came to helping my son. Otherwise, there may have been some hard feelings between us and he didn't want that. Money was not reason enough to create a rift between us. A troubled child was not reason enough to create a rift between us. He decided to wait it out. To wait for me to let go. He just supported me in the meantime. He gave me a shoulder to cry on. He loved me. He was patient. I felt lucky to have him.

As angry as I was, I struggled every minute of every day that my son was sitting in prison. He was cold and hungry. He was isolated. He was in jail. I didn't know if he was going to get beat up or picked on. Or worse, I didn't know if he was going to get raped. It was awful. He deserved to be in jail. He may have even deserved to get beat up, but he didn't deserve to get raped. How much could he take? Would I be getting a call that Tom was found hanging by his bed sheets in his cell? I quickly pushed the thought out of my head. I struggled with every thought. I could pay sixteen hundred dollars and get him out of jail. Get him to a safe place. But I couldn't do it. He had to get himself out of this one. It couldn't be me. That would just make him worse and I knew it.

Tom needed to grow up and appreciate what he had. He needed to see how bad life could be. How bad some people's lives were. He needed to realize how lucky he was to have a loving family. He needed to really appreciate his daughter, not just say he loved her. He needed to love her whether or not he was with her. He needed to show her by living as a responsible man. He needed to appreciate himself and all the gifts that God had given him. All the tools that he had been given to make it in life; his intelligence, his sense of humor, his athletic ability, his good heart when he wasn't manipulating people or influenced by drugs.

He needed to appreciate his overprotective mother. I knew that wouldn't happen until I let go. I didn't know if Tom had placed any blame on me for who he was, for where he was in life. I didn't know if he was angry at me for my overprotectiveness, my overreactions, my need to save him all the time. I didn't know what Tom thought. I never did. If he was angry at me, he still needed to appreciate me. He needed to see the good in me. The love within me. He needed to see that any mistakes that I had made, concerning him, were made with good intentions. He needed to see that I wasn't the only one to blame. Mostly, he needed to see that no matter who was to blame, he was responsible for his own life once he had become an adult.

Tom's response to my letter:

Mom,

Hey what's up? I just got your letter. I understand where you are coming from with your anger. Looking at myself, from where I am now, and looking at all the people I've hurt, I'm straight-up a piece-of-shit disappointment. I know that is what I've been for the past five to six years. I could write that I'm going to change, just wait until I get out, and beg for your forgiveness. I could promise to turn my life around, just bail me out. I could write a lot of that, but I won't.

You already know where I stand on what I want to do with my life. I don't expect help or forgiveness until I prove myself. I don't expect anything from you. You've done so much for me, and I have let you down. I feel like a piece of shit because of it and I'll leave it at that.

Now, to answer the two questions you have asked me; why didn't you pay your bills, and what did you think would happen to you? I don't have to think about that at all because I just have to answer the best I can and as honest as I can. The first week I didn't pay because we went camping. Gas cost a lot more than I thought. I ended up being broke after we got back, which put me behind two weeks. Then I screwed up with a few jobs. I priced them way too low and was almost working for free. Driving around constantly cost a lot of money. I was lying about how much work I had to everyone because I wanted to get my own company going, but it was really slow. I would get a check and put money aside to pay bills, but then I wouldn't get another check for a while and I would end up spending my money on gas and food. Then I got a job with that painting company. I honestly don't know what I did with my money for a couple of weeks. It just went, fast. Then I started smoking weed and doing coke. Most of my money went towards that for about two to three weeks. Then, I had that suicide attempt. I was driving so much, I would spend a hundred and fifty dollars a week, then blow the rest on going out, and towards the last few weeks on drugs.

I don't really know why I would do that. I don't really know what I was thinking. I don't think I was thinking. I know I would always be like, oh, I'll catch up next week, and then, oh, next week. Then I was so far behind, I turned to drugs and alcohol to forget all of the problems and bills and buried myself further. The more I think about it, I have to realize that I have a drug problem.

Now, what I thought would happen. I

thought, at first, I would just catch up the next check and everything would be fine. Then the next check was the same. I thought I might pay some late fees and catch up. Then, I started using drugs, and I don't think I cared what happened to me. I just hated life and wanted to get fucked up to forget. I didn't think you or dad would bail me out, but I probably didn't think of the consequences because you always do get me out of major jams. I didn't think I would go to jail this soon. I didn't think I would lose everything, including almost losing my life. If I had just stopped and thought about it, I would have realized what could happen.

But, finally it happened. I lost my car, my phone, and my freedom. The worst of it is, I lost my chance to see Lily and everyone else I love. I have to take it as a good thing. A chance for a new start. A new, old me. I think I answered your questions as honestly as possible.

Well, thank you for the drawing Lily did.

It made me smile. Were you going to send more pictures of Lily? I got the ones of her in the highchair and on the boat.

I love you, Mom, and I'm sorry for the pain I have caused. I know it probably doesn't mean anything but I really am, and I just have to tell you that. I can't imagine the pain you've been in, and that makes me feel like an ass-hole, a jerk, and a bunch of other things. I love you, Mom, forever. Write back!

Love, your son,
Tom

I thought Tom's letter was the only time he had been open and honest with me in many years. Still, I was afraid to trust him. It could still be manipulation. His honesty could be a set-up, I thought. Tom knew that his honesty would suck me back in. Then he would take advantage of me while I trusted him again. I didn't want to think about it that way, but I had spent so many years being played by him.

I wanted Tom's letter to be a new start for us. I wanted it to be a clean slate, so a clean slate is how I decided to take it. But it was only the beginning, and it wasn't a reason to bail him out of jail. I wanted to do that, more than anything, but I knew that I couldn't.

Not only did I struggle with my own doubts about leaving Tom in jail, but I had to keep talking his father into leaving him there. I thanked God that the logical part of my mind kicked in whenever I spoke to him. Phil hadn't lived with him long enough to realize how important it was for us to leave him where he was. He hadn't gone through what Dave and I had gone through with him. He hadn't been manipulated or lied to as much. In fact, Phil still believed what Tom was telling him. He didn't really get it, but he went along with the plan because he respected me and Dave. He always thought of me as a good mother, so he tried to trust that I was making the right decision because I loved my son. Phil knew how much I loved Tom. He just thought I was too intense, too overreactive.

Phil won out in the end. I could only hold him off for so long. Tom didn't serve his six months. He was released after only four weeks. Phil borrowed the money and gave up his two weeks of vacation, in lieu of pay, to come up with the money required to spring his son out of jail. He couldn't bear the thought of leaving him in jail through the holidays, through his daughter's first birthday, through his own birthday. Not when he could get him out for sixteen hundred dollars. The only thing Tom missed was Thanksgiving. Considering how much he loved to eat, and that he was so hungry in jail, it was a good holiday to miss. Other than a few weeks of his life, that was all he missed. Tom was coming home again.

I really thought that jail would have some impact on Tom. I thought he would never take a chance on going back. I was reluctant to think that his experience had caused him to grow up, but I thought he would do anything to avoid jail again. I thought he would run right out and get a job, but that didn't happen. He was just as stubborn and apathetic as he ever was. He did nothing. He pretended to look for a job while we were at work. We couldn't believe it. Jail had had no effect on him. It was like he was angry and he was going to show everyone how unfairly he had been treated. He didn't act angry. He never did, but it showed in his actions, not in his words. Dave and I were fed up by January. Tom had gone through all the money I had made from the sale of his belongings. His child support was paid, but he hadn't worked for it. We were done waiting for Tom to decide what job he would get or when. His vacation was over.

Dave and I set up a list of rules, with a timeline, for Tom to live by. Not rules that he could decide whether or not he wanted to live by. They were our rules. They were not meant to help him. They were meant to help us get him out of the house in a reasonable amount of time.

Rule number one: Get any job he could, immediately. We gave him a week. He was to save one hundred and fifty dollars a week toward a vehicle. His bills were to be paid every week and we wanted proof. He had to show us receipts.

Rule number two: Once Tom had a minimum of fifteen hundred dollars saved, he had to have a vehicle on the road, or April first, which ever came first.

Rule number three: Get a real job by May first. Not a part-time job. Not a job that paid cash. A real, full-time job, with a paycheck, and he was to have his child support payment taken out of his check.

Rule number four: Tom was to save one hundred and fifty dollars each week toward an apartment. By September first, he had to have an apartment. If he did not follow every part of every one of these rules, he had two weeks to find a place to live.

Tom agreed to the rules. He really didn't have a choice. If he didn't, he had to leave. By the third week, Tom decided to test the rules. He didn't show us the receipt for his child support payment. We told him he had two weeks to move out. I reminded him that the rules were not in place to help him. They were not meant to teach him anything. They really didn't have much to do with him at all. The rules were made to help me and Dave. I told him, "Tom, make no mistake about this, I have no problem throwing you out. That is the point of all this. There is nothing left to teach you, so if you think I'm not serious, you will see in two weeks because that is how much time you'll have to find another place to live." Tom came up with the receipt that night.

20

REUNIONS

Tom was angry with our arrangement for a while, but eventually, he came to accept the conditions and just went along with the rules without complaining. I knew he hated every second of it, but that made me happy. I knew the more he hated it, the more motivated he would be to move out. He was finally giving me something that I wanted. I finally understood what it would take to get Tom to do the right thing. He was following the rules and wanted to move out on his own.

Other things were getting better for Tom. His relationship with Angie was improving. They were getting along and he was seeing Lily more often. He was happier. Lily always made him happy. He was still pissed at me, but everything else was going well. He was saving money and paying his bills. Not that he had a choice. I was making sure of it.

Tom decided to go back to work with my brother. He didn't have much of a choice about what job he took, either.

He had a week to get a job or he would be kicked out of the house. He didn't want to paint anymore, but it was a job. There wasn't any health insurance, and the work wasn't always available, but it was a decent paycheck most weeks. I seized my opportunity to assure Tom's financial obligations were met. I asked my brother to give Tom's checks to me. If Tom wanted money, he would have to sign his checks over to me. I would put his savings in my safe and give the rest to him.

Tom was very angry about that arrangement, but he didn't have any choice, unless he wanted to live on the street and seldom be able to see his daughter. He felt that I had no right to take his money. I felt that I had an obligation to get him out of my house and out on his own. I didn't care how he felt about it. It was going to happen my way from that point on. I wasn't listening to his complaints. I wasn't negotiating any changes. I wasn't making any exceptions. There would be no second chances. It made life a whole lot easier for me. There were no guilt trips. There was no worry about making compromises. There were no decisions to be made. The rules were already in place.

I only wished I had handled things the same way earlier on. I wished I hadn't been so worried about Tom's feelings, Tom's happiness, Tom's perceived rights. I should have been worried about what kind of contributor I was helping to create for society. I should have been more focused on what Tom needed to learn to be a man, to be independent, to succeed in life. I shouldn't have worried only about making him happy and comfortable. That would have happened if I had put my foot down hard to begin with. I was always trying to be fair. I was always trying to be diplomatic. I had felt bad for what he had been through, and I had thought he deserved a break. I had hoped that he would do the right thing on his own, but he never did.

I hoped it wasn't too late for him to figure things out on his own. The problem was that his responsibilities were getting bigger. I didn't know if he could handle the adult life that he had chosen. I felt that I had blown my chance at teaching him how to be independent. It was up to him, alone.

Tom saved enough money by his deadline to buy a car. It took him a month to find one worth buying and get it on the road, but he had met the first goal. It was a step toward his independence. It was a step toward my freedom. The next step was a better job. I couldn't wait. I had hope for a more stress-free life.

Our annual family trip to the mountains was coming up in the second week of August. It was a time to put all of our differences aside. It was a week with no anger, no resentment, no pain, no nightmares, no anxiety. It was a week when our entire family, and some friends, could enjoy all the good qualities in each other.

Dave and I had started the trip for Tom after he lost his ability to play basketball. I needed something to keep us together no matter what Tom was going through. Tom loved hiking. He loved our tubing trips down the river. He loved having his grandparents around for the week, everyone spending time together without fighting. It was a time to regroup and tighten the bonds of our family.

Angie had always been a part of our trip, until the year after Lily was born. It was a stressful time between them. It was a stressful time in our family. It was the middle of the custody battle. Even with all the problems, Angie was missed that year. It felt like there was a piece of the family missing. Angie had been a part of making some of our favorite family moments.

Dave and I put all the past problems behind us, and with Tom's permission, we decided to invite Angie to come with us again. I knew it would take Angie a long time to trust our commitment to her. She had her pride. It was her daughter. It was her relationship with Tom. We had gotten involved and she felt that we had threatened her security.

It would take time for us to trust Angie as well, to trust that she would never hurt us like that again. I had faith. I had always loved Angie and appreciated her being in Tom's life. She was always good for him. She had kept him on the straight and narrow more than anyone else ever could. She was a good kid. She had had one miserable, nasty, lapse in judgment. Maybe it was post-partum depression. Maybe she listened to her mother or her lawyer too much. Whatever it was, we were willing to try to forgive and forget. Angie was too, so we all agreed to put the past behind us.

Tom and Angie weren't back together, but they had repaired enough of the damaged relationship to be good friends again. Tom was happy that everyone was getting along. We were all looking forward to making more happy memories for our family, especially for Lily.

Tom was worried that he would have to miss the trip. He had found his real job, operating machines in a juice factory. The job offered full benefits, and he would have a paycheck that he could have his child support taken out of every week. It was another big step toward our freedom. The only problem was, Tom wouldn't have a vacation for a year. Under most circumstances, he wouldn't care. He was usually a hard worker. It was one of his positive attributes that I had always held onto.

Our trip was very important to Tom. He didn't want to miss it, so he told his employer, before he started the job, that he already had a vacation planned and paid for. He needed that week off, unpaid. He was granted permission as long as he could find his own coverage. He was relieved. Tom had never missed the trip. He would find his coverage. No matter how bad things were, he was always there. He wouldn't miss it for the world.

As I was getting ready for the trip, Tom's friend Pedro was on his way out of the house. He stopped to talk to me, as he always did. He was excited to get home and get ready for his own trip. He told me that every year, he and a bunch of his friends went up to the Saco River for a long weekend. They rode canoes down the river and camped along the river bed on the way down. It was the first I had heard about it.

"You guys do that every year?"

"Yeah. We've been doing it for a while."

"How come Tom has never gone?"

"It's always the same time as your family trip."

"He should have told me. I could have changed the

date."

"He looks forward to going with you guys. He would rather be with you."

"You're kidding me?"

"No, really, he looks forward to it."

I couldn't believe it. I knew Tom loved our trip, but I didn't think it was enough to miss an annual trip with all his childhood friends. I didn't think it was enough to miss out on canoes filled with beer, or camping along the river bed, something he wanted us to do during our vacation. I felt bad that he had missed out on that opportunity for all those years. I couldn't believe that he had never told me.

Tom came up from the basement with an arm load of camping equipment. He was on his way back down for more, until I stopped him. "Tom. You never told me about the Saco River trip with your friends." Tom shrugged his shoulders to express that it was no big deal before heading back downstairs.

"How come you didn't say anything? I could have changed the date of our trip so that you could go."

"I would rather go to the White Mountains with the family. It's okay. I probably would have gotten in too much trouble with them anyway. They do a lot of drinking."

I shook my head at the first sign of insight I had seen in Tom in a long time. I felt a little sad that he knew he might not have enough control over his behavior. That he had to miss a trip like that because he was afraid of what he might do. I felt responsible for making him miss out.

"It's okay, Mom. I didn't miss out on anything. I love being with you guys." His words were genuine. I didn't sense any regret in his voice. I was proud of him. More than ever, I was looking forward to the mountains.

Tom bought a backpack to carry Lily on the hikes. He wanted her to experience everything with him. He was so excited to take her with us. Everyone else was a little nervous because of our past experiences hiking with Tom. We were afraid Tom hadn't outgrown his magooism yet.

Years earlier, Dave, Angie, and I spent our entire first hike announcing the obstacles in our path to Tom. Whoever was in the lead at the time would call out, "Tom, rock! Tom, root! Tom, bridge!" Tom would still trip sometimes. We would all laugh, including Tom. He had made some of our favorite memories because of his magooism. It wouldn't be fun watching him fall with Lily on his back, though.

Tom wasn't a clumsy hiker. He just didn't pay attention all the time. When the trail wasn't challenging, he would trip. During the years that we had called out the obstacles, he had also amazed us with his ability to navigate through the rapid, slippery, rock-filled rivers. It was more challenging. That's when he did better.

One summer, we came across a section of river that was difficult to cross. The protruding rocks were far apart, wet, and small for our feet to secure a good plant. One wrong step, and it was a long way down. Angie was scared. Tom told her to wait on a large boulder where she could comfortably sit. He told us that he would be right back.

We watched Tom walk off down river a ways. He came

back a few moments later dragging a large tree trunk behind him. He found the perfect spot to wedge the trunk across the river as he stood knee-deep in the cold, rapid water. He called for Angie. She hesitantly walked toward Tom's outreached hand. He patiently coached her along. "I won't let you fall. It's okay. I promise. You can do it. You can do it, Angie." Angie kept moving, slowly, across the makeshift bridge, secured by Tom's hand and encouraging words.

He was so patient and lovable. I thought, *how lucky is she?* He's so romantic. I felt so proud to have such a wonderful son. Angie made it across the river with the guidance of Tom's hand. She was so proud of herself. Her grin spread ear to ear as she jumped into Tom's arms when she was sure she wouldn't fall. It was a beautiful moment. We were in awe of Tom's sporadic capabilities. We were still afraid for Lily's upcoming adventure with her daddy.

Our minds couldn't let go of the memories of Tom's magooism. It was only one short year ago that Tom had made one of our funniest memories. Dave, Tom, our nephew Jonathan, and I hiked up to Lonesome Lake. We were staying in one of the Appalachian Trail huts at the top of the mountain. When we got to the hut, we read a sign that said there was a nature walk planned at dusk.

Tom couldn't wait for the walk. He was the oldest one in the bunch, but you wouldn't know it by his enthusiasm. He had to talk his younger cousin into joining in on his fun.

Tom had an amazing love for life when his brain wasn't infected by drugs. When he could let his troubles go. He found so much pleasure in new things. In all things. His essence brought happiness to everyone around him. How could such a happy person choose to live his life in pain and disappointment? He couldn't. He would come around. He had to. I knew it in my heart.

Dave and I sat outside our primitive hut, enjoying the warm, summer air. The glimmer of the moonlight reflected on the lake just enough for us to watch the subtle ripples move across the surface below. We were resting our weary muscles, recuperating before the hike down the mountain the next morning.

We could see the line of flashlights moving through the woods. We could hear the children's chitchat and laughter as the nature walk guide pointed out the different vegetation and wildlife habitats. Tom's voice was the loudest. He was so excited. I loved listening to his voice. He brought a smile to my face as I sat, relaxed, atop the mountain.

"Oh crap!!! I'm okay!" Tom cheerfully responded, before anyone even asked. We knew it was his voice echoing up to our ears from below. He had fallen. I knew it. Everyone started to laugh, including me and Dave. We couldn't see what had happened with our eyes, but we could see with our minds. We had been there many times already, pretty much on a daily basis. At home, Dave and I would hear Tom's footsteps start up the stairs, then we would hear a loud thud, then, "I'm okay!" We never even asked if he was okay. We couldn't because we were laughing. We couldn't because he would respond before we had the chance to. He just wanted us to know, right away, that he was okay. God, did I love him.

Tom and Jonathan came walking up the trail, toward the hut, a little while after the loud announcement of something gone wrong. Tom was soaking wet and covered in mud up to his knees. Jonathan was still laughing at him. Tom was still laughing at himself. "I didn't see the walkway. It was dark. I stepped off the wooden trail. I didn't know we were in the marsh."

"Isn't that what the flashlights were for?"

"I was looking at something."

"Obviously not where you were going. You're going to have to hike tomorrow with wet boots."

"I know. I'll be okay. We only have six miles to go." I could never get mad at him for his magooism. He was just so oblivious to his surroundings sometimes. There was nothing ill-intentioned in the boy, but I was scared for Lily.

We pulled onto the long dirt road that wove through the pines and over a branch of the Pemi River. We crossed the old, bumpy wooden bridge. We were rejuvenated by the scenery after our long ride. A quick stop at the office to check in and we were on our way to settle into what would be our home base for the next week.

After checking in, Dave and I pulled into our site. I waited while Dave scanned the area. He was figuring out where the tarp would go. He was figuring out where the tent and fire pit would go. I started to unpack while he did all the figuring.

Our sites were right on the river. It was a beautiful landscape. We could see the water flowing by. We could listen to its calming sounds at night. We had a week embedded within the pine-scented forest of the White Mountains. We were surrounded by breathtaking beauty.

We had a lot of work to do, but the payoff was great. We had beer and hard lemonade that had been packed in ice since that morning. It was the best tasting drink of the year. We had a week to hang out with our loved ones. We had river rides and hikes planned. We were surrounded by nature. The work it took to set up camp was worth it.

One of my favorite things to do was the river ride. I couldn't wait to fill the truck with people and rafts and head up river to our starting place. As much as Tom hated cold water, he would never miss the river rides. It was one of his favorite things also.

The beginning of the river ride was always the best part. It always started off with laughter because of Tom. He was always the last one in. He had to find just the right way to get onto his raft without any of the cold, mountain water touching his body. He always managed to do it somehow. He would hang his drink around his neck. His plastic bag, filled with some of his possessions, was held tightly between his teeth. He would stretch out his arms to balance his hands on the outer section of the raft. Then somehow, he would get his knees onto the closest section, pushing off first with his foot so he wouldn't remain stationary in the slow whirlpool where we began. The only problem was, he ended up going about a third of the way on his hands and knees, balancing the tube just right so he wouldn't fall into the water as we all laughed at his commitment to stay dry and warm. I couldn't understand why he loved it so much, but he did.

Tom would eventually fall off his tube and hit the icy water. After the initial shock, it wasn't so bad. I couldn't understand why he didn't just get it over with at the beginning. Every year, it was the same. Every trip we took, during the week, was the same. We all looked forward to the laugh. The year with Lily would be different. He couldn't worry about himself getting wet anymore. He would have to protect his baby girl from the cold water.

The beginning of the ride was my favorite part of the trip for another reason. After my laughter subsided, I relaxed and enjoyed some of the best scenery I had ever experienced. It was the slowest and most breathtaking section of the river. I spent the rest of the ride looking for the rapids.

Our starting point was also one of the widest sections of river. I would let my tube turn so I was floating backwards. The first glance at the enormous mountains behind us was truly amazing. It made me feel appreciative of every tiny river bed stone and enormous mountain range that I was privileged enough to experience. I was in no rush. I wanted to take in the beauty as long as I could. I had time because Tom was always the slowest, being stuck in the whirlpool with no use of his limbs to better navigate. We tried to stay together, but Tom always lingered behind. One limb off the tube would destabilize his position. He had to wait for the lazy river to drift him into faster water.

The river trip ended right at our camp sites, approximately two and a half hours after we started. It was perfect. Some of us were pretty buzzed by the time we got back. A couple of cocktails in the middle of the afternoon always hit a little harder than they did at night for some reason. It was off to the showers for all but two. Someone had to drive back up river to get the truck. Everyone else started getting ready for the nightly family congregation around the fire to eat, talk, and plan our hiking trips.

We planned a small hike, for all who were able, on day three. My parents and some friends stayed at the camp site. Dave, Tom, Angie, Lily, my brother's family, and I were all going. We needed to start out slow for Lily, so we chose a short trail to see how she would do. We chose Beaver Brook Trail. It was only two miles round trip from where we started, but it would be a steep climb through most of the terrain. I knew Lily would do okay. It was Tom carrying her that I worried about.

At approximately .7 miles into the hike, we could see a sign up ahead. I had a strong urge to turn around after I read it. Angie was with me on that. Most everyone else was up for the challenge. I wasn't worried about myself. I had hiked expert trails before. I was worried about Tom carrying Lily. This is why:

This Trail Is Extremely Tough.
If You Lack Experience Please Use Another Trail.
Take Special Care at the Cascades
To Avoid Tragic Results.

The sign was enough for me to want to turn around, but my fears were ignored. We forged ahead as the hike became steeper and steeper until we were at a near vertical climb. We reached a point where there was rebar drilled into the rock to use as hand and footholds. I had never seen that on a trail in the White Mountains before. I wondered what we would come across next.

I stayed behind Tom most of the way. I was amazed at his ability. It was an advanced hike and he had an extra twenty-five pounds on his back. He was the most sure-footed person in the bunch. I found it fascinating. Strap a child to his back and he could walk a tightrope. Take the child off and he'd trip over his own feet. He always kept me wondering.

We reached the Cascades. It was a magnificent sight. It was the tallest waterfall I had seen yet. Part of the trail crossed the stone alongside the waterfall. I imagined, in the spring, it would be impassable. With a smaller stream of water, the trail was visible. That section of trail is where I put my foot down. I would go no further.

To continue the hike, we would have to do a completely vertical climb approximately fifteen feet up, using only the re-bar for security. Any mistake and the fall would be injurious. The landing would be onto stone. Any further up and we would have to cross the edge of the waterfall where all the stone was steep and wet. One slip and it would be death. It was several hundred feet down the rocky mountainside.

I wasn't going any further with Lily. Neither was Angie, regardless of what everyone else wanted. We took turns staying with Lily below the vertical climb. Everyone but Lily had the chance to climb on the waterfall. I was more nervous watching Tom without Lily strapped to his back, but it would be a stupid chance to take with her.

We took in the sights as we ate lunch along the rushing water's edge. It was so peaceful out there in the wilderness. Lily's eyes were overwhelmed by the enormity of it. She loved it. She was outside, her favorite thing.

Tom and Angie decided to set up their own campsite even though they denied that they had gotten back together. It was nice for Tom to have his own site with his own family. They came to our site for breakfast every morning. Dave and I made a mean breakfast and we wanted to share it with them. It was one of the few times we ate so unhealthily. Dave made the omelets with all the veggies I had chopped and packaged before we left for our trip. I had the grilled English muffin duty as I kept an eye on the sizzling bacon. The best part of the breakfast was the home fries from the previous night's baked potatoes. I cooked them in the bacon fat. It was a once-a-year delicacy that we couldn't go without. It was a good way to start off the day when we had something physically challenging planned. The extra calories came in handy.

My site was the gathering spot on the fourth night of our trip. It was a different night. It was a good night. A lot changed that night. Tom and Angie introduced the rest of us to Jager Bombs; a mixed drink popular among young people. I wasn't crazy about the taste, but they were having fun teaching the older folks what and how to drink, so we all went with it.

We didn't realize, until deep into the night, what the combination of ingredients would do to us. The effects of the Red Bull made everyone want to talk, especially Tom and Angie. The effects of the Jagermeister lowered everyone's inhibitions, allowing everyone to say what they wanted to say. It was like a big therapy session. Tom and Angie had been on the fence about getting back together. Tom wanted, more than anything, to have his family together. Angie would have liked that also, but the fear of their past, of Tom's past, kept her from being able to commit.

While we were getting some serious work done with Tom and Angie, I needed some music in the background. I started to put on a CD, but Dave put a stop to it quickly. "You can't do that. It's two o'clock in the morning." I had no idea it was that late. I stopped what I was doing and went back to my seat to help work out Tom and Angie's problems. I felt like the group leader. I figured I had the most experience for the position. I felt like we were doing a lot of good for them. Dave felt the need to get something done between his input into their relationship, so he started to chop wood, at two o'clock in the morning. No more quiet than background music.

Tom told the family about all his hopes and dreams. He told us about his plans for the future and what he wanted to do with his life. How he was going to accomplish it. How he wanted Angie and Lily with him. They were great plans. He just needed to find a way to make them happen. Tom was determined to change his life. He wasn't going backwards anymore, or wasting his life away partying. We all believed him that night, especially Angie.

We resolved a lot of family issues on that fourth night. The after-effects of the Jager Bombs took a lot out of us. It took the rest of the trip to fully recover. There was no more alcohol after that night. There were no more hikes; only lazy trips down the river to relieve us from the August afternoon heat. Dave and I vowed never to do Jager Bombs again, even though we didn't really regret the events or the outcomes of that fourth night.

Tom was ready to move out on September first. He decided it was time for him to move on, to get out on his own, to take care of his own family. Tom and Angie decided, while in the mountains, to give it another try. They had a lot of history together. They had spent a lot of years loving each other. They had a child together and owed their daughter at least that much.

Tom and Angie rented a tiny, red, two-bedroom cottage in an old summer beach community. They were struggling. They struggled with their relationship. They struggled with their finances. They struggled with their time, trying to figure out how to raise a child, work, and go back to school all at the same time. They would find their way on their own. It wasn't my job anymore. I was just relieved that Tom had reached the fourth goal without having to be thrown out. I was getting my freedom back.

21

Reflections

My friends and family thought I would have Empty Nest Syndrome after Tom moved out. They couldn't have been more wrong. The day after Tom left was the day my peace of mind, ever so slightly, started to come back. I had lived seven years of my life in a state of anxiety and fear, but I was on my way back. I could feel it in my heart.

My life was good during those seven years. I had a great marriage. There was none better that I knew of. My husband and I were best friends. I received all the support I needed from Dave. I was in a respectable profession. We weren't rich by any means, but we did okay. We had good friends, and we loved to spend time on our boat. We had a granddaughter who we adored. The only thing that could have made my life better was for my son to be okay. I was grateful for Dave's support, but it hadn't been enough to take away my anxiety about Tom.

The longer Tom was out of the house, the better I felt.

Not knowing made all the difference in the world. I didn't want to know anymore. The only thing I could do was to let go. I had to let go, for my peace of mind. I couldn't do it anymore.

It didn't take me long to realize that not having Tom in the house was giving me my life back. I had no more sleepless nights. I no longer cried myself to sleep because of the fear that Tom would end up dead from an overdose or a car accident. I no longer lay in bed for hours, trying to get to sleep, because of the fear that Tom would get arrested or because he had dropped out of school. I no longer had torturous, intrusive thoughts racing through my mind. I no longer woke up at three or four in the morning, worried that something bad had happened during the night.

I noticed that I no longer had that terrible, prolonged anxiety that I sometimes needed a drink to settle. I didn't want to take potentially habit-forming medication or long term anti-depressants. I didn't want to take anything on a regular basis, so an occasional drink was my best option. Some days, I just needed something to take the edge off. I wasn't sure my anxiety was caused by Tom's behavior until he was gone, but my heart rate suddenly slowed and became rhythmic. My hands stopped sweating. My head stopped spinning. My mind was settling.

I no longer had panic attacks. My overwhelming need to get out from wherever I was, my car, my house, my place of work, was gone. It hadn't mattered where I was. It could hit anywhere, no matter how comforting a place I thought I was in. I didn't know why I had to leave. I would just get ambushed with an overwhelming need to run. I didn't know where I had to run to. I just needed air. The air outside was better, unless I was already outside. If I was outside, I needed different air. After Tom was gone from the house, I no longer had to run. The air became okay. My panic attacks were gone. My mind was at rest.

My life suddenly became what it should have been. I was happy. I could enjoy all the wonderful things I had in my life. I was able to really enjoy the love I had for my husband. I didn't feel guilty anymore because I was crying or feeling anxious. I didn't have the fear anymore that Dave would have had enough and want to leave. He was a positive, upbeat person. I had been afraid he would get fed up with all the problems that I brought into his life when he married me. I had been afraid he would leave. He didn't deserve what he was burdened with, but I didn't have a choice. I knew it wasn't fair to Dave, but I couldn't abandon my son because of it.

Dave had never said a word to make me feel guilty. I just knew it wasn't fair to him. He was always supportive. He always had his shoulder available for me. He would make me laugh when he could. He would hold me when I needed to be held. He would take me out when I needed the distraction of other people. Dave always knew what I needed to get through the day and he was always willing to provide it. That made me feel more guilty. He was so good to me. He made me feel like I was the most loved person in the world. I don't know how I would have gotten through those seven years without him. I no longer had to feel guilty, and I was able to appreciate Dave the way he should have been appreciated.

With Tom gone, I had time to reflect. I was able to look back over the years and put things into perspective. I had been too overwhelmed while living it. I hadn't always been able to think logically. I had thought more with my heart than with my mind.

Everyone loved Tom. He was a lovable person. He was affectionate. He could be the center of attention in any crowd, without even commanding it. He was charismatic. He had a sweet look about him. Anyone, and everyone, was an easy target.

I never knew if it was a manipulation that he had perfected to get away with whatever he wanted without risking losing people who loved him in the process. I didn't know if he honestly did have so many good characteristics, but was also so impulsive, at times, that it made him look like he was just being manipulative in the end. I wondered if he really couldn't help getting into trouble. Or if there was something wrong with his brain, something that he had no control over. I couldn't take the chance on it being manipulation. If it wasn't, it would have been awful to abandon my own child. I guess everyone felt the same way about him. Nobody ever let go. The kind of person Tom was made it too difficult for me, at the time, to see things as clearly as I needed to.

I let go too late. I never loosened the strings. I figured I couldn't go wrong if I did the most that I possibly could. I didn't even have to think about it. Being a loving, invested, determined, overprotective mother came naturally to me.

I was afraid of child molesters. I knew that statistics show it is usually someone known or close to the family. I was afraid someone would give Tom alcohol at his father's house. Or he wouldn't be watched carefully enough. Any time anything bad did happen, I rushed to Tom's rescue. Any time something bad happened, it reinforced my rigid beliefs that I had to protect my child at all costs.

I decided who could care for my child and who his friends should be. I spoke for him and fixed all his problems. I worried enough for the both of us. Being a single parent made it more difficult for me to let go of Tom. We were always together. I was his playmate when he was little. Tom didn't have siblings to play with, so I had given him all my attention. It was just him and I.

In spite of having one underprotective parent and one overprotective parent, Tom was a perfect child. Too perfect, I guess. He was polite and respectful. He was very well-behaved. Everyone wanted to take him for a visit when he was little because he seldom got in trouble. He was lovable and cute. Tom was a well-adjusted child who had the basic skills necessary to cope with stressful situations. I just hadn't allowed him to develop those skills. Tom had a great sense of humor. Everyone loved to be around him. He was charismatic from the time he was a little boy. Tom could have handled himself just fine, had he been given more of a chance.

When Tom was a teenager, I held on tighter. But that only drove him away further. The harder I tried to fix things, the worse things became. I held on so tight that I became desperate and hopeless. When Tom didn't listen to me, I yelled at him so that he would hear me. I yelled out of panic. My loud words only helped to drive Tom deeper inside himself, until he didn't even know who he was. Until he became whoever anyone wanted him to be. The more I tried to show Tom the road to happiness, the more unhappy he became. Tom was determined to continue on his path of self-destruction. I needed to let go.

Tom was screaming at me all the way along, but I couldn't hear him. I was so focused on doing the right thing for my child; I couldn't hear his unspoken words. The louder he screamed, the higher my panic rose, and the more deaf I became. The more obvious the signs that he needed space, the more my need to save him grew.

I never did hear him while he was growing up. Tom never did get what he so desperately fought for. He couldn't say it and I couldn't hear it. *Mom, just let go. Just let me live. Just let me learn. I will be okay. And if I'm not, the more I will grow, the more I will learn. I don't want to be a little boy anymore. I want to be a man. Please let me be a man. If you could just let go, it would be better for both of us. I promise. You would have peace in your heart and I could climb mountains.* Tom didn't know that is what he was trying to say to me through his actions. I wasn't able to decipher Tom's actions either.

I had racked my brain for many years trying to figure out what was wrong. I had put so much energy into finding an answer. I put so much emotionally draining effort and thought into figuring out what had gone wrong. The whole time, a piece of the answer was staring me in the face.

Stop. That was part of the problem. Just stop thinking so much. Stop draining your energy. Stop with the effort. Just stop. That was the answer. It was so easy. But it wasn't. It didn't make sense. My child was in trouble and I had to help him, protect him, teach him. I needed to fix him. It would have felt like a contradiction to let him fall further. I didn't know.

Tom was not an extension of me. It wasn't my job to help him all the time. Not the way that I did. Not to the extreme that I did. It wasn't my job, as a mother, to protect him all the time. Not for length of time that I did. It was not my obligation to teach him. Not when that teaching led him to remain too dependent on me. Not when it was my way instead of his. It was not my job to do Tom's thinking for him. It was my job to allow Tom to think for himself. If he didn't think, if he didn't act, I was to wait. He would do it all on his own. If given the opportunity, he would have. He wouldn't have had a choice. He might have fallen a few times, but he would have learned.

More is not always better. I tried to keep Tom in a bubble. He didn't need to do much for himself. He became dependent on the bubble that I created for his protection. I didn't allow Tom to fend for himself. I wasn't able to wait for him to do it on his own. I didn't give him enough chances to fail. He may have learned to fight harder if he had failed. I don't think he would have just lay there and died. I don't believe now that he would have rejected human nature to survive. Less, actually, would have been better. Not nothing, but less.

I had been determined to be a great mom. I would protect my son from anything bad. I would point him toward the right friends and only let a chosen few influence my child, unless I had no choice. There weren't too many people I could really trust. I didn't think about why or how he should learn to cope with all the untrustworthy people in the world. The risk was just too high for me. The consequences could have been too great.

My parents didn't make it their mission to make sure I was happy all the time. I don't know where I got the idea that was my job as a parent. Life isn't just about good times and getting what we want all the time. Life is full of ups and downs, challenges, and hard work. What was I thinking? Making life easy for Tom didn't help him. It hurt him in the end. I didn't want to hurt my child. I should have focused more on raising a self-sufficient, productive member of society. I was so wrapped up in protecting and comforting him that it blinded me from most everything else.

I cannot imagine being thrown into adolescence or adulthood without having had learned the coping skills necessary to deal with adversity. That would be petrifying. It's no wonder Tom expected everyone else to bail him out of every difficult situation. It's no wonder Tom wanted me to fix everything unpleasant in his life. I should have focused more on my own life and paid less attention to Tom's. I should have put more thought into what I was doing. Love wasn't just about comfort and happiness. I only had one chance to teach Tom how to become independent, and I thought I was doing great with my one chance. I didn't realize that Tom's mind just allowed me to take over, instead of learning to become more self-sufficient.

I should have just been a good enough parent. I should have realized that raising my child with love shouldn't have just involved the easy, coddling stuff. Loving my child is doing whatever I had to do for the good of my child. If that meant letting go, then I should have let go. If that meant laying down the law, then I should have laid down the law and followed through. If love meant I had to make a painful decision for me or my child, then I should have made the decision and stuck to it. I just didn't know that that was what Tom needed me to do.

I made Tom feel secure with me. I helped to make him feel insecure with life. I gave him structure and rules. I just abandoned the rules when he needed them the most because I thought he deserved a break. I can only hope at this point that Tom will find his way and maybe learn a little from my mistakes.

I would tell Tom to find a happy medium, if he would listen to me. I would tell him not to neglect his daughter, but to pay less attention than I did. I would tell him to just be a good enough parent. To have his own life so that Lily could develop her independence. Being just a good enough parent is being a good parent.

I don't blame myself for all of Tom's problems. I put the blame where it belongs. I didn't allow enough space for him to grow up or enough freedom for him to make decisions when it was appropriate for him to do so. I didn't allow enough opportunity for him to learn how to protect himself or to speak for himself. I did it for him. I knew best, or so I thought. I didn't let him be himself. My mistakes only swayed Tom towards the unhealthy coping mechanisms that he chose to use.

Because of Tom's easy-going personality, my overprotectiveness was perceived as more intense by him. We misunderstood each other. I didn't foster that wonderfully mellow quality in him, and he couldn't appreciate my intentions.

Tom is laid-back and tends to go with the flow of life's ups and downs. He lets the rights and the wrongs of the world just pass. I tend to fight. I protect and stand up for the people that I love. Most of my loved ones could appreciate my passion. To Tom, it was perceived as overreactive and overly dramatic at times. Those good qualities that we had in ourselves ended up being bad for one another, given our opposite personalities.

Some of the blame falls on his father. Phil was underprotective and exposed Tom to too many things. Some scared him and some confused him. Phil and I lived in two different worlds. There was no discipline or structure in his father's house. Phil's intentions were good. He loved his son, but he only had a few days a month with him and he wasn't going to spend them on unpleasantness. He should have done what his son needed, not what he wanted. We both had a lot to learn.

Some of the blame falls on Phil's family. Tom had a normal, structured, secure life in my family, with normal relatives. My parents were loving and always doting on Tom. His father's family was wild and crazy. It was a drastic and confusing contrast.

Bad things happened at his father's house and there wasn't much I could do about it. Phil's family had very poor judgment and insight at times. Their way of living was different from mine. It was different from what I wanted for my child. Tom found a way to cope and came to love his paternal relatives for who they were. They were interesting to him.

I place blame on traumatic emotional experiences. Tom needed to overcome a serious assault to his mind, to his emotions, to his identity. It may have all been easier if he was allowed to learn how to cope when he was younger. He was naturally equipped to cope with traumatic situations. His father and I just didn't realize how well, and we did nothing to foster that attribute. We unintentionally damaged it.

Tom was only eleven years old when he was victimized. What Tom didn't realize was that he was less a victim than he was a hero. What he did was purely amazing by anyone's standards. The special victim's investigator had made it a point to let me know that on the day that the assault had happened. It was the only time, in all his years as a police officer, that he had come across anything like what Tom did.

Nobody knows the exact details of that miserable night except for the people who were present in the children's bedrooms. Nobody needs to know all the details, but one is definitely worth attention.

When Eugene had illegally entered the house early that Sunday morning, he had preyed on the first child he had stumbled across. That child happened to be a nine-year-old little girl, with her six-year-old little sister lying comfortably asleep next to her. Somehow, the boys had become aware of what was going on. Tom, being the oldest, had the most insight of all the boys. He needed to protect his young cousins, so he had lured Eugene out of the girls' bedroom. He had gotten all the children out of harm's way, except himself. He had acted on instinct. He had acted quickly. The only problem was, Eugene had followed him. Tom had become trapped and alone with a child molester, leaving himself prey. He had taken the brunt of the trauma that night. By the time one of the children safely and courageously escaped into their parent's bedroom, it had been too late for Tom to be saved.

Tom took that pain willingly to save five other children from his same fate. Some didn't escape completely. Some did. They have Tom to thank for that. He was a brave young boy. He is a hero in my eyes. There are not many people who would have done the same. There can't be too many children that could have had the insight or the courage to do the same. If Tom never accomplished another thing in his life, except to recognize the incredible good deed that he is solely responsible for, I could not be more proud. He means something in this world. He made a difference that I have always been proud of.

I place blame on physical adversity. The injury that Tom suffered would scar his identity, possibly forever. After his traumatic shoulder dislocation, he was never able to play basketball the same way again. Basketball had been everything to him. He had been the local star athlete. Seeing Tom's face all over the front page of the sports section in our local newspaper had become a weekly event. If he wasn't on the front page, he had been listed somewhere within the paper. He had been the best.

He had had the most heart of all the players. His friends had looked up to him. Basketball had been his way of life.

By the third surgery, and the fourteenth dislocation, Tom had been permanently displaced from the thing he loved most. He was out of school, but he still could not move past it. He was lost. Basketball was the only direction he had considered. Only time would heal him. Only time would bring a replacement. He may have found that replacement in Lily. I can only hope.

I place blame on genetics. I do believe that Tom was born with the genetic predisposition to cope the way that he did. I also believe that with a strong family unit, and the most appropriate parenting for him, he would have developed in a more emotionally healthy way.

I had finally let go of Tom for my own peace of mind. What I didn't know was that it would be the best solution I could have come up with for my son's well-being. He seemed to be maturing while trying to make it on his own. Tom and his girlfriend were trying to raise their daughter together. They had their own family; a young family, a family that had to find their way. A family that looked like they may have to parent apart. They had decided that they couldn't make it together after all.

I didn't expect Tom to suddenly grow up because I had learned to let go. I knew it would be a long, hard road for him. I wanted him to learn how to fix the mistakes that I had made.

Mistakes that were all made with good intentions, but mistakes nonetheless.

I hoped I had let go with enough time for Tom to gain enough emotional growth to handle what the mailman brought to my home. I hoped he had enough strength to handle what the letter meant, on top of a broken relationship, on top of the fear of losing his time with his daughter again. He had never had the strength to handle such intense problems in the past without destroying himself first. I was scared for him.

I was afraid to tell Tom about the parole hearing. He was doing so well. He was struggling with the contentious break-up with Angie, but he was even handling that better than he had in the past.

Tom was maintaining his two-bedroom apartment. He wanted to make sure that he kept a good home for Lily. Angie was being reasonable about the custody arrangement after their second break-up. She and Tom went to court together to change the legal status to fifty-fifty custody so Tom could enthusiastically take on his responsibility. He was paying for a private school for Lily to go to three days a week, which she really loved. She was adjusting to her mommy and daddy not being together anymore. Tom was doing what he could to help her adjust.

I was so proud of his paternal instincts. He coveted every second he had with his daughter. His favorite time with her was the mornings. They got up together and he cooked breakfast for the two of them. They made their lunch together, then he brought her to school. He looked forward to coming home at night to spend more time with her. He had no problem setting limits or giving his affections to her. Lily told her daddy, at two-and-a-half years old, that he made her feel safe. Lily did turn out to be his new passion.

Tom was trying to figure out a way to go back to school. He wanted to get started on his goals. He was really moving in the right direction. I was petrified of sending him back to the life he had left behind.

I was petrified of going backwards myself. I couldn't. No matter what happened, I couldn't go back to the hell I had lived in for seven years. I couldn't go back to the anxiety, the panic, the insomnia. But I had no right to keep it from him. It was his right to know, his demon. It was up to Tom to figure out how to cope. I just needed to be there for him. I showed him the letter.

22

DEMONS

Just as I started to plug in my hairdryer, my cell phone rang. It was six-thirty in the morning. I was afraid it meant he couldn't go through with it. I knew he had to do whatever he needed to do and it was okay with me if he wasn't ready. I thought the hearing would be good for him, if he could get through it. I knew, someday, he would have to face his demon. I was hoping that it was time.

"Mom, I didn't have a chance to hook up my printer yet. I emailed you my statement. Can you print it out for me? I'm leaving in a minute." I let out a sigh of relief. He was still coming. He was running a little late, as usual. It was okay. This would be a difficult day. I wasn't surprised that Tom was disorganized. He was typically disorganized on a good day. This was far from a good day; at least this early on.

Just as I finished getting ready, Tom pulled into the driveway. He looked a little disheveled. His hair was cut, and his beard was trimmed close, the way I liked it. He was such a handsome young man when he took care of himself. His clothes were old and wrinkled, but on a day like we were facing, he did his best.

"Do I look okay? I brought a change of clothes in case I don't."

"You look fine, honey." It wasn't the time to criticize. Tom would need all the confidence he could muster and I wasn't about to take any of it away. He did look good. He matched. It wasn't important. He was there to face his demon.

It was a long ride to the Massachusetts Parole Board offices in Natick. I knew there would be a lot of traffic. We had to be there at nine o'clock in the morning; right in the middle of rush hour traffic. The traffic was the least of our worries. We could use the time together. Tom and I always had good talks when we took long rides. This ride was no different.

"I don't remember a lot of the details from that night, but I remember something he said to you. I remember it clear as day. I was only eleven years old. I don't know why I remember this, of all things. We were sitting around the fire. Eugene had just gotten there. He looked at you and said, 'Your father must have been a robber because he stole some diamonds and put them in your eyes.' I don't know why I remember that. I guess because you're my mom. I didn't like it."

"That makes sense. You were only eleven years old. You didn't like him. I didn't either. Ya know, I had no recollection of that until this moment." I could picture that night. I could picture sitting around the fire. I could picture Eugene sitting across from me. He was staring at me. Suddenly, I remembered his words. I could remember the way I felt about him. The words that came into my mind were untrustworthy, shady, and phony. He was trying to fool me into thinking he was interested in women. He was trying to fool me into thinking he was interested in me and not my son. He was taking any attention off his interest in my little boy. I didn't know his intentions at the time. I did connect my feelings of distrust with a negative energy, but I didn't know what that energy was. My instincts were right. I just didn't act on them the way I could have.

I didn't realize it then, but Eugene's words were meant to throw everyone off. If he were to hit on me, nobody would think he was really interested in our little children. He had put a lot of thought into how he would fool the parents: how he would gain access, when he would strike. He had thought about all this while we sat around the fire and talked, laughed and ate. While we had our guard down.

Neither Tom nor I wanted to dwell on what lay ahead of us. Neither of us needed to say it; we just took most of the time we had catching up on other things. We talked about Lily's first field trip that she would be going on the next day. Tom giggled quietly whenever her name was spoken. His face always lit up when he talked about his daughter. A smile would immediately appear on his face whenever he heard her name. His smile was made of pride. It was made of adoration. It said she was the best thing he had ever accomplished. She was his true happiness, his true love. I knew how he felt. I knew how precious that kind of love was. I knew how painful it could be, and I knew how wonderful it could be.

Tom and I made a lot of small talk while we sat in traffic. He was buying a new car. A new, used car. It was old. A 1986 Toyota Camry, but it only had eighty thousand miles on it. It was all that he could afford while trying to support himself and Lily. The car was a sensible decision. An affordable decision. Tom was finding his way on his own. He was growing up.

We reached the parole office fifteen minutes early. We waited for someone to open the secured glass door that led into the lobby. Once inside, Tracy, the victim advocate, greeted us and checked us in. She was a nice girl. I liked her. She really made me feel like she was on our side. She made us feel like she was there for us. Tracy asked if we had any questions. I couldn't think of any at the time. Tom couldn't think of any either. It's funny how anxiety can take over your mind and clog your thinking.

I took a seat in the last available chair as Tom stood beside me. I assumed they didn't expect too many people to show up at the hearings since there was only enough seating for six in the waiting room. We had to wait for security to check us through the metal detector. Once they did, Tracy led us upstairs to an office so that she could review the proceedings. She told us that if Eugene was granted parole, the district attorney's office would have six months to decide if they wanted to pursue him civilly. It could be up to six months that Eugene would be kept in jail until they made their decision. If he wasn't granted parole, the district attorney would follow the same procedure on Eugene's release date.

We asked Tracy what it meant to pursue civilly. She explained that on rare occasions, the district attorney could keep a sexual predator committed for a lifetime if they felt the predator was a high risk to society. She said it didn't look like that would happen in our case. She said that it seldom ever did happen.

We found out that Eugene had received a two-hundred-and-fifty day credit toward his sentence for participating in the sexual predators' treatment program. "That's not right. Why should he get time off for that?"

"It's a voluntary program. He doesn't have to do it. It's incentive to get them to participate."

"That's bullshit. It makes no difference if he goes through the program or he doesn't. It's not like it's gonna change him. It's just a way for him to look good for parole and get his sentence reduced."

"You never know. It might help some people."

"Pedophiles can't change any more than I can change my heterosexuality. It's in the genes. Pedophiles just have an evil, mutated gene. You could put me in jail for sleeping with a man. I would promise that I would never do it again, even if I thought I meant what I said at the time because I was afraid of going back to jail. I would still sleep with a man when I got out. It's the same drive. They can't change that. There's no proof that they can."

"I have to believe they can or I couldn't do what I do. I handle the whole sexual predators unit."

"I don't know how you do it. I couldn't."

Tracy told us that it looked good for us because Eugene had gotten in trouble recently. She couldn't really say how she felt the hearing would end. It was up to the parole board and she couldn't read their minds. We would just have to wait to get the answer to that question.

Tom and I already knew about the infraction from the prior conversations I had with Tracy. We were hoping that it would be enough to have Eugene's parole denied. The first time parole was denied, he had had forty-something infractions. This time, it was only one. We were worried that the parole board would look favorably on Eugene for participating in the sexual abuse predators' treatment program. We were hoping that they would see that he had waited ten years to begin the program and that it was only an attempt to look good for his release.

When we were finished with Tracy, another woman led us into another waiting room, next to the office where we had reviewed the case. It was just me, Tom and the woman. We couldn't be left alone, so she was brought in to keep an eye on us. The woman had the same ear piece and radio hooked to her waistband as the rest of the staff in the building. Tom and I each chose a magazine out of the three that were sitting at the center of the long, rectangular table situated in the center of the room. We began to thumb through our magazines as the woman decided to chat with us. She was pleasant enough.

She told us that it might be a long wait because they had ten or twelve hearings scheduled for that day. They had to bring the prisoners in by bus and leave them on the bus because they only had three holding cells. There was only one prisoner allowed per cell. I liked the idea of keeping them in the bus. I hoped that they would not keep the bus running. It was cold outside and I wanted Eugene to be cold. I wanted him to suffer any discomfort possible, even if it was just a minor little gift from God. I would take what I could get.

I could picture Eugene sitting in the cold, old, converted school bus, shackled and locked into the floor by his chains. I envisioned the prisoners crammed against one another. I hoped he was seated next to a prisoner who hated pedophiles and knew that Eugene was what he hated. Another possible little gift from above.

While Tom and I waited to be called, another couple entered the waiting room and sat at the opposite end of the table. Soon after, a single woman entered the room and sat next to me. I wondered what they were there for. I wondered what pain they had to suffer in their past. I wondered what had made them strong enough to return many years later to face their demons. I didn't know why they were there, but I wanted to cry for them anyway. I wanted to cry for what had happened to them. I wanted to cry because they were brave enough to be there.

I looked at Tom. I could see the worry on his face. I could see that he was trying not to show it. I was his mother. I knew. "Are you okay?" After all those years, I finally knew not to say too much. I knew enough to let Tom get through the day in his own way, to say what he needed to say, to use his own words, to feel his own feelings. I knew my place, as his mother.

I just needed to be there for what Tom chose to need from me.

"I'm okay." Tom gave me a little smile that said, *this is tough, but I'll be all right. Thank you for asking.* I knew he was okay.

"Did I sound like a crazy lady in there with Tracy?"

"Yeah, kinda. You just have strong opinions." Tom grinned at me. "I might have some of the same beliefs, but I just don't express them the same way." His smile told me he didn't resent me. He loved me. He just had his own way of expressing himself. I liked him better for it. I always loved him, but I didn't always know who he was. I had been so busy trying to force Tom into thinking my thoughts that neither one of us had realized that I actually liked it better when Tom had his own ideas, his own opinions. I loved it more when they differed from mine.

We were getting restless. It was ten am, an hour and forty-five minutes after we had arrived. We had no idea how long we would be waiting. I started to thumb through another magazine. I was disinterested. I wasn't reading any of the words when Tom got up to stretch his legs. He walked to the far end of the room to look out the window. "The buses are right out there."

I got up to take a look. I was surprised at what I saw. The buses weren't old, converted school buses at all. They looked like tour buses. "That's not fair."

"What?"

"They get to transport in those buses."

"I don't think there are recliners or anything like that inside. I'm sure they converted them."

"Yeah, you're probably right."

An hour after we entered the second waiting room, a man and a woman wearing the headpieces and radios came to get us. They were bringing us back downstairs. The woman led the way as she talked on her radio. "We're on our way down." The man stayed close behind us.

Tracy was waiting at the bottom of the stairs for us. "It's time. Do you have any questions for me before we head in?" Neither one of us had questions. We just wanted it to be over. Tracy walked into the hearing room with us. There was a long table at the head of the room where two parole board members sat. I recognized the woman from the first hearing. The man was new. He had a pleasant look. I didn't like that. It scared me. The man at the first hearing had looked tough. He had looked like a detective. That had made me feel more confident.

There was a small, square table facing the head table. There was one chair that I imagined was for whoever was testifying. Past the small table were two rows of long tables that also faced the head table. We sat at the second long table on the right side of the room. There was a woman sitting in the same row on the left side of the room. I didn't know who she was or what her purpose for being there was. I didn't give it much thought because I didn't have time. Just as Tom, Tracy and I took our seats, two security guards brought Eugene through the door.

He had lost a lot of weight since I had seen him ten years earlier. The first hearing was by teleconference so I had only caught a quick glimpse of him on the monitor. I didn't want to see him back then. This year, I was ready.

Eugene's hair was now clipped almost to his scalp, and he had no more facial hair. He looked so small. He no longer looked like a monster to me. He didn't look like anything to be afraid of. The two security guards sat Eugene at the small table and left all his chains and shackles attached to him.

After we were sworn in, Eugene was asked by the parole board if he had an opening statement. The only thing I wanted to hear out of his mouth was anything stupid that would contribute to his denial of parole. Anything else was a waste of precious air that could be better put to use by someone who deserved it.

"I just want to say that Tom shouldn't think that any of this was his fault. It was my fault." I was getting angry at his words immediately. I wanted to get up and kick him in the back of the head. It was only a fantasy. I was above that. I would have to use a different tactic to get back at him. I would have to rely on my words.

When Eugene was done with his brief speech, it was the parole board's turn for questioning. The pleasant-looking, large man did all the talking. It was all hinging on him to ask the right questions. I prayed he knew what to ask. I prayed he just hated pedophiles, no matter what Eugene did to try to get out of prison. "You've had 47 D reports. The last one was this past May. That's not something you do if you want parole. Would you agree with that?" He started off hitting Eugene right between the eyes. Maybe it would be all right.

"Yeah, but I've done a lot since then. I've learned a lot. I just got to Bridgewater when the last one happened. MCI was tense. I had to always watch my back. Bridgewater was different. It's much more laid-back. I still had a chip on my shoulder when I got there. I was defensive."

"Defensive? You were in someone else's cell." Eugene squirmed in his seat. I loved every second of it.

"You're in phase two of the treatment program. Is that right?"

"Yes."

"Do you think it would be beneficial for you to participate in the third and final phase?"

"Yes."

"So, you agree that it would be the best thing for you to get further treatment?"

"Yes."

"Then, don't you think it would be irresponsible of the parole board to grant you parole when you said yourself that the best thing for you is to continue treatment?" Wham! Bullet number two.

"I can continue to get treatment when I get out. Phase three takes two to three years. I won't be there long enough anyway."

"There are other programs you can participate in." The pleasant-looking man asked a bunch of questions about what Eugene's plan was if he were to be released. He planned to live with his father in Wareham and work part-time for his brother's construction company. He said he had his plan all written out. The pleasant looking man picked up a packet and held it out in front of him, "Yes, we have it right here. We read it over thoroughly last night." He looked over at the woman, "Do you have any questions?"

"I have no questions. I was here for the last hearing." There was no hesitation in her voice. There was nothing she wanted to hear. Nothing she wanted to ask. I could feel her disgust and I hoped my intuition was right. The security guards walked Eugene back to his seat.

The pleasant-looking man asked for the first person to come up and testify. It was time for Tom to be heard. Tracy walked next to him as he approached the small table. Tom stood quietly for a moment in front of the chair. The pleasant-looking man told him he could sit down. Then he quickly said, "You can do whatever you feel comfortable with." Tom held his hand forward, and out by his side. His gesture said, thank you, but I'm good right here. He was ready to give his statement.

"This man is evil. He needs to prey on little boys for control and satisfaction. That is pathetic. He controlled my life from a jail cell for many years. He did, and I'm not afraid to admit that now. I hated myself. I wanted to die at times. I was disgusted, violated, and just sick of thinking about what this monster did. Now he doesn't seem like a big, bad monster in my head. Just a puny little piece of crap, PEDOPHILE!" Tom's voice was loud, strong and confident. He was in control.

His words were angry, as they should be.

"I am all grown up now. He just seems pathetic and weak, a disgrace to humanity. He is the worst kind of scum there is. LITTLE BOYS. Defenseless human beings. He prowls and attacks so that he can be big and bad. He should sit in a cell forever for the crimes he has committed, and the pain he has made families endure. I feel strong now and I thank GOD that I have a great family. I have surrounded myself with people I love. I hold my head up high and I will not let this scumbag control me anymore. Never again."

My heart was thundering hard and rapidly. I was afraid to look down. I thought I might see my shirt beating to the rhythm of my heart's show of empathy. I could feel the lump in my throat begin to swell, blocking my breath from escaping my body. My palms began to sweat. I wouldn't allow my tears to come. I couldn't. I had to retain control for Tom because he did not want to cry in front of this man. It was important to him and I would not let him down. I looked down and to my right. I had to look away for a moment to focus on my breathing. I needed to slow my heart rate. Tom continued.

"Why should this pedophile get out of jail early? He's a PEDOPHILE! During my freshman year of college, I did a research paper on the recidivism rate of sexual offenders. I found, in many studies, that the rate runs over forty percent. That only counts the pedophiles that get caught repeat offending. I don't think a pedophile can be changed. If it were possible, they would have to become a completely different person. Go through treatment, show remorse, maybe apologize. This creep hasn't done any of that, to my knowledge. He has only completed part of his sexual predator treatment, and he just got into a fight a few months ago. He hasn't even accepted full responsibility for his actions. This pedophile is sick and twisted. He deserves to be in jail for as long as possible.

"Now, what I have to say to this pedophile is this: I will be there when you get released. I will be wherever you live, going door to door, and hanging up fliers that tell people of the sick, pathetic pedophile living around them. If you move, I will go there too. I will not give up making sure you don't do this again. You're a piece of shit and you deserve to rot in a prison cell! You will never have a normal life again. I will make sure everyone around you knows that you are sick. You are pathetic.

"I know that you will do this again. It kills me to think that another little boy will have to endure the pain that many others already have. Maybe next time, you will sit in a little cell, rotting away until the day you die. I will try everything in my power to prevent you from hurting another innocent little child while a parent has their guard down, or when you break into a house to create the opportunity yourself to SEXUALLY assault another little boy. You're a sick man. That's the bottom line. You will never be better. You are PATHETIC.

"Can you look me in the face and tell me why you did this to me and my cousins? I really would like to know what your sick and twisted thought process is like." Tom turned to go back to his seat, looking Eugene in the eye as he walked by. I was proud of him. I was relieved for him. He had done it. It was my turn.

I walked to the small table and sat down. I didn't think I had the strength to stand as Tom did. I took out my statement and began to read.

"I know that my purpose for being here isn't to keep this pedophile in jail. I know that I haven't been given the power to do that. I wish that were different, but it's not the way the system works. I do have other reasons for being here, though.

"One reason I'm here is to make it known that I'm not ever going away. I will be a constant reminder that someone is watching. Someone that cares about children. Someone who, even though this pedophile will be given the chance to destroy another child again, will do anything and everything within my rights to try to prevent that from happening.

"Another reason for me being here is so that he never forgets my son's name. So he doesn't forget our faces. He cared so little about what he did, that he couldn't remember the names of the boys he hurt so badly. He showed no remorse the last time we were here. He was defensive and made excuses. He blamed the parents, like there is a reason for what he did that makes it okay. This pedophile believed that if parents are distracted, he has the right to rape their little boys. That is a sick mind. That is a sick statement to make to the parent of one of those little boys. That is not the kind of mind that this society needs on our streets. This pedophile has an evil, freakish thought process. I am more powerful than him, though. He won't ever be able to forget us. I won't let him.

"I don't want this pedophile to know the power he had over my son for so long, but I need to tell the parole board how my son's pain didn't end because this person went to jail. The last time I sat here at this hearing, my son was lying unconscious on his father's bathroom floor from a suicide attempt. He had a letter to the parole board nearby."

My hands began to tremble, shaking the paper I held between my hands. Tears stung my eyes. I stopped for a brief moment. I would not allow my tears to fall from my eyes. I rested the edge of my hands on the table to disguise my tremor. I resumed my speech.

"The letter begged the board to not let this pedophile out of jail. It begged the board not to let this pedophile hurt any more children, because Tom knows, with absolute certainty that he will hurt again. The letter said that his suicide was the most powerful way he could make people believe how important it is to prevent any more children from suffering in the same way.

"I am so grateful that my son didn't die that day. He struggled to gain control over his life. Today, Tom is different. He is strong. He is happy. He is hopeful. He refuses to give this freak another minute of control over his life, his thoughts and feelings. This pedophile is not worth the dirt on the bottom of our shoes. I hope that this hearing is empowering for my son. That he can feel strong and rise above all of this.

"The third reason I'm here is to remind the board that he did nothing to show remorse. He did nothing to show that he wanted to change, not that he ever could. He didn't participate in any programs offered until recently. He should be required to finish the treatment program since he does have two more years on his sentence. This pedophile has been found with pornography, has gotten into fights, as recently as five months ago, and he hasn't shown any signs that he won't do this again.

"To let this pedophile out of jail before his sentence is fully carried out is unfair. It's unfair to the children he has already hurt, and it's unfair to the children he will hurt in the future. This pedophile already blew his chance. He's made a very late, half-assed attempt at showing he should be released. Half-assed because he was just recently found in someone else's cell, who he had a physical altercation with. He hasn't changed. He blew it.

"I know, in my heart, that this pedophile will strike again. He will get his opportunity in two short years. Please don't give him the chance before the time we have been promised. Please give my son his two years to keep getting stronger. He needs that time. He deserves that time. I know that my statement can't contribute to your decision, but this pedophile's actions can. Just remember, he already blew it.

"I have three questions for the pedophile." I had to direct my questions to the parole board. They nodded their head, signaling me to go ahead.

"One. Do you feel that you deserve to be in jail for what you did, and if so, when did you start to feel that way?

"Two. What are the names of the little boys you sexually assaulted?

"Three. If being out on bail for raping your retarded nephew wasn't enough for you to change, and going to prison for sexually assaulting four more little boys wasn't enough to change, what did make you change, if you changed at all?"

When I finished, I stood, facing Eugene. I stared at his eyes as I made my way back to my seat. He couldn't meet my eyes. He wouldn't meet my eyes. I wasn't giving him what he wanted. I was determined to keep the control he wanted to take away from me. He couldn't have it.

Tom's face showed pain. He didn't look as strong as he had a few moments earlier. There were no tears, but I could tell the wall was crumbling. The blood had drained from his face just a bit, leaving small areas of visible circulation just under the skin. His lips barely pouted now with a man's pride. But what tugged at my heart the most was his eyes. Eyes that danced with life, more often than not, had fallen flat and sad. Sad eyes that I had seen for the first time ten years earlier. They were back again.

I reached over and gave him a little pinch on the outside of his thigh. I didn't care if he cried, but Tom wanted, more than anything, not to. Dave told him to pinch the inside of his thigh as hard as he could. He would have to pinch hard enough to be unable to think about anything but the pain he had just inflicted upon himself. It would hurt, but it would keep him from crying. Tom was doing fine on his own, using his mind. My little pinch was just a gesture of support. He kept his tears from flowing.

It was time for Eugene to go back to the small table to make his closing statement, if he chose to do so. He did decide to make one last-ditch effort to convince the parole board that he should be granted the opportunity to be released into society. His statement was weak. He just repeated the same thing he said in his opening statement. He told Tom not to blame himself. Then he made an attempt to answer my questions.

Eugene started to list the names of the four boys. He got hung up on the last one and had to start his list again, getting it right the second time around. He said that he spent a lot of time writing about them. I knew the only writing he did was a list of their names because he knew the question would come up. He was asked the same question by the parole board at the first hearing two years earlier. He didn't remember their names the first time and it angered the board, so he had made a list. It wasn't impressive. Eugene didn't answer my other two questions, and he did not apologize to Tom.

The pleasant-looking man resumed his questioning. He asked if there were any more boys that he had sexually abused. Eugene answered yes. He admitted to raping his mentally retarded nephew and another boy. He was then asked how many boys, in all, have there been. Eugene didn't answer. "We don't need names. How many in all?"

"About twenty." Everyone's mouth dropped. My eyes met the eyes of one of the security guards. We mouthed the word *wow* to each other. The dummy was trying to be honest to prove his case for early release. Pop! Bullet number three, I hoped.

The parole board was done with their questioning. It was time for Eugene to leave the room. The board asked us to stay seated. After Eugene left the room, the woman sitting on the left side of the room approached the head table. The three were whispering to each other. When they finished talking, they asked for me and Tom to approach their table.

"We don't want you leaving here not knowing," the female board member said. "I'm glad you came this year. You did well. Don't let him take any more of your life." Tom appreciated her kind words. "We're denying his parole."

Tom had faced his demon. I watched the burden shed from his body and fall to the ground as he exited the hearing room. The life started to fill back into his eyes. He had done something good for himself. He was healing.

We drove home, quiet for a little while. We were both lost in our own thoughts. I was tired and hungry. I felt like I could sleep long enough to make up my ten year deficit.

"Twenty little boys. I wish there was something we could do about it, but we have no names." Tom's quiet continued for a few minutes. "Under oath." Tom's quiet continued.

"I know what we can do. He's from Wareham, right?"

"Yeah."

"We can put an ad in the Wareham newspaper. We can ask people to come forward to help keep this pedophile in prison. He's already there, so it will be easier to come forward. I wish we had a picture of him."

"We can get one. The press put his picture in the paper when he was arrested for your case. We can look back through the old articles and find one."

"That would be perfect. The picture would be from the right time. Someone would recognize him."

"Tom, that's a great plan."

When we got back to my house, Tom hugged and kissed me, and thanked me for everything. He was off to be a contributing member of society. I walked upstairs to lie down on my bed and blissfully drifted off to sleep with a quiet mind.

Tom is happy again. He's as happy as he was when he was a little boy, except he is a man now. He's the man he was always destined to be. He just had a few roadblocks thrown in his way, but he has found a way to conquer them all. He came through his crises a stronger, more compassionate person.

Tom has his karma back. He's fun to be around. He doesn't miss a family function and he brings all his friends to join in on our celebrations. He loves his family more than anything and wants to share that happiness with everyone he can.

Tom is working hard at figuring out a way to reach his goals. He's taking some classes at the local community college, when he can afford to, when he can find the time. He wants to work with children someday and hopes to start his own unique business that is very much needed for children. It's a perfect goal for him. He is the most patient person I have ever known. He's great with kids and they love him. The teachers at Lily's school think very highly of him. He volunteers sometimes to help out when there is a special occasion. He keeps the children busy so that the teachers can get done what they need to do. He doesn't realize the knack he has. It just comes naturally to him. Maybe because he's a kid at heart.

I know Tom will reach his goals. It just might take awhile. Working full time and raising his child takes up most of his time. It will be easier for him when Lily is in school full-time. For now, he'll do what he can and concentrate on the good things he has in his life.

As much as Tom hurt people, he never intentionally set out to hurt anyone but himself. He was angry and lost his ability to care about anything because of what had happened to him. He has always had a good heart, a good sense of humor, and he has always felt a commitment to family. Tom was always meant to do great things, he just got lost for a little while. He has risen above all of his adversity and is embracing life with everything he has. He now has more than he ever lost, and so do I.

Tom has found his new passion, a passion that makes basketball pale in comparison. He has full legal and physical custody of Lily. The more he has her, the better and happier he is. The more well adjusted Lily is. Tom is an incredible father and he enjoys every second of parenthood. Lily is an incredible little girl who adores her daddy.

I hear him laugh with his daughter often, just as I laughed with him. He finds great enjoyment in everything that she does. She is a happy, sometimes oblivious, little girl. She is a lot of fun to be around, just like her father. She is smart, lovable, and wonderfully magnetic.

Watching Tom and Lily together gives me déjà vu. The way she tightly wraps her arms around her daddy's neck, gazes deeply into his eyes, and gives him giant kisses puts a sincere smile on his face. Her contagiously happy disposition draws Tom and everyone else around her in to stay. When she just walks through the room and falls over nothing, then yells, "I'm okay!" before anyone can ask, it puts laughter in our bellies. It's amazing how two simple words can be passed on through the genes. It's uncanny. It's magooism all over again, and Tom finds as much pleasure in it all as I did. I wonder if he realizes what a wonderful, love-filled journey he is in for. A journey that, no matter how painful it can be at times, is worth every second of life with the love of your child in your heart. A love you can never again live without.